# FRENCH EXISTENTIALISM
Consciousness, Ethics, and
Relations with Others

## VIBS

Volume 87

Robert Ginsberg
**Executive Editor**

**Associate Editors**

G. John M. Abbarno
Mary-Rose Barral
Kenneth A. Bryson
H. G. Callaway
Rem B. Edwards
Rob Fisher
William C. Gay
Dane R. Gordon
J. Everet Green
Heta Häyry
Matti Häyry

Richard T. Hull
Joseph C. Kunkel
Vincent L. Luizzi
Alan Milchman
George David Miller
Peter A. Redpath
Alan Rosenberg
Arleen Salles
John R. Shook
Alan Soble
John R. Welch

a volume in
**Nordic Value Studies**
**NVS**
Heta Häyry and Matti Häyry, Editors

# FRENCH EXISTENTIALISM

## Consciousness, Ethics, and Relations with Others

Edited by
James Giles

Amsterdam - Atlanta, GA 1999

∞ The paper on which this book is printed meets the requirements of "ISO 9706:1994, Information and documentation - Paper for documents - Requirements for permanence".

ISBN: 90-420-0488-6
©Editions Rodopi B.V., Amsterdam - Atlanta, GA 1999
Printed in The Netherlands

# Contents

|  | Editorial Foreword | 1 |
|---|---|---|
|  | Acknowledgements | 5 |
|  | Introduction<br>*James Giles* | 7 |
| ONE | The Duality in Sartre's Account of Reflective Consciousness<br>*Elizabeth Murray Morelli* | 19 |
| TWO | Merleau-Ponty and the Sensory<br>*Edmond Wright* | 33 |
| THREE | French Existential Ethics and the Creation of Value<br>*Matthew Kieran* | 59 |
| FOUR | The Ethical Concept of "Assuming" in the Existential Philosophy of Sartre and Beauvoir<br>*Terry Keefe* | 87 |
| FIVE | The Origins of Beauvoir's Existential Philosophy<br>*Margaret A. Simons* | 107 |
| SIX | Sartre's Critique of Humanism<br>*Juliette Simont* | 125 |
| SEVEN | Marcel, Hope, and Virtue<br>*Philip Stratton-Lake* | 139 |
| EIGHT | Sartre, Sexual Desire, and Relations with Others<br>*James Giles* | 155 |
| NINE | Useless Passions?<br>*Thomas Jones* | 175 |
| TEN | Struggling with the Other: Gender and Race in the Youthful Writings of Camus<br>*Christine Margerrison* | 191 |
|  | About the Contributors | 213 |
|  | Index | 215 |

# EDITORIAL FOREWORD

Existentialism in France is one of the most sustained attempts made by philosophers of that country to find an alternative to the objective idealism of Hegel on the one hand and naturalistic objectivism on the other. Yet all three of these movements are initiated by a desire for concreteness of one sort or another. The concreteness of Hegelianism is that of concresence, growing together. Itself motivated by a drive to overcome opposition, the Hegelian dialectic progresses by the absorption of dualities into higher-level unities. The concreteness of naturalism is paradigmatically that of tangible solidity, of the stone which Dr. Johnson kicks in order to refute Bishop Berkeley. But this sensory concreteness lends itself to conceptualization in ever more general abstract forms and structures. The claims to fundamentality either of this concrete experience or of the ideas of the so-called primary qualities adduced to explain it are challenged by both Hegelian phenomenology and by the phenomenology of Edmund Husserl.

Sartre draws on both of these phenomenologies, the phenomenology of spirit and the phenomenology of perception. This is what gives rise to the tension distinctive of his account of the human condition. The end toward which the Hegelian dialectic aspires is compared by Hegel himself to the thinking of thinking which Aristotle ascribes to divinity. This would be the absolution from a history conceived as the interiorization and remembering of something which is in the first place external. Sartre retains this ideal in which the in-itself and for-itself would become one. But whereas Hegel's self-styled philosophical Christianism sees the Passion achieving its ideal with the individual subject "realizing" itself—in the gnosiological, ontological and, indeed, financial senses of that word—as Self, the passion as described by Sartre is bound to suffer frustration. This is because Sartre, while endorsing Hegel's formal characterization of the end of human existence as "for-itself-in-itself," endorses also Husserl's principle of intentionality to the effect that all consciousness is objective consciousness of something other than itself, even if at the same time it is non-objective consciousness (of) itself: self-consciousness. The identity of this self-consciousness is no more than that which it borrows from its determining itself as other than the object of which it is conscious. The total transparency of Aristotelian *noêseôs noêsis* and of Hegel's adaptation of this is replaced by a partial transparency of a for-itself noetico-noematically "othering" itself against an in-itself which is totally opaque.

The concreteness which Sartre and other French existentialists and existentialistes seek to save is that of the inhabiting of a world with others which Husserl calls the *Lebenswelt*; Sartre's and Merleau-Ponty's approaches here are the basis for the discussions in Chapters One and Two of the present volume. Phenomenological existentialism purports to show how the way of ideas pursued either rationalistically or sensualistically deviates and derives from the ways of being in the world as "existed," where this verb is transitively parsed. This transitive and transcending syntax of existence follows from the intentionality signified by the hyphenation of noesis-noema. Now Husserl's descriptions of the many ways of consciousness—paving the way, along with Franz Brentano and again Aristotle, for Heidegger's analyses of the many ways of being—are Cartesian meditations. For they inherit Descartes's double use of the words *cogitatio* and *pensée* to refer both to reflective cognitive thinking and to any of the states of consciousness upon which one may reflect: states of intellectual awareness, but also imaginings, willings, feelings, and so forth. The liberation from intellectualism which existentialism in France effects is facilitated by the most intellectualist philosopher of that land. This is an irony that would have delighted the Danish ironist Kierkegaard, whose attempt to subvert Hegelian and any other kind of systematicity is a further inspiration for philosophers of existence in France, thanks in particular to the transmission through Heidegger of Kierkegaard's notion that truth dwells in "subjectivity."

How do you transmit such a notion? How do you share it with someone? How do you propound it? How can the attempt to express it in philosophical propositions not be as self-defeating as the desire to unite consciousness and its object? Is it surprising that on the eastern side of the Rhine Heidegger finds himself having recourse to an idiom which is essentially poietic or a meditation on poetry and that on the other side Marcel, Sartre, Beauvoir, and Camus, as pointed out in the Introduction, supplement their more recognizably philosophical treatises by writing novels and plays and biographies—or supplement these latter by writing philosophy?

The Kierkegaardian ancestry of French existentialism—which itself makes the study of French existentialism also a study of Nordic thinking—manifests itself too in the manner in which its preoccupation with salvation differs from that of Hegel. One may mention only Marcel's soft spot for British Hegelianism to begin to understand why his "Christian existentialism" (a title he repudiated for his own thinking anyway) was eclipsed and rendered unfashionable by the "atheistic" version of Sartre. During and in the aftermath of the Second World War any kind of totalism was suspected of carrying a threat of totalitarianism. Even Kantian humanism could seem to risk an idolatry of a moral law under which human beings are cases, albeit with equal indefeasible rights. Once more the concreteness and uniqueness of this and that human being are endangered. But the existentialist road to the protection of human singularity and freedom all too often begins and ends with the first person singular, whether as the *mig, mig, mig* of Kierkegaard fixated on the salvation of his soul, or as an egologism, if not egoism, where I am required to assume within the circle of my own projecting the contingency of my being hurled into existence alongside others, and where this assuming is a subjective-existentialist rejigging of objective-idealist and objectivist-materialist

*Foreword*

*aufheben*. But by what or by whom or by Whom is this assumption required? By nothing other than myself who, on Sartre's account at any rate, am nothing but nothingness. As shown in Chapter Three, there are obvious difficulties with this view. So the preoccupation with saving myself has to be qualified by the rider that any essential content possessed by this self is due to the self's own existing of what it thus transitively exists. The essentiality is accidental. The self, as Nietzsche says, is no more than a grammatical fiction. I, as Arthur Rimbaud says, am another—*Je est un autre*—down there in the past sedimented by my choices, choices which cannot be justified by appeal to any ground that is not in principle itself a ground on which one has chosen to stand and which one could in principle choose to quit. In principle, essentially, necessarily, necessity, essence, and principiality or firstness come second.

Here, repeating what Kierkegaard's one-time hero Schelling did to Hegel, necessity is made contingent upon contingency. And contingency is subjected to the necessity of each singular person's being condemned to be free. Decision is contaminated by undecidability. Contaminated and leavened by it. For French existentialism, far from being a philosophy of despair, and becoming in Marcel (as Chapter Six makes clear) and in Sartre's later Marxist version of it a philosophy of hope, is a declaration of the dignity of woman and of man, not simply under the moral law, as that dignity is defined by Kant, but, in both senses of the preposition, *before* the law.

One could therefore say that a "deconstruction" of essentialism takes place both in phenomenological existentialism such as one finds in the writings of Sartre, where homage is still paid to the dialectical negativity operative in the methods of Hegel and Marx, and too in existential phenomenology such as is practiced in the writings of Merleau-Ponty, where the ambiguity of incarnation (see Chapter Two) is more pivotal than opposition and where Descartes's answer to Princess Elizabeth of Bohemia blunts the edge of his dualism. At least, one could say what I have just said if the word that I scare-quoted in saying it is taken to mark a work of mourning which, neither reifying the past or the passed nor expecting the future to be logically or causally deducible from it, recollects what it lets go *pour mieux sauter*. Especially at the passing of the millenium, the millenium which saw the birth of French existentialism, it is gratifying to have that service performed as attentively and comprehensively as it is by the studies contained in this volume.

John Llewelyn
Formerly Reader in Philosophy
University of Edinburgh

# ACKNOWLEDGEMENTS

Earlier versions of most of the chapters in this volume were originally presented at a conference of the British Society for the History of Philosophy in 1996 at Madingley Hall, University of Cambridge. I therefore express my graditude both to the staff of Madingley Hall, particularly Linda Fisher, and to the officers of the Society, particularly Stuart Brown and Pauline Phemister, for their help in organizing and holding the conference. I also thank Linda Chusid and Terry Keefe for translating Chapter Six, Terry Keefe for his further help and support at various stages in the preparation of this volume, the Executive Editor Robert Ginsberg for his time and effort with the copy-editing, the Special Series Editor Matti Häyry for his kind help in bringing this book to publication, and Cherry Ekins for her invaluable editorial assistance. I also express my gratitude to Sylvie Le Bon de Beauvoir for her permission to print passages from Simone de Beauvoir's 1927 Diary. Finally, I give a special thanks to John Llewelyn, both for writing the Foreword and for his continued support.

James Giles

# INTRODUCTION

## James Giles

French existentialism is a school of thought which belongs at once to both French philosophy and existential philosophy. It is the intersection of these two traditions which gives French existentialism its distinctive style and approach. This is not to say that any French philosopher whose philosophy can be described as existential is therefore a French existentialist, at least not in the specific historical-philosophical sense in which the term is normally understood. This is because the term "French existentialism" in its common usage normally refers to a certain philosophical movement which, beginning in the 1930s, culminates in the reaction of a group of French, and mainly Parisian, intellectuals to the horrors of German wartime occupation, and which eventually subsides in the early 1950s under a burgeoning wave of French Marxism. Thus, French existentialism is clearly related to a specific epoch and even a specific geographical location. This historical-geographical placing of French existentialism is further underlined by the fact that the major leaders of the movement also knew each other well and frequently worked together. Indeed, two of the major French existentialists, Jean-Paul Sartre and Simone de Beauvoir, were both lovers and life-long companions. And this is why it would be something of a misnomer to call, say, Blaise Pascal (1623-1662) a French existentialist. Although he is French and shows many existential themes in his writings, he is nevertheless a philosopher who lived and wrote in the seventeenth century and is consequently pursuing his existentialism with quite different concerns in mind and under quite different assumptions from those that characterize the group of thinkers of the 1940s.

It is for similar reasons that the distinctive concerns and focus of the French existentialists are often lost when, as frequently happens, discussions of existentialism fail to distinguish between French existentialism and the existentialism of German, Scandinavian, Russian, and other thinkers. In this way the contributions that are particular to the French existentialists are often submerged into a more general view of existentialist thought. None of this is to say that there are not important similarities between the French existentialists and earlier French thinkers or existentialists from other cultures. Nor is it to say that the French existentialists were not strongly influenced by these other philosophers. It is rather to say that the style of philosophy developed by the French existentialists shows a uniqueness and cohesion which marks it off in important ways from other schools of thought. It would be a mistake, however, to conclude that because French existentialism made its appearance and flourished during a certain epoch that its insights have little relevance for contemporary philosophy and thought. For as is evidently true, all philosophical ideas are in some sense tied to the specific social and historical milieux in which they appear. But their being so tied does not mean they cannot speak to a broader base of human experience.

When one considers the diverse range of philosophers who are often referred to as existentialists, it is difficult to see what exactly such thinkers have in common. Because of this difficulty, Mary Warnock argues that what distinguishes existentialism from other types of philosophy is essentially its practical focus.[1] Existentialism is a philosophy which is meant to be have practical consequences in our day-to-day lives. Thus, although many non-existentialist philosophers might want us to intellectually consider the view that human beings are, say, free to make ethical choices, the existentialists' concern here is rather that we experience our free will as a concrete reality and that such an experience has consequences in how we choose to live our lives. It is in a similar way that other commentators argue that existentialism is a method of doing philosophy rather than a particular subject matter within philosophy. Although this may be true of existentialists in general, when it comes to the work of the French existentialists, there seems to be a definite focus on a particular subject matter, namely, the nature of concrete human existence. It is, therefore, the human being and those concrete aspects of his or her lived experience which are the subject matter of French existentialism. Thus, Beauvoir's ground-breaking book, *The Second Sex,* was written, she tells us, simply because "one day I wanted to explain myself to myself." Likewise, Gabriel Marcel claims that his existential philosophy grew out of his own personal experience, a fact aptly reflected in the title of his work, *Metaphysical Journal*. This is also the basis of his famous claim that "we do not study problems of philosophy, we *are* those problems."

This focus on the lived experience of the existing individual also helps to explain another of the distinguishing marks of this school of philosophy; namely, its literary method. While many contemporary philosophers seem to feel that standard philosophical prose based on the argumentative essay or treatise is the only proper means for doing philosophy, many of the French existentialists make liberal use of the different genres of writing—including philosophical prose, fiction, drama, the diary, and biography—to present their ideas. Thus, of the five leading figures in French existentialism (that is, Sartre, Beauvoir, Maurice Merleau-Ponty, Gabriel Marcel, and Albert Camus), only Merleau-Ponty keeps to philosophical prose as a means for presenting his philosophy—which might help to explain why some commentators have chosen not to see Merleau-Ponty as an existentialist. However, even a cursory consideration of his work will show that he is intimately concerned with the same issues and deploys much the same approach as the other French existentialists do in their non-literary works. Beauvoir and Camus, on the other hand, are quite partial in their use of literature over standard philosophical essays and treatises. The use of such a method is not, however, without an underlying purpose. For it has its origins in what is the paramount concern of French existentialism; namely, the concrete existence of the individual. And fiction, drama, and biography are well-suited to laying bare the structure and vicissitudes of such an existence. This primary concern for the experience of the individual also helps to explain why those areas of philosophy which seem only distantly related to the immediate concerns of human existence—the problem of universals, and the philosophy of science and mathematics, for example—have received little attention from the French existentialists.

On the other hand, those areas which seem directly relevant to human life have received intensive study. Three such areas of existentialist enquiry are the nature of consciousness, ethics, and relations with others. These areas, which form the three main themes of this book, are all interrelated aspects of the human condition which are continually present to us through our daily lives. To exist as a human being is to be conscious, and it is through consciousness that we perceive the world about us, that which we take to be ourselves, and our relation to others. It is also through consciousness that we think, contemplate, undergo emotions, and struggle with our ethical concerns. In studying the nature of consciousness many of these philosophers employ phenomenological techniques in their investigation—techniques which aim at a purely descriptive account of the contents of consciousness. Not only does phenomenological investigation seek to eliminate or at least suspend various theoretical commitments—commitments which can distort our perception of the data—but, further, it seeks to disclose the lived experience of the individual: a disclosure of paramount concern to French existentialism.

The point about experiencing our ethical concerns brings us to our second theme; namely, the ethical dimension of human existence. Ethics, or the question of how I ought to live, what I ought to value, and how I should relate to others, is also an ever-present feature of human existence. Some philosophers have tried to argue that ethical questions only arise in specific circumstances, such as when I am faced with a particular dilemma about whether or not I should keep a promise. From the point of view of French existentialism, however, every action implies a commitment to a certain value or set of values. Each time I act, I have necessarily decided on one action rather than another, and in doing so I have shown that I value one action, or the consequences of one action, over others. The problem of what action I ought to take or what things I ought to value is particularly acute when it comes to our relations with others. For that which above all other aspects of our world fills us with happiness, sorrow, fear, or longing, is other people. Consequently, the question of my relations to others is one which is brimming over with ethical concerns. Related to these ethical concerns is also the question of the nature of our relations to others. Behind the question of how we ought to live with others is the question of how we *do* live with others, and why our relationships take the particular paths they do. Because of their focus on the lived experience of the individual, existentialist accounts here often take the form of phenomenological descriptions of how a person undergoes particular types of relations to others. It is through their richness that such accounts are able to disclose the structure of a relationship and the hopes, fears, and desires that drive it. Here we are able to see the intricacies of human interaction and of the relations that the various interpersonal attitudes have to one another.

French existentialism's focus on the concrete experience of the individual is one which clearly has a French ancestry, going back at least to the skeptical fideists of the sixteenth century. Michel de Montaigne (1533-1592), for example, saw his skeptical essays as being essentially a self-portrait, a picture of his personal attempts to deal with his skepticism. Similarly, Francisco Sanches (1551-1623) and others argued that knowledge could only be gained on a personal level with the individual turning his or her gaze inward to the facts of inner experience. This focus on the inner existence of the individual as a way to knowledge reached one of its best-known expressions with the reflections of René Descartes (1596-1650), who, wanting to discover whether or not humans could ever have indubitable knowledge, began by turning his focus inward to his own consciousness and systematically doubting his own thoughts until he arrived at something he felt he could not doubt; namely, his own existence. This conclusion is expressed in his famous claim, "I think, therefore I am." One can wonder just how particular or "individualistic" such an "I" could be—an I about which nothing can be known save that it exists and thinks—but still the technique of focusing on the individual is clearly present. Descartes, it should be noted, also had a strong interest in mathematics and physics (as did Pascal). This, however, only shows the breadth of his interests (another feature common to the French tradition) and does not affect the fact that he also started his skeptical investigations by the exploration of concrete experience. The interest in science is one which ties in with another but separate tradition in French philosophy; namely, the philosophy of science.

This reliance on concrete experience is also found in the works of Pascal. Although Pascal strongly rejected much of Montaigne's and Descartes's approach to philosophy—seeing Montaigne's skepticism as a mask for his atheism and Descartes's use of reason as inadequate—he nevertheless was in full agreement with their focus on the particular experience of the individual. For Pascal, however, it was the experience of the "heart," as he called it, rather than that of reason that was of importance. Too much of human existence is, contra Descartes, unclear and indistinct for reason to be of much use. The answer is to be found by reflecting on the intuitive experiences of the heart, experiences that need no reason to support them. It is worth noting here that a similar concept is also found in Jean-Jacques Rousseau's (1712-1778) notion of "sentiment." Sentiment is likewise a human faculty through which one undergoes experiences—such as the experience of my own existence or freedom—which stand outside the realm of logical proofs but whose veridicality, he thought, are known immediately.

The importance of immediate experience was also argued for by the spiritualist philosopher Maine de Biran (1766-1824), who sought to base his entire philosophy on the immediate knowledge the individual has of his or her own volitional efficacy. Although we can never perceive causal power, we nevertheless have a direct and intimate awareness of such a power whenever we will to act. This awareness of our own volitional power, our willed effort, is the most fundamental awareness we have. And, according to Maine de Biran, it is through the use of this awareness that one comes to interpret and understand all other categories of existence. Maine de Biran is criticized here by Sartre who argues that the experience of a "willed effort" does not really exist. Sartre's critique, however, is based on his own phenomenological investigation, and thus, despite his disagreement about the existence of such a volitional power, is nevertheless in agreement with Maine de Biran about what counts as a testing ground for such a view; namely, an exploration of the concrete experience of the individual.

The views of Maine de Biran were upheld by his follower Félix Ravaisson-Mollien (1813-1900). In his attempt to propagate the views of his mentor, Ravaisson unleashed an attack on the positivism of the time. During the nineteenth century science was making significant advances. This had the effect of encouraging many philosophers to attempt an imitation of scientific methodology. Ravaisson, however, argued that the internal world of the mind could not be studied by the scientific methods used for observation of the external world. This is because conscious phenomena do not exist in the spatial and objectified way that the objects of the external world do. Among other things, the world of the mind contains within it its own individuality, something unliving matter necessarily lacks. Thus, argued Ravaisson, any attempt to adopt a scientific methodology in the study of the mind would necessarily distort our understanding of its nature.

Ravaisson's notion of an internal and personal world which cannot be explained in terms of the external world is a theme which was pursued by Henri Bergson (1859-1941). Here again we find the same emphasis on personal experience. For Bergson the realm of individuality is found in the time of inner experience, something he calls "duration." Duration is different from the time of the external world. For while external time can be seen in terms of events which occur "earlier than" or "later than" other events, with no essential relation to any particular point, in duration time is always seen from a particular point, namely, the present in which the individual exists. That is, duration always involves a reference to one's own temporal existence, and consequently time here is, like one's existence, intrinsically directional.

Further, unlike external time, duration is not precisely measurable, nor are past, present, and future—which intermingle and flow like the waters of a stream—clearly distinct. It is this duration that constitutes the innermost individuality and uniqueness of each person.

In this progression of ideas, ideas which focus on the fundamental role of lived experience and the importance of the individual, one can easily discern the basis of French existentialism. I have only touched on a few French philosophers, but hope nevertheless to have given an idea of the continuity of French thought and the roots from which French existentialism eventually sprang. This continuity of French thought is one which has been noted by various scholars. William Barrett, for example, tells us, "French culture has in these matters a marvelous sense of conservation. The most inbred of cultures it is nevertheless among the richest because it preserves and elaborates what it has in its own kitchen." This is not only true of French philosophy but, as the reference to "kitchen" might lead one to suppose, it "is also the spirit of French cooking, which does not throw away anything but uses it to create a stock—the fundamental element in cooking."[2]

It would be a mistake to suppose, however, that French existentialism was not affected by ideas from outside France. On the contrary, French existentialism was strongly influenced by the ideas of philosophers like Georg Wilhelm Friedrich Hegel, Søren Kierkegaard, Friedrich Nietzsche, Edmund Husserl, and Martin Heidegger. But one of the likely reasons why the ideas of these thinkers made such an impact on French existentialism is because the way to an acceptance of their ideas had already been opened up by earlier French thinkers like those who have just been discussed. Thus the French philosophical interest in concrete experience and the human condition provided a receptive ground for the development of Hegel's account of the slave and master relation. For even though Hegel himself showed little concern for the lived existence of the individual, his ideas about the slave-master dialectic provided a basis from which the French existentialists could construct their accounts of concrete human relations. In a similar way, one of the reasons why Kierkegaard, who was himself influenced by Pascal, had such an effect on the French existentialists is because his attack on the idea of objectivity and his account of subjective truth and inwardness fit well with and elaborate in new ways the concept of the individual and concrete experience, ideas which, as we have seen, were already in one form or another part of the French tradition. The same is true for the individualism of Nietzsche and his idea of a master morality in which the noble person conceives of the concept of good "spontaneously out of himself." Such a view harmonized with earlier French ideas about the sovereignty of the individual and pointed the way to French existential ethics and the idea of the creation of value. Likewise, Husserl's account of phenomenology, with its bracketing the question of existence and its systematic focus on the experience of ideas, also echoed the French interest in individual experience and, through its rigorousness, gave the existentialists a systematic framework for exploring human existence from the perspective of the existing individual.

The same can also be said of Heidegger, who had a special influence on Sartre. Heidegger's project of giving an account of existence from the perspective of the individual, or what he calls "*Dasein*" (there-being), is a project which has important affinities with the ideas of, among others, Maine de Biran, Ravaisson, and Bergson. And it is natural therefore that Sartre, who was also much influenced by Bergson, should show an interest in the philosophy of his senior contemporary Heidegger. However, despite the views of some commentators, there are important and basic differences between the philosophy of Sartre and Heidegger. Thus, although Heidegger, like Sartre, is normally referred to as an existentialist (though he himself rejected the label), his avowed interest is not, like Sartre, human existence, but rather what he calls "being." Thus, Heidegger's reason for embarking on his famous analysis of human existence in *Being and Time* is foremost because he feels that only through such an analysis can he arrive at an understanding of what is his primary interest: non-human "being." This is not to say that *Dasein* does not play a major role in Heidegger's philosophy; for according to Heidegger the existence of being depends on the "opening" or "clearing" in being that is offered by *Dasein*. Still, the overall focus of Heidegger's approach is on being itself. This primary interest in being, rather than in human beings, is perhaps also one of the underlying reasons why Heidegger rejects the notion of consciousness—a notion which is fundamental to the French existentialists—in favor of the notion of *Dasein*'s relation to the world, a relation he terms "being-in-the-world."[3] Also fundamental to the French existentialists' analysis of the human condition are the notions of gender, sexuality, and race, notions which are also of current philosophical concern. Heidegger's *Dasein*, on the other hand, is presented as genderless, non-sexual, and raceless. With this it is understandable why another French-reared, though not existentialist, philosopher, Emmanuel Levinas, could attack Heidegger's philosophy as being impersonal and non-ethical.

Although the French existentialists have been quite creative in dealing with each of these interrelated areas, there are nevertheless, as with all attempts to deal with such fundamental problems, numerous difficulties besetting their accounts. The purpose of this book is therefore to engage philosophically the ideas of the major French existentialists—namely Beauvoir, Merleau-Ponty, Marcel, Camus, and, because of his central and leading role in the movement, particularly Sartre—in a critical manner in an attempt to elucidate both their shortcomings and their contributions to contemporary thought. Because of the broad approach taken by the French existentialists, this engagement will also make use of contemporary research in such areas as the psychology of perception, developmental psychology, sexology, feminism, gender studies, cultural studies, and literary theory. For recent discussion in these fields provides new material with which to evaluate the arguments of these philosophers. This evaluation is done by each of the volume's contributors focusing on how one or more of the French existentialists deals with one or more of the themes of consciousness, ethics, and relations with others. Thus Elizabeth Murray Morelli and Edmond Wright look at the problem of consciousness and perception; Morelli exploring Sartre's account and Wright exploring Merleau-Ponty's. In the chapter, "The Duality in Sartre's Account of Reflective Consciousness," Morelli examines Sartre's phenomenology of consciousness and attempts to elaborate on the nature of reflective consciousness as described by Sartre in his early works. She starts by criticizing some of the distinctions Sartre draws between types of consciousness and attempting to revise them. She then raises the central question of her chapter: can one's present reflective act be given to itself in the present? Sartre, Morelli, points out, seems to give a negative response here, but his answer remains ambiguous. In attempting to pursue this question, she explores how Sartre imports his notion of duality in the witness/observed model of ordinary reflective consciousness into his account of reflective consciousness. She concludes by trying to show how the difficulties inherent in this approach might be avoided by using a non-dualistic model.

In "Merleau-Ponty and the Sensory," Wright also examines an existentialist account of the phenomenology of consciousness, but here the existentialist is Merleau-Ponty and the consciousness examined is sensory consciousness. Wright's examination deals with Merleau-Ponty's rejection of the notion of a nonconceptual sensory base for perception. Working from the Gestalt psychologists' dismissal of the notion of an internal sensory mosaic, Merleau-Ponty argues for a "living" relationship between the body and its environment, stressing the inter-subjective nature of perception which enabled its continuous adjustment. Wright argues that although Merleau-Ponty's conclusion can be sustained, the premise in which he rejects a non-conceptual base leads him to inconsistency.

The theme of ethics is then introduced by Matthew Kieran in "French Existential Ethics and the Creation of Value." Here Kieran critically examines what an existential ethic may look like and whether it could prove adequate. He does this by setting forth a general account of French existentialist ethics and exploring both the traditional criticisms raised against them, and recent attempts by existential scholars to deal with the inadequacies of the existentialist account. The virtue of French existentialism is its emphasis on the spirit in which the action is chosen. Indeed, the recognition of my own self-conscious existence and freedom justifiably precludes me from murdering or oppressing others. Furthermore, as distinct from Kant, the French existentialists, particularly Sartre and Beauvoir, hold that there are necessarily numerous distinct and particular moral ideals we may freely and blamelessly choose to pursue. Yet, Kieran argues, despite the recent attempts by Catalano, Golomb, and others, existential ethics can only hope to be partially adequate because of the fundamental failure to recognize, at least regarding certain basic general principles of categorical morality, that there are the right sort of things our motivations and actions should be directed toward.

A different approach to existential ethics is taken by Terry Keefe in "The Ethical Concept of 'Assuming' in the Existential Philosophy of Sartre and Beauvoir." Here we are given a philosophical analysis of a central (and largely overlooked) concept which is fundamental to the ethics of Sartre and Beauvoir. The concept of "assuming"—as in "assuming responsibility"—is one which is employed by both Sartre and Beauvoir in a variety of senses. To find the most coherent interpretation, Keefe examines all Sartre's uses of this concept in both *Being and Nothingness* and other philosophical writings up to the end of the 1940s. He then explores the question of whether Beauvoir merely inherited the concept from Sartre, or whether she uses it in her own distinctive way.

Keeping with the thought of Beauvoir, all three themes of this book—consciousness, ethics, and relations with others—are then dealt with by Margaret A. Simons in "The Origins of Beauvoir's Existential Philosophy." Simons here analyzes Beauvoir's recently discovered 1927 diary, tracing the origins of Beauvoir's philosophy to her philosophical reflections on her own experience. In recounting her struggle against despair and the fragmentation of self in the diary, Beauvoir affirms her commitment to doing philosophy, defines a literary philosophical method valuing concrete lived experience, and lays the groundwork for a theory of consciousness as nothingness and a theory of a narrative self. The theme of ethics is apparent in Beauvoir's early concern with the temptation of self-deception in religious faith and her affirmation of the value of lucidity, that form the core of her condemnation of bad faith. Beauvoir's interest in relations with others is evident in her philosophical theme of the opposition of self and others. Simons rejects a Sartrean context for reading this opposition as the problem of solipsism, arguing instead for reading Beauvoir's ethics as addressing what the feminist psychologist Carol Gilligan defines as the central moral problem for women: that of reconciling adulthood and femininity.

Another idea which plays a central role in existential ethics is the idea of humanism. Sartre's ambivalent relation to this pivotal existential idea is discussed by Juliette Simont in "Sartre's Critique of Humanism." The purpose of Simont's chapter is to articulate the numerous criticisms of humanism which are scattered throughout Sartre's work, while exploring the assumption of a humanism which belongs to Sartre himself. In doing so Simont attempts to answer the question of whether the humanism portrayed in *Existentialism and Humanism* is a retreat from the somewhat harsh views in *Nausea* and thus designed to reassure those who have been frightened by the radicalism of the work. Or is there really a form of specific universality in the humanism which Sartre advocates which is itself irreducible to the types of human universality which he criticizes?

In the final chapter on the theme of ethics, "Marcel, Hope, and Virtue"—a chapter which also ties over to the problem of relations with others—Philip Stratton-Lake examines the work of one of the most neglected French existentialists, Gabriel Marcel. As Stratton-Lake shows, however, Marcel offers some important and original contributions to a philosophical analysis of the concept of hope. According to Stratton-Lake, on the standard account, where hope is analyzed in terms of a desire for something plus a belief that the thing desired is in some degree obtainable, it is not at all clear why hope might be seen as a virtue. And yet it commonly is so perceived. Marcel, however, claims that hope cannot be understood in accordance with the standard account. He thus offers an alternative existential account which, Stratton-Lake argues, enables one to see why hope may rightly be considered as a virtue.

With this we come to focus on the third existentialist theme of the book: relations with others. In my chapter on this theme, "Sartre, Sexual Desire, and Relations with Others," I try to give a detailed critique of Sartre's account of interpersonal relations and the role played by sexual desire in such relations. Sartre begins his account by dividing human relations into two primary attitudes, the first including love and masochism, and the second including indifference, sexual desire, sadism, and hate. There are, however, many difficulties with this account. A central difficulty is that although sexual desire is first presented as being merely one more of the various attitudes, Sartre later argues that it is an attitude which is somehow present in all other attitudes. However, as given by Sartre, these two accounts are inconsistent with each other. Drawing on the work of developmental and social psychologists, an account of human relations and sexual desire is given which shows how, once the ontogenic aspect is taken into consideration, a sense then exists in which all the attitudes to others are, as Sartre says, instances of sexual desire.

One type of relation with others which has received much attention in French existential writing is the relation of love. Sartre's well-known views on love and the problems that these views face are discussed in Chapter Nine, "Useless Passions?" In this chapter Thomas Jones shows how, for Sartre, we engage in the conscious project of love in order to realize a value. That value is being loved—we love in order to be loved. But, says Jones, one ought to consider sexual desire more explicitly in the phenomenology of love. A consideration of Merleau-Ponty's concept of embodied consciousness reveals that love is not only a conscious project, but that it is also the organization of prepersonal and organic sexual desire into a conscious project. One should also consider how Sartre's view presupposes a cultural organization of love in the form of our culture-specific tradition of romantic love. A further problem, argues Jones, is that Sartre does not consider the possibility of the authenticity of love. Seeing love as authentic friendship allows one to conceptualize a passion for others that is not ontologically doomed and useless.

Two aspects of relations with others which are of concern to the French existentialists—notably Beauvoir, Sartre, and Camus—are the aspects of gender and race. In the last chapter in the book, "Struggling with the Other: Gender and Race in the Youthful Writings of Camus," Christine Margerrison offers an in-depth criticism of how these concepts affect the early literary efforts of Camus. Here we are introduced to the literary approach of one of the major French existentialists and see how he attempted to deploy literature as a means for analysis of human relations. However, as Margerrison shows, the youthful Camus's biased attitude to the notions of gender and race produces a distorting effect in his accounts of relations with others. For, as a consideration of these early works suggests, that which underlies Camus's notion of the other is the notions of the other gender and the other race. Margerrison shows how the encounters with the other portrayed in these early works are typically given as encounters with the Arab world of French Algeria, or with women—women as either mother figures or as sexual partners. The vulnerability that Camus portrays in both these encounters—or rather struggles—with the other is one which is intimately linked with the issue of sexuality—the natural property of woman as a sexual partner. This sexuality is then projected on to the "colonial other." Although such a portrayal of human relations focuses on but one area of human interaction, it nevertheless does so in a way that enables one to gain an understanding of how an existing individual might construct and deploy a map of the interpersonal world.

The arguments in this book, it is hoped, will help to bring forward the specific focus and concerns of the French existentialists and, through an engagement with their ideas in terms of current philosophical thinking, explore their insights into the nature of human existence.[4]

## Notes

1. Mary Warnock, *Existentialism* (Oxford: Oxford University Press, 1971), pp. 1-2.

2. William Barrett, *Irrational Man: A Study in Existential Philosophy* (New York: Doubleday Anchor Books, 1962), p. 114.

3. See Joseph P. Fell, *Heidegger and Sartre: An Essay on Being and Place* (New York: Columbia University Press, 1979).

4. I thank John Llewelyn for his helpful comments on this introduction.

# One

# THE DUALITY IN SARTRE'S ACCOUNT OF REFLECTIVE CONSCIOUSNESS

## Elizabeth Murray Morelli

Sartre is indisputably the pre-eminent French existentialist. Yet my focus in this chapter is not on Sartre as an existentialist, but on Sartre as a phenomenologist. Not every existentialist employs the rigorous scientific method founded by Husserl, and clearly Sartre's own creativity was not confined to phenomenological enquiry. Nevertheless, not only are his phenomenological descriptions richly nuanced and valuable in themselves as contributions to a contemporary understanding of consciousness, but, further, they are foundational to his existentialism.

But what has Sartrean phenomenology to offer philosophy as it is practiced today? Contemporary philosophy is in the curious position of finding itself "after philosophy." Some philosophers are no longer interested in defending their enterprise against the charges of present-day Callicles; they are declaring philosophy obsolete. If truth is relative, objectivity a sham, metaphysics impossible, and authenticity suspect, then what is there for philosophers to do? Should we be content, as some suggest, to be professional story-tellers who serve only to sustain a perhaps pointless conversation? Husserl's response to the crises of the sciences earlier in this century was to seek a ground in the field of immanence. It was within conscious intentionality that he sought the well-spring of historically emergent commonsense, scientific and philosophic principles, theories, and systems. If we have grown weary of conflicting arguments and ideologies, it seems we can do one of two things. We can despair of the search for truth altogether, and abandon philosophy as a discipline, or we can follow the lead of those thinkers in the twentieth century for whom the scandal of philosophical conflict serves to re-animate, rather than to eliminate, their philosophical desire for the truth, and who turn our enquiries to that realm which gives rise to all philosophical positions—the realm of conscious intentionality.

Sartre's phenomenological enquiries into consciousness are to be found in his early works, such as *The Transcendence of the Ego*, *The Psychology of the Imagination*, and *Being and Nothingness*. It is his account of consciousness—particularly reflective consciousness—to which I now turn.

The question, "What is reflective consciousness?" brings to mind Augustine's epigram regarding the nature of time: "If no one asks me, I know; if I want to explain it to someone who does ask me, I do not know."[1] The special difficulty of giving an account of reflective consciousness was lamented by Kierkegaard:

> The most concrete content that consciousness can have is consciousness of itself, of the individual himself—not the pure self-consciousness, but the self-consciousness that is so concrete that no author, not even the one with the greatest power of description, has ever been able to describe a single such self consciousness, although every single human being is one.[2]

While Kierkegaard apparently despairs of giving an account of this consciousness, Sartre applies his own great power of description to the task. But before we examine the key elements of his description, let us consider a problem that arises at the heart of Sartre's account of reflection, a difficulty that calls into question the very possibility of the phenomenological project.

## 1. A Problem with Reflective Consciousness

What access do we as phenomenologists have to reflective consciousness? This question does not concern unreflective conscious activity like, for example, hearing the phone ring or imagining one's friend, because our access to that kind of consciousness is clearly through reflection. The question regards the access we have to the reflective consciousness itself with which we investigate conscious intentionality. According to Sartre, both Descartes and Husserl consider reflection to be a type of "privileged intuition because it apprehends consciousness in an act of present and instantaneous immanence."[3] The certitude sought by the Cartesian introspective method and the evidential apodicity foundational to Husserlian phenomenological method depend upon the "presentness" of the reflective act, its simultaneity with the consciousness reflected on. Sartre proceeds to show, however, that "reflected-reflecting" as given is not possible: "But the totality 'reflected-reflecting,' if it could be given, would be contingency and in-itself. But this totality cannot be attained."[4] In his earlier work, *The Transcendence of the Ego*, he seems to suggest the opposite: "There is an indissoluble unity of the reflecting consciousness and the reflected consciousness (to the point that the reflecting consciousness could not exist without the reflected consciousness)."[5] There appears to be a discrepancy in Sartre's position. Is reflective consciousness simultaneous with the consciousness of which it is conscious, or is it not? On the one hand, he says that the two constitute an indissoluble unity, and on the other hand he says that such a totality as given is not possible. One might resolve this problem by explaining that the passage from *Being and Nothingness* regards how we come to know reflective consciousness and the passage from *The Transcendence of the Ego* regards what reflective consciousness is in itself. If we stick with the assertion that reflective consciousness forms a unity with the consciousness reflected on, we can then ask how is this known? If it simply must be the case because of the very nature of consciousness even if it cannot be given to us as such, then our knowledge of this unity would seem to be the result of a kind of Kantian deduction. If we are to claim some phenomenological knowledge of this indissoluble unity, we must have some conscious access to it. Yet Sartre says that reflected-reflecting cannot be given. Perhaps the key to resolving this seeming discrepancy lies in the difference between reflected-reflecting as a unity and reflected-reflecting as a totality. The unity is asserted but the totality as given is denied. The unity of reflective consciousness and the consciousness reflected on may be both ontologically necessary and phenomenologically possible, while the reflected-reflecting as a totality cannot be given. To be given to consciousness is to be an object for consciousness, but for reflective consciousness to be given as an object would be for it to be wrapped up as a complete package, a finished totality. As such, reflective consciousness would be a perfected in-itself for consciousness, and no longer the on-going consciousness which it is. So, Sartre can be consistent when he claims that reflective consciousness must be united with the consciousness that it reflects upon, and that this unity as a totality cannot be given to consciousness as an object.

An ambiguity has crept into this preliminary discussion. Before we can reformulate our original question regarding access to reflective consciousness, this ambiguity must be addressed. When Sartre writes of the reflected-reflecting, he has in mind the unity of reflection with some original *cogito*. But reflective consciousness itself, that is, reflecting on some *cogito*, must also be accessible to conscious reflection or else this whole discussion would be speculative or deductive. The *cogito* reflected on need not be some perceiving or imagining or feeling, it could be a reflecting. Such a possibility may evoke for the reader an image of the receding curve of reflections created by two opposed mirrors, but reflective consciousness does not entail an infinite regress. Sartre dismisses the conceptualist difficulty of an infinite regression of consciousness at the very first step: "Moreover, there is no infinite regress here, since a consciousness has no need at all of a reflecting consciousness in order to be conscious of itself."[6]

We can refine the initial question regarding access to reflective consciousness. If reflective consciousness, as unified to the consciousness reflected on, is not given as an object to consciousness, what consciousness of reflective consciousness can we have? To put the question in terms of temporality: is it possible to be conscious of reflective consciousness at the same time one is reflectively conscious, and not after the fact through recollection? Before we take up the question directly, let me suggest what difference it makes. Laboring over fine distinctions in the field of conscious intentionality may be intellectually stimulating and challenging, but it may also have about as much impact as discovering that one faint star in a distant galaxy is actually two. The question of the nature of reflective consciousness is, however, the question of the evidential ground of phenomenological enquiry. In his commentary on *Being and Nothingness,* Joseph S. Catalano characterizes the gravity of Sartre's treatment of the nature of reflection: "Sartre realizes that, to a great extent, his entire ontology is here at stake, for reflection is the only means by which the nature of consciousness and the entire ontological description of the for-itself are revealed to the for-itself."[7] If there is some flaw or some minor adjustment to be made, then, in Sartre's account of reflective consciousness, it would have far-reaching repercussions for his ontology. Beyond Sartrean scholarship, the question of the nature of reflective consciousness bears upon our very access to the subject matter of phenomenology.

## 2. Consciousness and Reflective Consciousness

Consciousness for Sartre is always both intentional and self-conscious. Two kinds of consciousness are distinguished: unreflective (also termed pre-reflective) and reflective. Both unreflective and reflective consciousness are characterized as intentional and self-conscious. Both kinds of conscious act are directed toward objects, which stand outside of or over against consciousness. One possible object of consciousness is the self, which is of particular interest in an enquiry into reflective consciousness. But the self *qua* object of intentionality does not enjoy privileged status. It is as transcendent as any other object. The self-consciousness essential to consciousness is not an intuition, objectification, or knowledge of the self. It is, rather, consciousness's awareness of itself. The statement, "Consciousness is self-conscious," is analogous to the statement, "The oven is self-cleaning." As no self in addition to the oven need be present for the oven to be self-cleaning (after all, that is the whole point of this technological innovation), so no self need be posited for consciousness to be self-conscious.

While Sartre characterizes the nature or essence of consciousness as intentional and self-conscious, he nevertheless stresses the non-essential nature of consciousness. The essence of consciousness is to have no essence. Consciousness is not any kind of thing; it has no constitutive components, strata, or compartments. Consciousness is wholly transparent. It follows that it is pure fiction to suppose a dimension of consciousness that is inaccessible to us, that is unconscious. Ontologically, consciousness is the nothingness Sartre names the for-itself. Consciousness has no interior for Sartre:

> If impossible though it be, you could enter "into" a consciousness you would be seized by a whirlwind and thrown back outside, in the thick of the dust, near the tree, for consciousness has no "inside." It is just this being

beyond itself, this absolute flight, this refusal to be a substance which makes it consciousness.[8]

Thus, while Husserl writes of the field of consciousness within which acts and noematic correlates are given, Sartre sets out to dismantle the "illusion of immanence."[9]

Now that we have reviewed the outlines of Sartre's account of consciousness in general, let us turn to the specific nature of reflective consciousness and to its characteristic intentionality and self-consciousness. Sartre defines reflective consciousness in *Being and Nothingness* simply: "Reflection is the for-itself conscious of itself."[10] While reflective consciousness is positional inasmuch as it posits the consciousness of which it is aware, the consciousness which is the object of this reflection may be either positional or non-positional. In most passages in which Sartre describes reflection he has in mind reflection on a non-positional consciousness; for example, consciousness becomes aware of itself as absorbed in counting matches or looking through a keyhole. But the consciousness that reflection becomes aware of may also be itself positional, for example, consciousness becomes aware of itself doing phenomenology, reflecting on reflective consciousness.

The puzzle of reflective consciousness, for Sartre, is that it comprises a duality—the reflecting and the reflected on, and yet reflective consciousness is an ontological identity. A single transparent consciousness with no interior is simultaneously reflective of itself. Sartre encapsulates the paradoxical nature of reflective consciousness in the following: "Here once again we meet that type of being which defines the for-itself: reflection—if it is to be apodictic evidence—demands that the reflective *be* that which is reflected-on. But to the extent that reflection is *knowledge*, the reflected on must necessarily be the *object* for the reflective; and this implies a separation of being."[11]

The intentionality of reflective consciousness is that it is of the consciousness which it is. If it were not, then there would be no absolute givenness as the evidential ground of phenomenological method. And, allow me to restate that we are not only concerned with reflective consciousness of unreflective acts, but also with reflective consciousness of reflective acts themselves. Otherwise Sartre's own account of reflective consciousness would be either deductive or speculative, but not phenomenological.

## 3. Reflection on Reflective Consciousness

The duality at the heart of the unity which is reflective consciousness can be teased out by examining distinctive features of this consciousness. In order to do this, we can employ three distinctions drawn from the intentionality analysis of Bernard Lonergan, whose approach is similar to Husserl's in that his starting point is the data of consciousness although his ultimate position is critical of phenomenological immanentism.[12] The first distinction regards the relation of consciousness to intentionality. The second is a distinction between reflective consciousness as simply experienced and reflective consciousness as known. And the third is a distinction between two senses of object of consciousness.

First, Sartre's differentiation of reflective and unreflective consciousness arises in the context of his critical analysis of Descartes's and Husserl's treatments of the intentional act or *cogito*.[13] The *cogito* is first and foremost an operation or act. How this act is qualified by what kind of consciousness, and whether or not this act is necessarily attached to an ego are secondary. The secondary nature of the relation of the *cogito* to the ego is the focus of Sartre's critique of Husserl. But the secondary nature of the kind of consciousness that qualifies the intentional act is glazed over. Instead Sartre identifies consciousness with the intentional act. As Hazel Barnes explains, "consciousness is the activity of revealing; that is, of reflecting, of intending." Consciousness is neither entity nor substance, but rather "Consciousness is real as activity."[14]

I do not dispute what Sartre calls the "essential principle of phenomenology," adopted from Brentano and Husserl, that "all consciousness is consciousness of something."[15] However, we can question the legitimacy of identifying consciousness with the intentional act. Conversely, we can affirm Sartre's view that every intentional act is self-conscious without identifying the act with consciousness. Consciousness and intentionality can be inseparable without being identical. To employ Lonergan's terminology, consciousness and intentionality are "notionally distinct" but not "really distinct." It would be more accurate to speak of both as characteristics of the act. We could agree with Sartre that all conscious acts are intentional, but add that all intentional acts are conscious, and that it is the act that bears these two characteristics.[16] While this clarification may seem to be a simple logical or categorical distinction, it has, as will be seen, ramifications for the analysis of reflective consciousness. It might appear, however, that the distinction between the intentionality and the consciousness of the act presupposes the foundational role of the act, which in turn seems to conflict with Sartre's account of the constitution of actions in *The Transcendence of the Ego*.[17] To adequately reconcile how the act can be a constituted transcendent and also that of which consciousness and intentionality are characteristics, we must introduce yet another distinction. Sartre suggests a distinction between active consciousness and simply spontaneous consciousness.[18] This distinction is similar to Aristotle's distinction in *The Nicomachean Ethics*, Book 10, of act as *kinesis* (process) and act as *energeia* (whole act). The act to which Lonergan refers would correspond to Sartre's simply spontaneous consciousness, which I take to be more like Aristotle's *energeia*. Act as process is the constituted transcendent.

Granted this characterization of the intentionality and the consciousness of the reflective act, we are in a better position to examine a further distinction Sartre makes. In *Being and Nothingness*, in addition to distinguishing unreflective consciousness and reflective consciousness, Sartre further distinguishes pure and impure reflection. He defines pure reflection as "the simple presence of the reflective for-itself to the for-itself reflected-on."[19] Sartre here defines this form of reflection in terms of the *consciousness* of the reflection, for he refers to the "presence" of the reflective to the reflected. His account of impure reflection, on the other hand, is in terms of the *intentionality* of the reflection. Impure reflection is that reflective for-itself acting in bad faith by attempting to identify itself with the reflected-on which it has objectified. This distinction between pure and impure reflection is problematic because the basis for the distinction is logically inconsistent; it shifts from the consciousness of the reflection to the intentionality of the reflection. So far as one identifies consciousness and intentionality, no inconsistency will be discerned.

Phyllis Morris helps to clarify an earlier differentiation of forms of reflective consciousness offered by Sartre in *The Transcendence of the Ego*. In the course of analyzing the self-deceiver's consciousness, she points out that the distinction between unreflective consciousness and reflective consciousness is not to be confused with the distinction between non-positional and positional consciousness.[20] Unreflective consciousness, such as that found in ordinary perceiving, is non-positional, while reflective consciousness may be non-positional or positional. To say that unreflective consciousness is non-positional is to say that neither the self nor the object are posited as such. The non-positional consciousness is self-conscious, but no self is objectified; similarly, the non-positional consciousness is intentional, but its necessary content is not objectified—that is, made into an explicit object distinguished from the subject. Both subject and object in immediate consciousness are implicit. non-positional reflective consciousness is positional in relation to the object it intends, but it is merely self-conscious in relation to itself. For example, I can doubt what a friend tells me as she speaks, and my focus can be wholly on the subject matter discussed or on her manner, not on the fact that I am doubting. This would be a case of the "spontaneous doubt" Sartre describes in *The Transcendence of the Ego*.[21] This doubting remains present to itself as self-conscious, but it is not itself the object of any intentional act. Positional reflective consciousness, on the other hand, is positional in relation to both the object intended and to the consciousness intending. In positional reflective consciousness both the object and the consciousness become explicit:

"Reflection is the for-itself conscious of itself."[22] This positional reflective consciousness conforms to Sartre's definition of pure reflection.

This interpretation could give rise to the objection that every instance of consciousness is both non-positional and positional: non-positional in relation to itself and positional in relation to its object. On this reading the distinction of a non-positional reflection and a positional reflection would be half-true on two counts. But to say that every consciousness, although self-conscious, is non-positionally aware of itself is to deny the possibility of the reflection Sartre describes in *Being and Nothingness*: "Reflection is the for-itself conscious of itself."[23] And to say that every consciousness is positional in relation to the object is to import a naive notion of intentional object, one that overlooks the constitutive role of consciousness. Ontologically, the object of consciousness is more primordial for Sartre than the for-itself, for the for-itself first constitutes itself as not being the thing.[24] But this does not mean that the object is explicit *qua* object in every consciousness.

Further, a distinction between experiencing and knowing should be explicitly maintained throughout an analysis of reflective consciousness. However, as the focus of Sartre's analysis shifts back and forth from the consciousness of reflection to the intentionality of reflection, so there is also a vacillation between experience and knowledge in his discussion of reflection. In the passage from *Being and Nothingness* quoted above, we find an example of this vacillation: "But the totality 'reflected-reflecting,' if it could be given, would be contingency and in-itself. But this totality can not be attained."[25] To refer to reflective consciousness as given is to refer to it as experienced, as immediate. To refer to reflective consciousness as a totality of reflected-reflecting to be attained is to refer to the object of an intentional pursuit, the pursuit of inquiry and reflection, which is mediate. One may deny the possibility of the totality reflected-reflecting as known, without denying the possibility of the totality as given, that is, as undifferentiated immediacy. Lonergan, for example, articulates how knowing is a structure of conscious and intentional acts, not any one act, such as perceiving or understanding, and not, more generally speaking, simple experiencing.[26] Furthermore, a clear distinction between experiencing reflected-reflecting and knowing reflected-reflecting may reveal that both phenomena are possible.

In order to pursue the question of reflective consciousness as a kind of knowing, let us introduce the third distinction, that of two senses of object. In the passage from *Being and Nothingness* quoted earlier Sartre states, "to the extent that reflection is *knowledge*, the reflected on must necessarily be the *object* for the reflective; and this implies a separation of being."[27] Why does knowing necessarily involve a separation of being? Sartre is presupposing here, as he does in his account of conscious intentionality in general, a notion of object which is fundamentally empiricist. It is the notion of object as over against the act, as standing before the act. This notion of object presupposes what Lonergan terms an "ocular model" of knowing. The empiricist assumes that all knowing must be modeled on what takes place in the act of looking. Sartre, as a phenomenologist following in the tradition of Husserl, criticizes the naive assumptions of the natural standpoint, but not thoroughly. An ocular model of intentionality is carried over into the critical position. Sartre is in agreement with Husserl that the object of consciousness is constituted through conscious intentionality, that it is not already out there to be seen. However, there is still operative in the notion of the *Anschauen* of phenomenological method a kind of picture thinking that places the object at a distance from the act. In looking, a distance is required between the looking and the looked at. But the range of possible conscious and intentional acts includes acts different in kind from looking. Not all conscious acts are like looking. Consequently, the relation of the intentional act to its object need not require a distance between the act and its object. A prime example of an intentional act not like looking is the act of inquiry. In questioning an object is intended, but it is not an object there to be seen, or constituted in the act as there to be seen. The object is carried in the intentionality of the act. What is true of the intentional object of inquiry is true of the intentional object of understanding and judging as well. In fact, Sartre says as much in Chapter One of *Being and Nothingness*, when he gives examples of the non-being, the nothingness, implicated in different kinds of conscious acts. But the idea of an intentionality with no object over against it is not consistently elaborated in his account.

We have, then, two senses of object: the ocular object and the intentional object. These are not two kinds of object, but two theoretical interpretations of the object of conscious acts. In light of this distinction, we can understand the object of reflective consciousness to be reflective consciousness as intentional object, and as such it need not be conceived of as necessarily at a distance from the reflective consciousness as act. We have seen that for Sartre, due to an implicit ocular notion of object, reflective consciousness as knowing implies a separation of being. But we can still ask how it is possible for there to be an act of reflective consciousness which has as its intentional object the self-same act of reflective consciousness, because the reflective consciousness as intentional object supposedly is intending its own object already.

## 4. The Temporal and the Dramatic Structure of Reflective Consciousness

Both Husserl and Sartre attest to the possibility of experiencing reflective consciousness of reflective consciousness. In *The Idea of Phenomenology* Husserl writes: "Every intellectual process and indeed every mental process whatever, while being enacted, can be made the object of a pure 'seeing' and understanding, and is something absolutely given in this 'seeing.'"[28] His phrase "every intellectual process" logically includes the act of reflective consciousness. In *Being and Nothingness* Sartre vividly describes pure reflection as "that lightning intuition without relief in which the reflected-on is given without a point of view for the reflective."[29] That this experience can be given is not in question, but how can we account for its possibility?

We can find a solution to the difficulty of a simultaneity of distinct reflective acts given as a unity by turning to Sartre's conception of the temporality of reflective consciousness. Discussing accounts of the *cogito* found in Descartes and Husserl, Sartre explains that this act was interpreted as a reflective operation, "an operation of the second degree...performed by a consciousness *directed upon consciousness*, a consciousness which takes consciousness as an object."[30] If the consciousness which is an object is a prior act of consciousness, no difficulty arises in accounting for reflection. But when the consciousness which is the object of reflection is the self-same consciousness, then we face the difficulty of a simultaneous duality of consciousnesses. We find a clue to the problem of accounting for the simultaneity of reflective consciousness of reflective consciousness in Sartre's *The Psychology of the Imagination*. In his critical analysis of Leroy's definition of hypnogogic vision, Sartre comments: "There is an organization of instantaneous consciousnesses into the intentional unity of a longer consciousness."[31] He proceeds to describe the temporal structure of hypnogogic imagination. If Husserl is correct in finding the structure of internal time-consciousness to be universal for all conscious acts as well as contents, then reflective consciousness as reflectively experienced should have a similar temporal structure to the hypnogogic imagination. Reflective consciousness is comprised of the act reflected on and the act reflecting, and these two are retained and given as simultaneous in a now constituted as distended through short-term memory and anticipation. Yet this solution still leaves us with two clearly distinct reflective acts even if they are suspended in a specious present. But the reflected-on and the reflecting must be identical, according to Sartre, if we are to have an apodictic ground for phenomenological investigation.

So, let us turn to a consideration of the dramatic structure of reflective consciousness and, specifically, to the characteristic self-consciousness of reflection. Sartre suggests, although he does not say as much, that the consciousness of reflection is a heightened self-consciousness. Consider the following passage:

> The reflected-on is profoundly altered by reflection in this sense that it is self-consciousness as the consciousness reflected-on of this or that transcendent phenomenon....It may best be compared—to use a concrete

example—to a man who is writing, bent over a table, and who while writing knows that he is observed by somebody who stands behind him.[32]

What happens when one is busy at work, writing, and another walks into the room? The very presence of that other transforms one's level of awareness. One is now not merely intellectually or creatively involved, but also dramatically involved, for now there is a witness. The man who is writing and becomes aware that he is being observed as he writes simultaneously becomes a role-player. He now plays at being someone who is at work writing. This added dramatic dimension commonly causes some interruption in creative effort, and some difference in the intensity of self-awareness. Sartre employs this image to convey the structure of reflective consciousness. The intensification of self-awareness that may occur in such a case occurs also in reflective consciousness itself.

The difference in the quality or intensity of reflective consciousness can be illustrated by another example. Consider the case of showing a visitor around one's home town. I have seen all of these sights before, but the presence of this other witness heightens my awareness of the familiar, making it seem novel (no matter how oblivious or uninterested the visitor may actually be). I am not directly the object of the other's intentionality; we are both seeing the sights. In this instance, the heightening of self-awareness is a function of the co-viewing of the sights. One might want to object that my self-awareness is only intensified because I feel myself to be responsible for the sights seen, and in that sense it is me that is seen in and through the sights. In that case we would again have the original model of one being observed by another. With this complication in mind, let us change the example, then, to any case where one is sharing sights with another—traveling companions for example. It still holds that the presence of another with whom one experiences something intensifies, or at least alters, the self-awareness that qualifies that experience.

In both the original case of being observed by another and the case of observing with another, the quality of self-awareness is intensified by the presence of another. In the first example, one's self-awareness is increased by becoming the object for the other, by being for the other. As Sartre explains: "The reflected-on has then, in a way, already a consciousness (of) itself as having an outside or rather the suggestion of an outside; that is, it makes itself an object for."[33] In the second example, one's self-awareness is increased by sharing an object with the other, by being with the other. We can name these two models of the dramatic structure of reflective consciousness, the witness/observed model and the ensemble model. In both models the quality of the self-consciousness characteristic of reflection is heightened because of the dramatic structure inherent in reflection.

Although descriptions of being-with along the lines of the ensemble model can be found in Sartre's work (see, for example, the description of joint intentionality involving the young Sartre and his mother in *The Words* 34), he employs only the witness/observed model in his description of reflective consciousness. In light of the distinctions made earlier in this chapter, we can now employ the ensemble model to attempt a brief sketch of reflective consciousness.

In introspective reflection a subject-pole and an object-pole can be differentiated, the act of reflecting as intentional and the act of reflecting as conscious. This distinction can be made so far as we do not identify consciousness with the intentional act. As conscious, the act of reflecting is self-conscious, as is any intentional act, and thereby accessible to introspective reflection. As intentional, the act of reflecting has an object, an intentional object, the act itself. The act of introspective reflection, then, as an intentional act has as its object itself as conscious. If we allow for the possibility that the heightened self-consciousness is a function of being with oneself, as the ensemble model would suggest, then the experience of reflective consciousness does not necessitate any distance from oneself. Reflective consciousness can be given as both concomitant and coincident with itself (how it is that reflective consciousness can be known through acts of reflection is a further question).

This description of the dramatic ensemble of the reflecting and the reflected-on in a single, self-same reflective act poses a problem for Sartrean ontology. For it is on the basis of his witness/observed description of reflective consciousness that he characterizes the for-itself as essentially non-coincident. On the other hand, this alternative account secures at least the evidential ground of phenomenologies of reflection.

In this chapter the theme of consciousness as a central element in French existentialism was explored in terms of Sartre's account of reflective consciousness. We now turn to another French existentialist's account of another sort of consciousness; namely, Merleau-Ponty and sensory consciousness.

## Notes

1. St. Augustine, *The Confessions*, trans. John K. Ryan (New York: Doubleday, 1960), p. 287.
2. Søren Kierkegaard, *The Concept of Anxiety*, trans. Reidar Thomte (Princeton: Princeton University Press, 1980), p. 143.
3. Jean-Paul Sartre, *Being and Nothingness: An Essay in Phenomenological Ontology* (1943), trans. Hazel E. Barnes (New York: Washington Square Press, 1966), p. 212.
4. *Ibid.*, p. 130.

5. Jean-Paul Sartre, *The Transcendence of the Ego* (1936–1937), trans. Forrest Williams and Robert Kirkpatrick (New York: Farrar, Straus, and Giroux, 1957), p. 44.
6. *Ibid.*, p. 45.
7. Joseph S. Catalano, *A Commentary on Jean-Paul Sartre's Being and Nothingness* (Chicago: University of Chicago Press, 1974), p. 126.
8. Jean-Paul Sartre, "Intentionality: A Fundamental Idea of Husserl's Phenomenology," trans. Joseph P. Fell, *Journal of the British Society for Phenomenology*, I:2 (May 1970), pp. 4-5.
9. Jean-Paul Sartre, *The Psychology of the Imagination* (New York: Citadel Press, 1991), p. 5.
10. Sartre, *Being and Nothingness*, p. 212.
11. *Ibid.*, p. 213.
12. See Bernard Lonergan, *Insight: A Study of Human Understanding* (1957), *Collected Works of Lonergan*, vol. 3, eds. Frederick E. Crowe and Robert M. Doran (Toronto: University of Toronto Press, 1992); Bernard Lonergan, *Method in Theology* (New York: Herder and Herder, 1972), ch. 1.
13. Sartre, *The Transcendence of the Ego*, pp. 43-54.
14. Hazel E. Barnes, "Sartre's Ontology: The Revealing and Making of Being," in *The Cambridge Companion to Sartre*, ed. Christina Howells (Cambridge: Cambridge University Press, 1992), pp. 16-17.
15. Sartre, *The Transcendence of the Ego*, p. 44.
16. See Elizabeth Morelli, "The Feeling of Freedom," in *Religion & Culture: Essays in Honor of Bernard Lonergan, S. J.*, eds. Timothy P. Fallon and Philip Boo Riley (Albany: State University of New York Press, 1987), p. 102.
17. Sartre, *The Transcendence of the Ego*, pp. 68-71.
18. *Ibid.*, p. 68.
19. Sartre, *Being and Nothingness*, p. 218.
20. Phyllis Sutton Morris, "Sartre on the Self-Deceiver's Translucent Consciousness," *The Journal of the British Society for Phenomenology*, 23:2 (May, 1992), pp. 103–119.
21. Sartre, *The Transcendence of the Ego*, p. 69.
22. Sartre, *Being and Nothingness*, p. 212.
23. *Ibid.*, p. 212.
24. *Ibid.*, p. 242.
25. *Ibid.*, p. 130.
26. See Bernard Lonergan, "Cognitional Structure," in *The Lonergan Reader*, eds. Mark D. Morelli and Elizabeth A. Morelli (Toronto: University of Toronto Press, 1997), pp. 380–386.
27. Sartre, *Being and Nothingness*, p. 213.
28. Edmund Husserl, *The Idea of Phenomenology*, trans. William Alston and George Nakhnikian (The Hague: Martinus Nijhoff, 1964), p. 24.
29. Sartre, *Being and Nothingness*, p. 224.
30. Sartre, *The Transcendence of the Ego*, p. 44.
31. Sartre, *Psychology of the Imagination*, p. 57.
32. Sartre, *Being and Nothingness*, p. 214.

33. *Ibid.*, p. 214.

34. Jean-Paul Sartre, *The Words*, trans. Bernard Frechtman (New York: Vintage Books, 1981), p. 102.

# Two

# MERLEAU-PONTY AND THE SENSORY

## Edmond Wright

### 1. The Story

To say that I was going to tell you a story might raise a few eyebrows. Yet you must have heard many a philosopher, particularly of the English-language establishment, saying something like "The story Kripke tells is rather different...," or "That's one kind of story that told about the referent...." It is a current and familiar idiom in the professional patois, but its presence, I would say, is not without a significance that escapes those who use it. What could a story about a French existentialist like Maurice Merleau-Ponty be? Well, it could be about something in his actual life, such as his being taken for Sartre by mistake by an eager young would-be existentialist who wanted to hear his latest argument for the distinction between the *en-soi* (being-in-itself) and the *pour-soi* (being-for-itself). But it could also be about his thought, if one could show that his animus against that distinction led him first to a healthy emphasis upon a dialectic that bridged that gap and then to a false interpretation of it which prevented him explaining that very dialectic—for would not that have the character of a tragicomedy?

For what is a story? Simply, someone is in pursuit of a certain goal, and everything in the situation appears to conspire to make them think that something or someone will either—if it's a tragedy—contribute to that end, or—if it's a comedy—hinder that end. From the hearer of the story's point of view the clues the protagonist is depending on are discovered to be wildly misleading, and there are others he or she is missing which point in a contrary direction. The conclusion, in the simplest case, comes when the protagonist realizes the mistake—the mis-take. A brief example will illustrate; one of Aesop's fables:

A wolf thought that by disguising himself he could get plenty to eat. Putting on a sheepskin to trick the shepherd, he joined the flock at grass without being discovered. At nightfall the shepherd shut him with the sheep in the fold and made it fast all around by blocking the entrance. Then, feeling hungry, he picked up his knife and slaughtered an animal for his supper; it happened to be the wolf.

The wolf is the protagonist in pursuit of a goal, the killing of the sheep. The core element subject to his would-be favorable interpretation is his own false appearance in among the flock, which he regards as one that will guarantee an ample satisfaction of his desires. The rival clue in the situation, the one to which he was blind, was the perspective of the other, the shepherd, that included all sheep in a gaze that saw them as possible food. This was the tragic pattern, for, though the wolf thought he was going to achieve a high satisfaction, it led to the cessation of all his desires. Notice how important motivation is to perceiving, how it governs how one chooses what one sees.

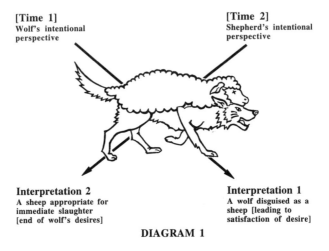

**DIAGRAM 1**

There was something ambiguous, which from one point of view promised the satisfaction of the protagonist's desires and from another denied them (see Diagram 1). Isn't this something with which Merleau-Ponty would heartily agree? For at the core of all his writings on perception was the engagement of the body with all its desires and fears, a feature he believed had been neglected by both rationalists and empiricists.

## 2. The Riddle

Exactly the same pattern shows itself in the Joke, the Pun, and the Riddle. Take the primary schoolchild's riddle (based on a pun): Question—"Where did Humpty Dumpty put his hat?" Answer—"Humpty dumped 'is 'at on the wall." There is a central region of ambiguity, namely, the whole of the answer. From one point of view, the context evoked by the mention of the name "Humpty Dumpty," what we hear is the well-known first line of the nursery rhyme. However, the question as a whole indicates another context, one of interrogation (another of Merleau-Ponty's interests in philosophy), in which we are asked to find where Humpty Dumpty's hat has been placed, and the assumption of the question is that we are expected to know or to be able to find out. These two clues to rival intentional contexts enforce rival interpretations. Again there was a dominant, out-in-the-open context, which drew the hearer in one direction, in this case, the hat question; again there was a faint clue to another interpretation, this time one that we should have been aware of. We, as the victim of the joke, are in the protagonist's position, misled by a strong wrong clue as to what will satisfy our current desire, and upstaged by a faint right clue which shows us that we should have known better. It can be diagramed as follows. The answer has also been shown in International Phonetic Alphabet, from which it can be seen that there are two versions differing very slightly in phonemes and also in morpheme separation. Such fudging is common to jokes, which in this match many a cause of misapprehension in actual sharing of perceptions. We can see this pattern overlapping with what others have said of humor generally: Kant, who saw it as arising from a shattering of expectations;[1] Schopenhauer, for whom it was based on some incongruity;[2] Bergson, who made salient the apparent automatism of the protagonist who was acting blindly against his own interest;[3] and, perhaps the most recent, the Polish philosopher Bohdan Dziemidok,[4] who sees in all humorous situations a deviation from a norm. One interesting feature of this joke, which can be generalized to many another perceptual situation, is that, in changing from the earlier interpretation to the later, the very entityhood of the so-called things—the words we heard—changed (see Diagram 2).

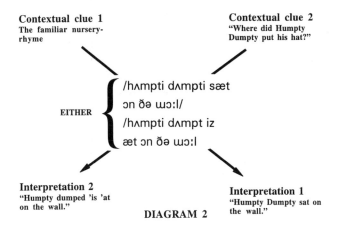

DIAGRAM 2

For instead of six words, "Humpty Dumpty sat on the wall," we heard seven, "Humpty dumped his hat on the wall." In altering our intentional perspective on a region of being, there is no guarantee that any object, any entity—and that could include a self—will retain its singularity. As the sixth-century Indian philosopher Dignaga said, "Even 'this' can be a case of mistaken identity."[5]

### 3. Merleau-Ponty's View of the Sensory

This is a story about Merleau-Ponty, and so, if it follows the pattern, there should have already been some faint clues as to how his theory of perception might be reinterpreted—not as in the adversarial manner of much of English-language philosophy of the twentieth century, with the aim of proving his philosophy false, but rather of showing how, if he had been more loyal to some of his major claims, he might have reached an explanation of the dialectic he was so much in search of. Indeed, it is because he took up too adversarial a position himself concerning the empiricists and rationalists that he blocked himself off from making the move that might have freed him. His critics have rightly condemned him for attacking the vague Aunt Sallys, the Empiricist and the Rationalist—with capital letters—without giving chapter-and-verse from those he opposed. If he had, he would not have found it so easy to set up his Aunt Sallys.

Take, for example, his claim that the associationists among the empiricists neglected the bodily drives that lie behind our percepts. George Eliot's husband, George Henry Lewes, was a philosophical anthropologist of no mean breadth of scholarship. He insisted upon an associationist view, but one that had to take account of what he called "the Law of Interest," which he states as follows: "It has long been observed that we only *see* what interests us....The satisfaction of desire is that which both impels and quiets mental movement." He concluded that this "discredits the old idea that the senses directly apprehend—or mirror—external things";[6] compare Richard Rorty's claims about the empiricists and their "mirror" fallacy.[7] William James, too, wrote of "the transformation of the world of our impressions being effected in the interests of our volitional nature."[8] But Merleau-Ponty claims that the classical philosophy ignores the intentional element.[9] Or take the American critical realist Roy Wood Sellars, who argued for a basic field of pure sentience like many another sense-datum philosopher, but with this difference: that his evolutionary bent prevented him from ignoring the part played by feedback in adjusting our percepts—he called it a "from-to" relationship—so that he proposed a cortical sensory field that was responsive not to external *things* but to the *energy-distribution* of light-waves over the whole of the retinas.[10] None of these empiricists have theories that meet the requirements of Merleau-Ponty's definition of Empiricist: on the contrary what they say overlaps with claims of his own. He insisted throughout both on the part played by bodily motivation in perception and on the continual adjustment of our concepts as we move through time.

Other critics have complained about the lack of convincing proofs, clear references, and precision in his definitions, about his failure to give succinct explanations and summaries, about his wordiness and the frequency of assertion without argument.[11] No doubt there is some substance in these accusations, and it has undoubtedly contributed to his neglect in English-language philosophy. But many thinkers at the moment would strongly second one of his main objections to empiricism, that there is no such thing as a level of pure sentience, no bare sensation, no "anoetic" experience,[12] or "raw feel,"[13] no sensory field that is "non-epistemic,"[14] or "non-conceptual,"[15] or "non-doxastic."[16] In this regard one can instance Rorty,[17] Donald Davidson,[18] Gilbert Harman,[19] Hilary Putnam,[20] and John McDowell.[21] All of them refuse to accept the notion of a level of pure sensation from which interpretations are made. Davidson, for example, uses an argument he could have developed straight from Merleau-Ponty. One can organize a cupboard, Davidson says, because in it there are identifiable shoes and shirts to be placed on the shelves in the places selected, but nothing is to be organized in the case of a level of pure sensation. "How would you organize the Pacific Ocean?", he mockingly asks.[22] But this is Merleau-Ponty's position, too, for when the philosopher sets to work to analyze perception, he finds that preceding all conscious judgments and selections is a pre-objective level, not of pure sensation, but of one in which the body has already sorted out the sensory material according to bodily interests (see Chapter Nine, where Thomas Jones discusses this notion in relation to sexual desire). Merleau-Ponty calls this "primordial experience."[23] In its engagement with the environment, the body has already established a range of habitual Gestalts which guide it surely in action. Merleau-Ponty was here influenced by the Gestalt psychologists to the point that, although he rejected their assumption that science would be able to explain the Gestalt mechanism, he accepted unquestioningly their claim that all perception is shot through by the figure/ground phenomenon.

At no point, he argues, should we fall into the empiricist error of thinking that objects are given in their entityhood and passively imprint themselves upon the mind, linking themselves together by given relations of resemblance and contiguity, as if it were nothing but a matter of behaviorist stimulus and response, nor can we make the rationalist error of arguing that what the mind does is make deductive inferences from the Kantian "blind intuition." Merleau-Ponty, in his characterization of the empiricist argument, sees the specter of solipsism in any account that puts a veil of sensation in between the subject and the world. He considers it a definite advantage that his position escapes the solipsist accusation, for how can the skeptic's argument take a hold if the body is already in engagement with the world, if things are to be seen as "already there" in an inextricable relation with the body in a given situation?

Furthermore, he believes that the process of pre-objective Gestalt-selection precedes any scientific objectification. The scientific object is thus an idealization. Science itself is consequent upon this bodily engagement. Empiricism makes the mistake of idealizing the *en-soi*, taking objects as foundational: rationalism, of idealizing the *pour-soi*, taking intentionality to be the foundation of knowledge. Not until the body's primordial union of the two is accepted can the character of perception and knowledge be understood. Both empiricism and rationalism ignore the intersubjective play that occurs in the praxis of knowing. An articulation of being exists that we are all involved in, a construction in which truth is rather created than found. In the pre-objective world lies a bond with the other that has to be taken into account. "Each subject's field," he says, can be "a further structuring of the other's."[24] This allows for any object to be further explored, to acknowledge that there is a richness of experience which outruns any current understanding, allowing a dialectical adjustment. The other works with us in a "consummate reciprocity" in structuring reality, so that it is impossible to think of him only as a "bit of behaviour."[25] Merleau-Ponty often returns to the metaphor of "commerce" for this interaction, which suggests a negotiation about what is to constitute common reality, and this is obviously out of key with any view that wants to make the ego sovereign in knowing. The visual field is full of tensions that instigate questioning, problems that present themselves to be solved. Here he is very close to George Herbert Mead and John Dewey, both of whom stressed that it is discrepancies between action and result that lead to changes of percept,[26] and to Roger C. Schank and Chip Cleary,[27] who say "Everybody needs to be creative in response to abnormalities," but they do not stress the mutual participation that Merleau-Ponty takes as essential. He called his approach a "genetic phenomenology" because he wanted to draw attention to the continual learning that we are all busy with together; indeed, it is learning that he believed both empiricism and rationalism ignored. As he puts it, "Empiricism cannot see that we need to know what we are looking for, otherwise we would not be looking for it, and intellectualism fails to see that we need to be ignorant of what we are looking for, or equally again we would not be searching."[28] Merleau-Ponty, as you see, is not afraid of paradox, which he finds "at the heart of creativity."

## 4. The Origin of "The Object"

Now if we are to move on in our story, there must come a moment in which much in the protagonist's interpretation of the ambiguous region can be conceded, but certain doubts begin to show themselves. Merleau-Ponty's commitment to the dialectic can be seconded, but one may legitimately ask whether his system provides a place for it. It is not enough to issue a declaration of support. At the time he wrote it, it might only be taken as a sign of solidarity with a left-wing view, and, in addition, there are remarks in the long rambling paragraphs of *Phenomenology of Perception* that do not fit well with it. We need only home in on one controversial topic, the status of the Object, the Thing. The world, in his view, is "not a sum of objects."[29] In the perception of an object a synthesis takes place which is not an intellectual recognition. There is always more to be discovered than what is shown in the present percept, and the other can help us and we help him toward that further discovery. He puts it thus: "our certainty about perceiving a given thing does not guarantee that our experience will not be contradicted, or dispense us from a fuller experience of that thing."[30] But there is a contradiction there that he is not aware of. He is claiming here that some further experience may lead us to a fuller experience of the same thing. Though he says that he does not believe that there is a "vacant X," a *Ding-an-Sich*, behind the perceived object, nevertheless he believes that some, even if adjustable, "some*thing*" lies there waiting a better Gestalt-play upon it. The point has been recently reiterated by a defender of his, Roger McClure: "What I see is the thing itself as an originary *it* ."[31] Merleau-Ponty anticipates James J. Gibson[32] in claiming that, under the endless variations of perspective we have upon a thing, lies an invariant: he puts it thus, "I grasp *in* a perspectival appearance, which I know is only one of its possible aspects, the thing itself which transcends it."[33] My perception, he believes, "accedes to things themselves, for these perspectives are articulated in a way which makes access to inter-individual significations possible."[34] But it is precisely here that his explanation ceases, for he does not tell us how inter-individual significations for two or more perceiving human agents work together in a common practice.

For part of an answer here we can go to a sociologist who was much influenced by phenomenology, Alfred Schutz, and a psycholinguist, Ragnar Rommetveit. They both independently arrive at a similar conclusion about human communication. It is that, in order to communicate about a portion of the world of which we are largely ignorant, that is, pass on some information about that portion to the other, we have to act to each other *as if we have already precisely defined the reference to that region to our mutual satisfaction*. The environment being what it is, this can only remain a project. No safe claim can in fact be made that the two agents perceive and understand some portion of the real in exactly the same way. Even Kant acknowledged this: "To one man...a certain word suggests one thing, to another some other thing; the unity of consciousness in what is empirical is not, as regards what is given, necessarily and universally valid."[35] Nevertheless, the two would not even get an partial overlap on the unsafe portion unless they behaved for the nonce as if they had already achieved a complete one. Schutz calls it the "Idealization of Reciprocity":[36] the two act on a hypothesis they know can never be substantiated, namely, that, if they were to exchange perspectives, each would still perceive the supposedly single referent in exactly the same way. If they "interchanged their standpoints," as he phrases it, all would be as before, we might say, give or take a few *irrelevant* criteria. Once this tentative overlap has been established, then the one who has information to pass on will, paradoxically, cancel that agreement by showing that the presumed perfect superimposition of understanding was actually not as they had mutually pretended it to be. Using the hoary example of "The cat is on the mat," if this is a real statement being used in actual time and the Hearer has just asked "Where is the cat?" then the statement by the Speaker of "The cat is on the mat" can be analyzed in the following way: it is as if the Speaker is saying, "You know that cat we both know about in the same way?"—"Yes," says the Hearer, entering into the Idealization of Reciprocity—"Well then," says the Speaker, "we don't know about it in the same way, for it is on the mat." Incidentally, a question is thus an indication to one's social partner that one wants one's concept of a portion of the continuum updating. As I have pointed out elsewhere,[37] this analysis of communication gives ordinary language the character of the Liar Paradox, for it seems to perform that very paradox—an agreement that a language is shared followed at once by a demonstration that it isn't. As will be understood from the earlier analyses, this is also the pattern of the Story and the Joke. Rommetveit's formulation of the same principle as Schutz's is as follows: "we must take a perfect intersubjectivity for granted in order to achieve a partial intersubjectivity."[38] One can say that this makes all the passing on of newly-discovered information creative: as Schank and Cleary say, creativity is the "intelligent misuse" of the knowledge structures underlying cognition...when scripted knowledge does not directly apply, people find some knowledge that does not quite apply and then see how they can modify it. In other words, they intelligently misuse it.[39]

This is the paradox that "lies at the heart of all creativity." How does this bear on Merleau-Ponty's view of the Object? If this is correct, what we have to do is act toward each other as if we have already achieved a satisfactory overlap of reference, just in order to get a rough-and-ready grip on a portion of the real. But the strict implication then is that *there is no logically single referent before us*. It will be surrounded by a haze of vagueness.

Now the logically-minded among us might say, as David Wiggins in fact does,[40] that "all our vaguenesses with respect to an object match exactly"; but I am sure you will see that that is no more than a Schutzian invitation to join in the Idealization of Reciprocity, for a little thought will show that there is no such assurance. On the contrary, even though we in all trust might take for granted that nothing the other understands but has not made mutually salient could be to one's own disadvantage, our social partner may in all innocence be understanding something that might lead him to act in a way that is of great danger to us and our interests. After all, the term "take for granted" includes those slippery words "take for," and what do they mean? Do we not use them thus, say, of a figure in the fog, "I took him for his brother," that is, "to take for" is to accept an illusion of one thing for another thing, and what in this case is the illusion we are *taking for* real?—Why, our *granting* something—and what is "to grant?"—It is to say that there is nothing in the case that will be to our disadvantage, discomfort, or actual hurt, for our *body* is involved. Merleau-Ponty said that "this *presumption* on reason's part" (his italics), this postulation of "a totally explicit knowledge," was "the fundamental philosophic problem."[41] Schutz and Rommetveit have pointed the way to its solution.

Here is another story, this time to illustrate the process of perceptual reference as played by two agents. Albeit a story, it can be taken as a logical generalization for the nature of all reference, which has been such a conundrum for philosophers, a real philosophical riddle. Two military observers are on the watch one evening. Their task is to keep an eye open for enemy missiles; they. have an anti-missile launcher of an antique type, which is guided by them directly but which is rather slow to respond to a new directional setting once it has been aimed, so they have to be very speedy with their initial reactions. One is called Short (he happens to be short-sighted); his companion is Sharp (he happens to be sharp-sighted). The day has been peaceful and, as evening approaches and the sun is setting (Time 1), Short says to Sharp, "What a beautiful cloud!" This is what lies before them in the west, a long band of water vapour, a stratus cloud, which has faint fringes on each side of it (see Diagram 3).

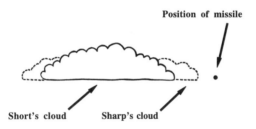

DIAGRAM 3

Those faint fringes are invisible to Short but visible to Sharp, though neither of them is aware of this difference in their sensory registration. Nevertheless, Sharp readily agrees: "Yes. What a beautiful cloud!" The fact that Short was particularly impressed with the tint in the central part of the cloud and Sharp by the delicacy of the fringes was irrelevant in this case. They had both achieved a common reference by their own rights. There was "one" object before them, and Short had managed to make salient something about it to Sharp which he had not noticed before and which brought him pleasure. They had achieved a common understanding about it. "To all intents and purposes," as they might have said, a communication had gone through about a commonly-recognizable portion of nature. We must add, "to all mutually salient intents and purposes." The very phrase itself in common use carries with it a scintilla of doubt, for "to all intents and purposes" is often used in situations in which we think some substitution is involved—for example, "To all intents and purposes, he was the bank manager."

However, to get back to our story: at Time 2, Sharp, who is not at that moment responsible for directing the anti-missile launcher, notices an approaching enemy missile and he immediately alerts Short. "Where is it?" cries Short. "At the edge of the cloud on the right!" shouts Sharp (at the spot shown by the black point to the right in Diagram 3). Short now aims at "the edge of the cloud on the right." One need not describe the consequences at any length, but merely add—end of Short and Sharp.

What the story illustrates about reference is that the selections we privately make from the continuum of nature and that we endeavor continually to keep in public co-ordination are dependent upon the percepts we have individually made from our own sensory fields, and that these selections are driven by motivation as the essential initial feedback, which can be later updated by communication from another. However, these selections can only ever be viable, that is, apparently confirmed by the circumstances that have existed up to that point in time. Our common understandings can only be sustained by the tests that one has so far applied, and there is no guarantee that all criteria relevant to a new situation will already have been made salient to both parties. This is the point that has been made repeatedly and with great clarity by the psychologist Ernst von Glasersfeld.[42]

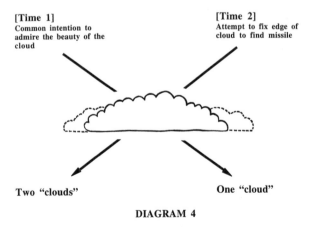

DIAGRAM 4

We can now enlarge the diagram to show, as before with the riddle, above the ambiguous "cloud," the rival contexts of interpretation, and, below it, the rival meanings produced by them (see Diagram 4).

Merleau-Ponty, if he were here, might now quote a passage from *Phenomenology of Perception* in which he virtually says all that Schutz and Rommetveit have said:

> The tacit assumption of perception is that at every instant experience can be coordinated with that of the previous instant and that of the following, and my perspective with that of other consciousnesses—that all contradictions can be removed, that monadic and intersubjective experience is one unbroken text—that what is indeterminate for me could become determinate for a more complete knowledge, which is, as it were, realized in advance of the thing, or rather which is the thing itself.[43]

But this is the Story of Short and Sharp: they did all that Merleau-Ponty could have expected of them, but what caught them out? A difference in sensory registration which had not been obvious to either of them. The reciprocity cannot be "consummate," it can only be the *mutually hypothesized* consummate co-ordination that is never achieved. Merleau-Ponty did say "as it were," and, interestingly, used the word "text" of the idealization. Of poor Short and Sharp, although their Gestalts from their point of view had embraced all they could see in their visual field, nevertheless there was a sensory feature that was not captured in the public word. But Merleau-Ponty's claim for a dialectical structure is correct. He is right to insist that there is a "certain fundamental divergence, a certain constitutive dissonance" between agents that allows for a creative dialectic to occur.[44] What can now be understood is that it will not work unless he concedes that there is a sensory level which is not capturable in the terms that we use in our public language. Émile Brehier criticized Merleau-Ponty for not giving due place to the sensory immediate,[45] yet Merleau-Ponty repeatedly stressed the inexhaustibility of the sensory. What he should have gone on to conclude, and inconsistently did not, is that it is differently inexhaustible for each body. If it is, it is therefore not capturable in the common object-term two agents are using for what they *take to be* the same portion of the continuum that is of motivational concern to both. Merleau-Ponty should have heeded his own term "play" in his phrase "intersubjective play," for play is precisely created by the provision of a clue to a rival context that transforms the meaning of a portion of the continuum (take the chimpanzee's special grin that indicates that the attack on his fellow is not a real one[46]). A precisely similar diagram to those above can be used to analyze play. Indeed, the highest moments in a game are those in which player A has just produced what every one thinks is a winning stroke (judging by the "strong wrong clue"), but player B, being a master, perceives the very weakness created by that winning stroke (only faintly indicated and thus missed by those over-impressed by the wrong clue) and takes advantage of it to everyone's delighted surprise. Consider judo, in which one party takes advantage of the opponent's momentum as that opponent makes an apparently irresistible attack. The Game, the Story, the Riddle, the Joke, and the Statement are all exactly alike in this, and it is no "family resemblance."

## 5. The Non-Epistemic Sensory Field

Other remarks of Merleau-Ponty show this loose thread. "Reflection," he says, "can never make me stop seeing the sun rise and set."[47] But that is empirically false. Holding your eyes focused strictly upon me, try now to see what is to left and right of you, without moving your head. As Josiah Royce pointed out long ago, a region exists which is "crowded with unknown impressions."[48] When I put this point recently to an audience of Australian tough-minded materialists, I was told that those were regions of "faint belief," but that is no answer, for I may just have come into an unknown situation and have no idea what is to left and right of me. A faint sun might be in that very region, unrecognizable by me. As regards the sun directly viewed, let me be just waking up in a tent in a strange place, and on the first dozy opening of my eyes, I have no idea what is before me, because, I have no idea of where I am, and part of my vision is made up of a doubled image of part of a sleeping-bag near my nose, part of a rucksack seen sideways with my right eye only, and the rising sun moving horizontally because I am lying down. My Gestalt-system may be prompt enough to show me a funny face made out of this jumble of *qualia*, but I could easily fail to perceive the sun, though I sense the whole energy-distribution field perfectly well (in the manner of Sellars). My *philosophical* reflection can show me that pure sensation is a reality after all. An intellectualist error is to believe that we never have any sensing without perceiving. On waking in that tent I may not even pick out the funny face, but just stare blankly for several moments.[49] As for the sun's rising and setting: once when I was in the Scottish Highlands and was watching the sun "set" behind a range of mountains fifty miles away, by imagining that I was on a rising platform like a vast lift, I saw, not the sun setting behind the Earth, but *the Earth rising over the sun.*

Nor is it true that the Gestalt-system must always be at work. According to my own theory of the mind[50] and that of the neurophysiologist Gerald Edelman,[51] Gestalts are characteristically driven into the bare sentience by pain and pleasure, and subsequently, having been thus embedded in memory, accompanied on their reappearance by fear and desire, but it is the case in the advanced mind that they can be played with, tested out on the sensory evidence without any necessary fear or desire that implies present immediacy of action. If one has a virtual-reality hood over one's eyes, and the engineer feeds a computerized random succession of colors and shapes on to the screens, a phantasmagoria like an endless screen-saver, one certainly does not have to play "faces-in-the-fire" or its equivalent. The very speed of change might defeat one so that one is left with the non-epistemic experience, the raw-feel, the possibility of which so many philosophers, locked in their normal habits of perceiving, have denied. I, like many another person, experience what the psychologists call hypnagogic visions before going to sleep. These visions are best described as being like the randomized screens I have just mentioned. In my tired state, I sometimes just let the succession flow before me without any perceiving—after all, how could I keep up with it? I would have to be thinking something like, "That wheel hub like the satellite in Stanley Kubrick's film *2001* has already turned into an aster that is more like a plastic Catherine wheel or a cobra seen from above that is a spiky button, if it hadn't already turned into a starfish," and so forth, but the rate of change is such that I cannot always keep up with it. At such moments, I am experiencing the bare sensation. Daniel Alroy's recent arguments take up the findings of recent experiments with the direct electrical stimulation of the visual cortex, in which no one could have any doubt that non-epistemic sensory experience, which he correctly calls "inner light," was being produced.[52] One could also call in support the new books *Colours* by Barry Maund of the University of Western Australia[53] and *Subjects of Experience* by Jonathan Lowe of the University of Durham.[54] Maund has an argument to show that the connection between the "inner light" and the photons that arrive at our retinas is entirely contingent; these photons could just as easily excite a sound. Indeed, research has been carried out in which a ferret's optic nerve was switched to its auditory cortex and its auditory nerve to its visual cortex.[55]

Other empirical facts could be cited. When Merleau-Ponty considers double vision, it does not occur to him that the fields of the two eyes are in fact different at every point. This fact enables our cortex to produce the internal stereoscopic space. Those computer experts who are responsible for the "Magic Eye" cards know this well, for the alternate bands which appear identical to the passing glance are quite different from each other, representing one eye's perspective as against another's. One can actually see this difference for oneself if one looks closely enough at the stereoscopic squares made by Bela Julesz. But those differences are not to be described by any terms derivable from any Gestalt I may be perceiving. The condition of the field needs entirely another mode of description, possibly by an account of the point-states of the matrix, just as one might give a precise account of the state of a television screen by listing all the intensities for each glowing phosphor cell without having to mention anything about what the screen happened to be showing. I have called this the "field-determinate" level of description as distinct from the "object-determinate" level of familiar recognitions.[56] For example, one might list all the point-states of a "Magic Eye" picture without ever referring to the fact that what it shows when its bands are combined by the cortex is a picture of a dog howling at the moon. This underlying field of bare sensation is "the Pacific Ocean" that Davidson thought impossible, but now, like "stout Cortez," he should be looking at it "with a wild surmise." He has only to close his right eye leaving his left eye open, then close his left eye and keep his right eye open. A change will occur in the bare sensation that is not describable in the terms he might use to describe any objects he might see before him, and that change is detectable. In my own case, the right eye shows a blurred field as against the left eye's clearer one, and the left eye sees reds better than the right. My hands look pinker to my left eye; it disturbs the direct realist to ask him "Which is the right color?").

A further visual oddity explicable under the present theory but not by those who deny the existence of the bare sensation is that of the "Wallpaper Illusion," first noticed by Charles Brewster,[57] which is Brewster's anticipation over a hundred years before of the principle of the "Magic Eye" pictures. Consider a pattern that has vertical bands, for example, on wallpaper or corrugated iron. Brewster noticed that on some occasions, when the eyes were focused on something closer than the corrugated iron, that the right eye's field moved across the left eye's field such that, instead of a correct superimposition of the fields of two eyes as far as the iron was concerned, the superimposition was *out of phase by one vertical band* (this is what occurs with the "Magic Eye" pictures). The result is strange: the pattern is as recognizable as ever, but the normal 3-D effect is enhanced (for corrugated iron, it would make the ridges and hollows more sharply defined in our internal stereoscopic space). Here, one is no longer looking at "an object," for the whole field is falsified from the epistemic point of view. According to any objective theory, reality has vanished, yet something is left. Those who take the field as endlessly explorable evidence, as in the present theory, can still learn useful facts from that presentation. I have an ordinary (non-3-D) photograph of Notre Dame cathedral in Paris. When I squint the left tower on to the right tower, I see a 3-D representation of a single tower *which does not exist in reality*, and so would be described as an "illusion" from the objectivist point of view. But taking this 3-D field—whatever its condition—as a source of evidence, I can learn much more about the sculpting of the towers that is not evident in the actual two-dimensional photograph (for the two towers in that photograph were presented from different angles).

## 6. The Dialectic as Mutual Correction

At the center of these diagrams, therefore, is evidence awaiting interpretation. The "pre-objective" is thus what Merleau-Ponty's term says it is: it precedes objectification. One might say "Existence precedes objectivity," and, if objectivity is created by the Idealization of Reciprocity, one might say that the "ideal essences" of objectivity are preceded by existence—even "Existence precedes essence." Gestalts are evolved attempts at the guidance of action, individual to each of us. Their immediate operation is utterly automatic. For, on feeling a pain, one cannot stop oneself selecting the Gestalt on those colors, sensations, and shapes, firming them into the percept (say, of a candle flame), nor fearing that percept when next it occurs, even in what one might call an "illusory" form. This is similarly true for a Gestalt projected by a pleasurable experience, which becomes attended by desire.[58] Merleau-Ponty, quoting Koffka, said: "The light of a candle changes its appearance for the child when, after a burn, it stops attracting the child's hand and becomes repulsive."[59] But Merleau-Ponty did not pursue the implications of this far enough, for the key point is that this might have been the first time the child applied a Gestalt to its sensations to produce that very percept, a Candle, and it would have illustrated what Edelman and I claim here, that motivation is what projects perceptions into the previously knowledge-free sensory fields. This is what "primordial experience" is, not a field already provided with percepts. This explanation fits readily into the evolutionary account of knowledge, "genetic epistemology,"[60] which sees the organism faced with the problem of producing action-guiding concepts when faced with an environment it knows nothing of, not even of what is to be selected as "an object."

Thus, in this theory of perception, a separation of the *en-soi* from the *pour-soi* certainly exists, but it has none of the dire consequences Merleau-Ponty envisaged. The non-epistemic sensory field can be said to part of the *en-soi*. What it can be taken to be evidence of is equally a part, and these are both bare existence: the *pour-soi* is involved in all objectivities, "essences," including that of the self, for they are shaped by this motivation-process from that sensory experience. That portion of the *en-soi* that is the sensory field exists in a brain in an individual body, providing a special access for each of us to energy-distributions around us, and, since the *pour-soi* Gestalt-projection system is also individually triggered by each person's own motivation-experiences, it is no surprise that "cognitive dissonances" occur from person to person, or, as Hans-Georg Gadamer would put it, differing "horizons" to be "fused."[61] His insistence on the part played by "tradition" can now be seen as no more than an exhortation to join in the Idealization of Reciprocity. It matches, too, Paul Ricoeur's notion of speech as the "intentional transgression of the situation."[62]

The dialectic arises because we have to update each other's Gestalts,[63] however habitually embedded they may be—like that of the sun. Let me update one more for you about the sun: it is always illusory. J. L. Austin would have comfortably taken it as a prime example of a safely common object, but it is never where we think it to be, not only because our sight of it is eight minutes old, light taking that time to travel from the sun, but because the Earth's atmosphere refracts the rays from it so that it is always displaced in the sky from what would have been its actual position. One has to be an astronaut and go outside the atmosphere to escape that distorting effect. We may even think that our subsequent recognitions of common objects are "automatic"—one may say that, but only with the sense of *prompt*, not that of *determined*. The laying down of percepts under a "regime of value"[64] *is* automatic in the "determined" sense, as we have just seen (which is perhaps a reason why Merleau-Ponty placed objects, "sensory things," in the "pre-objective"), but the adjustment of them is not. We do that as the Joker does, by providing the all-important second clue to a new relevance, a new interpretation according to interest and purpose, which effects the metamorphosis, both of the percept and the motivation that went with it. So no wonder we find serious philosophers speaking of the "conundrums," "puzzles," and "riddles" they face in their profession. Witness William James, who, in speaking of the paradoxes that the notion of the Absolute gave rise to, that rationalist presupposition of the convergence of word and world, concluded, "The whole thing remains a puzzle, both intellectually and morally."[65] One can also note the fascination of the philosophical mind with riddle-situations, from Gottlob Frege's "Phosphorus" and "Hesperus," to Husserl's mannequin/woman, Wittgenstein's "Continuing the Series," Willard V. Quine's "Gavagai," Putnam's "water" and "watter," Davidson's "frightening the burglar" and "opening the door," Michael Dummett's "baby-switch," Gareth Evans's "Madagascar," Kieth Donnellan's "Smith's murderer," Terence Horgan's Clark Kent and Superman, Fred Dretske's "last movie to be shown at the Strand Theater," Brian Loar's bus and orchestra conductors, Tyler Burge's Claras, and so on. From the point of view of this argument, all these are evidence of the nature of the informative Statement as having the Riddle-Story-Joke Pattern. What these philosophers did not realize was that in using the word "conundrum" itself they had a clue to the riddle pattern that attends all dialectical resolutions. They did not understand that one can be serious about jokes. One asks whether Merleau-Ponty might not have approved of this riddle analysis, for he says, "The other's words, or mine in him, do not limit themselves to vibrating like chords the listener's machinery of acquired significations or to arousing some reminiscence. Their flow must have the power of throwing me in turn toward a signification that neither he nor I possessed before."[66] This kind of riddle-resolution is precisely our evolutionary advantage both over those organisms which are unable to change their responses, and over the higher animals, who, able to update their own percepts, are unable to pass on their discoveries to their species-fellows, for we have the power to effect the updating via language from individual to individual. Not all the informative exchanges end up as did those of Short and

Sharp. Merleau-Ponty's metaphor of "commerce" is appropriate in this riddle sense, for in any instance of buying and selling there is a "presumptive" equivalence of monetary value which is not regarded as the same by the buyer and the seller. Money is thus an excellent metaphor for the linguistic statement in use, for the sentence contains the move, as described above, that shifts from a presumed idealization of reciprocity to a new adjustment of referential value. William James used it to emphasize how there always has to be a final appeal to the body's sensory fields:

> Truth lives, in fact, for the most part on a credit system. Our thoughts and beliefs "pass," so long as nothing challenges them, just as bank-notes pass so long as nobody refuses them. But this all points to direct face-to-face verifications somewhere, without which the fabric of truth collapses like a financial system with no cash-basis whatever. You accept my verification of one thing, I yours of another; we trade on each other's truth. But beliefs verified concretely by somebody are the posts of the whole superstructure.[67]

Finally, when the mutual correction goes through and is shown by its testing-out on the real to deliver the desired result, the updating of a our Gestalt shows (1) that the other has access to what caused our own sensings; (2) that an external continuum exists (even though the present objectification remains only viable); (3) that the other exists as a corrector of our percepts and concepts (even though our concept of him or her—and of ourselves—remains only viable); and (4) that our sensory fields exist as fields whatever we happen to be selecting from them (open-eye views, after-images, mental images, dreams, hallucinations, pressure-phosphenes, migraine fortification-patterns, and so on). Thus we can be sure of existence, so solipsism is no threat for this approach as Merleau-Ponty feared, even though every entity remains forever provisional.

## 7. The Resistance to the Dialectic

Some philosophers (the most recent example is Richard Woodfield[68]) have questioned Richard L. Gregory's theory that all perceptions are hypotheses constructed from a separate sensation-level[69] on the ground that Gestalt-projection bears no resemblance to logical inference. This you will recognize as a repeat of Merleau-Ponty's attack on the rationalist/intellectualist, who, he thought, reduced perception to an inference from evidence. As Woodfield says, "Monkeys do not make guesses when they leap from tree to tree." But one has to see the metaphorical point of Gregory's use of the word "hypothesis." The essential feedback provided by the motivation system is automatic, as we have seen, but, nevertheless, it only works tentatively, and that is its central advantage, for it can be updated at any time, either immediately as a result of some further motivation-feedback, or, in the human case, by communication (for the latter, there may be, on some highly self-conscious occasions, processes of logical inference literally involved). So a Gestalt-projection does partake of the nature of a hypothesis in that it is only viable, open to adjustment at any time should the feedback of an unexpected pain or pleasure result, or should a social partner give us warning of pain or promise of pleasure. In a sense, all communication of knowledge works on a basis of warning or promise, and rhetoric upon the dialectical skill of indicating those contextual clues that will suggest the needful change of our Gestalts.

Not until it is accepted that a field exists which is open to rival interpretations can the process of dialectic and of communication itself be understood. This very process of correction, which shows that the other has a kind of access to that most intimate of experiences, our non-epistemic sensory fields, provides the proof of there being an external world and other minds. That proof is not provided by Merleau-Ponty's "pre-objective," the well-engrained Gestalts we picked up as a child. It is the mutual correction of objectifications that proves the existence of the external, not the specious actuality of mundane objects. Sometimes the most familiar, the coziest object turns uncanny; hence, those stories in which the most harmless of things (say, a doll) turns into something fiendishly threatening, reminding us that all our perceptions are only viable, hypothetical in Glasersfeld's and Gregory's sense. The objectless viscosity of the field as such is prime evidence of existence beyond any solipsism. Call it the *en-soi* if one wishes, but there is nothing "monstrous, flabby, disorganized" about it, nothing "terrifyingly, obscenely naked" as Sartre saw it.[70] This bare evidence that awaits interpretation we come to learn is shared, through their own bodily sensory access, by others. Merleau-Ponty should have read his Helmholtz,[71] his Lewes,[72] and his Sellars,[73] and, one might add, his Nietzsche, with less adversarial an eye. He could have learned from Kant, Schopenhauer, and Bergson on humor, for it is there, and in tragedy, that we get the dialectic of desire and fear with all its splendors and miseries. The initial faith must exist that allows the co-ordination to go through, the "presumption" behind all rationality that Merleau-Ponty was eloquent about, but we must be able to produce a metamorphosis in the other's interpretation of his or her own sensory evidence. One can say that Hegel was right in recognizing the endlessness of dialectical correction, wrong in taking the presumed endpoint, the Absolute, as a reality instead of a projected, never-to-be-achieved point of convergent understanding, Schutz's and Rommetveit's "Idealization of Reciprocity," that is, something literally "pre*supposed*." So, first the tentative trust, and then the correction. Otherwise there is the danger of being stuck with an unintelligible, an uncanny, field.

But the prejudice that we are faced by an array of mutually common objects is extremely strong. McClure provides an example in his assertion that seeing is always and essentially pre-propositionally believing in "a something I am seeing."[74] The origin example can be found in Edmond Husserl's idea of the "determinable $x$."[75] McClure is both right and wrong. He is right because there is no perceiving without the motivation module in our brain projecting a unary Gestalt on to the sensory field, so if a child has developed to the stage when it can "see something," he or she will certainly "believe" that there is a something he or she is seeing. Once established in the practice of perceiving, we at most times range over a sensory field applying our Gestalt module, whose job it is to create apparently discrete entities from the sensory flux at the behest of pain and pleasure, desire and fear. But he or she is wrong if this is to be taken as involving two claims, (1) that it is impossible to sense without perceiving (which has been seen to be empirically false), and (2) that there is nothing in our perceiving which escapes our understanding, even to the boundaries of "the" entity we are supposedly identifying.

I think the misconception also arises from carrying the Idealization of Reciprocity too far. We are led to think that the sensory evidence must always have been safely sorted for mutual identification. It is tempting to think that there is no risk involved, that we have nature securely tamed, even to the counting of every "separate thing" up to one. We ourselves do have our one thing before us, as Short and Sharp individually did, a one thing that, up to that point, has caused us no surprises. But to play the Idealization of Reciprocity game properly, we have to keep in mind the fact that the common identification is what *pro tempore* we are mutually pretending, that one's own "one thing" cannot ever be wholly the other's "one thing." The point is to be ready for a correction from the other, for that is precisely how an informative communication is made, and this co-operative performance does imply risk.

The risk, as notably in the case of Short and Sharp, can extend to the entityhood of "what" is perceived. When Hamlet's Gestalt-camel, when he was looking at the cloud with Polonius, changed into a weasel, it was not necessarily all of the camel that changed into all of the weasel. Using the *Fliegender Blätter's* Duck-Rabbit as our sole example tempts us into thinking that the whole of one Gestalt changes into the whole of another on all occasions, but that is not the general case. To use another Shakespearean instance: when Duke Theseus' "bush" turned into a "bear" because the person he was describing was "imagining some fear," it was not the case—especially because of that motivating fear—that every part of the Bush-Gestalt became all of the Bear-Gestalt, for perhaps there was a projecting branch which appeared as part of "the bush" but was taken as part of the background when the fearful Bear-Gestalt was dominant. So even the word "this" as referring to a "particular," McClure's "something," or Husserl's "determinable $x$," is not a reliable term in this analysis, as Dignaga said long ago. But this is what we discovered in the analysis of the Humpty-Dumpty joke with its six or seven words, that no reliance could be placed on the boundaries of things, for they are part of the convenient common assumption, the same that David Wiggins made, that all our vaguenesses overlap perfectly. Many a conjuror takes advantage of our almost irrepressible tendency to go on seeing "one" thing.

Merleau-Ponty cannot have it both ways; he cannot go on claiming that the sensory provides "an infinity of perceptual aspects"[76] and then believe that objects are given to us in ontological discreteness. William James called the dictum, "Things belong to discrete and permanent kinds," a "postulate of rationality."[77] What the modern neorationalists forget is that it is a postulate, especially those who are tempted to believe in "natural kinds." Merleau-Ponty had not given up this "intellectualist" prejudice. To believe—and not merely mutually assume—that we have for any identification achieved a perfect objectivity which has selected a given discrete portion of the continuum, exactly the same portion for both of us, is a narcissistic illusion, a complacent self-reassurance, whether we idealize our own interpretation or the apparently public one. It is not an accident that "to count" means both *to enumerate* and *to matter*. We have to assume a perfect objectivity in order to achieve co-ordination of our differing perceptual-intentional perspectives, but we must never believe it; otherwise, we would never have the scope for the essential mutual correction.

Wasn't this the moral of all stories?—that it is dangerous to be obsessed with one strong wrong clue in the context to the point where one perception is held to in the belief that it alone will guarantee some current utility. And the story is resolved, the joke is out, when a second, fainter, clue becomes plain to the protagonist and he or she is forced to perceive anew—in the comedy, shifting to one that ceases to be threatening; in the tragedy, seeing the hopeful interpretation transmogrified into a presence that promises despairing loss. We the readers, the audience, have fortunately been in possession of the double truth for most of the time, and this has been tremendously consoling. So this is the outcome of this story, for it warns against taking any identification, including that of yourself, as more than viable.

## 8. Conclusion

The dialectic raises the ethical question of what faith in the other has to be. As Emmanuel Levinas has brought out in moral philosophy, a radical otherness in our social partner resists a final description, and we have to take responsibility for that fact even though a perfect reassurance escapes us. As he puts it, "the I does not construe the Thou as object, nor ecstatically identify itself with the Thou for the terms remain independent,"[78] which connects with the point made here that neither the public nor the private meaning can be absolutely privileged. A similar insight shows itself in the psychoanalyst Jacques Lacan's insistence that language, the Symbolic, can never wholly capture the Real,[79] neither from the synchronic, the publicly agreed, point of view, nor from the diachronic, the privately adjusted, one. This point was indirectly glanced at too in Sartre's claim that the other's surprising objectification of ourselves could bring a shock of shame.[80] And it explains Merleau-Ponty's own assertion: "We are not reducible to the ideal consciousness which we have of ourselves any more than the existent thing is reducible to the signification by which we express it."[81] This is embraced in what that wise empiricist Sellars insisted upon: "Being is one thing and knowledge is another."[82] The implications for some fashionable theories in modern philosophy are radical. If the above argument is correct, then Donald Davidson's attack upon the separation of "scheme" and "content," which he calls the "third dogma of empiricism,"[83] cannot be upheld, nor can Putnam's claim that "there are things and we think about them" be sustained without considerable qualification.[84]

So a story has been told about them as well as about Merleau-Ponty, one trusts of the genial comic variety. He wished to privilege the body, give it a place in the dialectic of which he was in search, but he held too timorously to the objectifications of the public language to allow a proper place to be given to the non-epistemic sensory evidence that the body automatically and neutrally provides. In this, he was still "intellectualist," still attributing to nature what is part of the human projection system, its knitting together of unary Gestalts from the sensory continuum. He prevented himself reaching his goal because of his fear that accepting an inner sensory field would draw him into the old empiricist camp, in which human judgment disappeared into associationist determinism. But the case is that it is out of the dual operation of the bare sensory evidence and the motivated Gestalt-projection system that evolution moves up to the human level of allowing mutual correction via the informative Statement—the Joke, the Story—to be made by individuals of the very words that have so far supposedly determined them. No wonder we are fond of games.

Let me conclude with a joke told by Gerald Edelman, who used it to emphasize the semantic creativity of language. Since interpretations can shift, as they did with Aesop's story, we can do the same with this. Two American Jews, Saul and Reuben, are visiting Israel, and they are keen to savor the uniqueness of that novel and interesting country. They therefore decide to go to a night-club to appreciate the entertainment that is on offer. The most successful act of the night turned out to be an Israeli comedian. As he told his jokes, all in Hebrew, the audience were in fits of laughter, with tears running down their faces. Saul, sitting there with a straight face, suddenly realized that

Reuben was as overcome as all the rest of the audience, being almost on the floor with laughter. "Hey, Reuben," he said, "how come you are laughing at the jokes? I didn't know you knew any Hebrew!"—"I don't," replied Reuben, "It's just that I trust these people." Here is a joke that makes fun of that taken-for-granted faith that is the initial move in the Statement, the Joke, or the Story. For Reuben, the non-epistemic remained exactly that, perfectly non-epistemic, that is, absolutely unintelligible. He trusted beyond the level of trust, forgetting that, in order to partake in the language game, he must be ready to check any assertion on his private sensory field himself, for one day the need to correct the public language might be crucial.

## Notes

1. Immanuel Kant, *The Critique of Judgement*, trans. James Creed Smith (Oxford: Clarendon Press, 1957), p. 199.

2. Arthur Schopenhauer, *Die Welt als Wille und Vorstellung*, vol. 2 (Leipzig: Brockhaus, 1859), p. 99.

3. Henri Bergson, "Laughter," in *Comedy*, ed. Wylie Sypher (New York: Doubleday Anchor Books, 1956), pp. 61-190 (see pp. 66-74).

4. Bohdan Dziemidok, *The Comical: A Philosophical Analysis* (Dordrecht: Kluwer Academic Publishers, 1993), pp. 35-40.

5. Bamil Matilal, *Perception: An Essay on Classical Indian Theories of Knowledge* (Oxford: Clarendon Press, 1986), p. 332.

6. George Henry Lewes, *Problems of Life and Mind*, two volumes (London: Trübner, 1874), I, pp. 121-122.

7. Richard Rorty, *Philosophy and the Mirror of Nature* (Oxford: Basil Blackwell, 1980).

8. William James, *The Writings of William James*, ed. John McDermott (Chicago: Chicago University Press, 1977), p. 89.

9. Maurice Merleau-Ponty, *Phenomenology of Perception*, trans. Colin Smith (London: Routledge and Kegan Paul, 1970), p. 52.

10. Roy Wood Sellars, *The Principles, Perspectives and Problems of Philosophy*, (New York: Macmillan, 1970), p. 125.

11. See, e. g., Mary Warnock, "Review of Merleau-Ponty's *Phenomenology of Perception*," *Philosophical Quarterly*, 14:57 (1964), pp. 372-375.

12. Roy Wood Sellars, *The Philosophy of Physical Realism* (New York: Macmillan, 1932), p. 88.

13. Herbert Feigl, "The 'Mental' and the 'Physical,'" in *Minnesota Studies in the Philosophy of Science*, vol. 2, *Concepts, Theories and the Mind-Body Problem*, eds. Herbert Feigl, Michael Scriven, and Grover Maxwell (Minneapolis: University of Minneapolis Press, 1958), pp. 370-497.

14. Arthur W. Collins, "The Epistemological Status of the Concept of

Perception," *Philosophical Review*, 76 (1967), pp. 436-459.

15. Gareth Evans, *The Varieties of Experience* (Oxford: Clarendon Press, 1982).

16. Jack S. Crumley II, "Appearances Can Be Deceiving," *Philosophical Studies*, 64 (1991), pp. 233-251.

17. Rorty, *Mirror of Nature*, p. 154.

18. Donald Davidson, "The Myth of the Subjective," in *Relativism, Interpretation and Confrontation*, ed. Robert Krautz (Notre Dame, Ind.: University of Notre Dame Press, 1989), pp. 159-172 (see pp. 161-164).

19. Gilbert Harman, "The Intrinsic Quality of Experience," in *Philosophical Perspectives*, vol. 4, *Action Theory and Philosophy of Mind*, ed. J. Tomberlin (Atascadero: Ridgeview Publishing, 1990), pp. 31-52 (see pp. 34-40).

20. Hilary Putnam, "Reason without Absolutes," *International Journal of Philosophical Studies*, 1 (1993), pp. 179-192 (see pp. 186-187).

21. John McDowell, *Mind and World* (Cambridge, Mass.: Harvard University Press, 1994), pp. 3-23.

22. Donald Davidson, "On the Very Idea of a Conceptual Scheme," in *Enquiries into Truth and Interpretation* (Oxford: Clarendon Press, 1984), pp. 183-198 (see p. 192).

23. Merleau-Ponty, *Phenomenology*, p. 433.

24. *Ibid.*, p. 354.

25. *Ibid.*

26. George Herbert Mead, "Social Consciousness and the Consciousness of Meaning," *Psychological Bulletin*, 7 (1910), pp. 397-405; John Dewey, "The Reflex Arc Concept in Psychology," *Psychological Review*, 3 (1896), pp. 357-370.

27. Roger C. Schank and Chip Cleary, "Making Machines Creative," in *The Creative Cognition Approach*, eds. Steven M. Smith, Thomas B. Ward, and Ronald A. Finke (Cambridge, Mass.: MIT Press, 1995), pp. 229-247.

28. Merleau-Ponty, *Phenomenology*, p. 28.

29. Maurice Merleau-Ponty, *The Primacy of Perception, and Other Essays on Phenomenological Psychology, the Philosophy of Art, History and Politics*, trans. William Cobb (Evanston, Ill.: Northwestern University Press, 1964), p. 12.

30. *Ibid.*, p. 20.

31. Roger McClure, "Seeing," *Journal of the British Society for Phenomenology*, 25 (1994), pp. 85-95 (see p. 92).

32. James J. Gibson, *The Senses Considered as Perceptual Systems* (London: Allen and Unwin, 1968).

33. Maurice Merleau-Ponty, *The Structure of Behaviour*, trans. Alden S. Fisher (London: Methuen, 1965), p. 187.

34. *Ibid.*, p. 219.

35. Immanuel Kant, *Critique of Pure Reason*, trans. Norman Kemp Smith (London: Macmillan, 1964), sec. B140, p. 158.

36. Alfred Schutz, *Collected Papers*, vol. 1, *The Problem of Social Reality* (The Hague: Martinus Nijhoff, 1962), pp. 3-47.

37. Edmond Wright, "The Entity Fallacy in Epistemology," *Philosophy*, 67 (1992), pp. 33-40.

38. Ragnar Rommetveit, "On Negative Rationalism in Scholarly Studies of Verbal Communication, and Dynamic Residuals in the Construction of Human Intersubjectivity," in *The Social Contexts of Method*, eds. Michael Brenner, Marsh Brenner, and Marilyn Brenner (London: Croom Helm, 1978), pp. 16-32.

39. Schank and Cleary, "Making Machines Creative," p. 230.

40. David Wiggins, "On Singling out an Object Determinately," in *Subject, Thought and Context*, eds. Philip Pettit and John McDowell (Oxford: Clarendon Press, 1986), pp. 57-72 (see p. 70).

41. Merleau-Ponty, *Phenomenology*, p. 63.

42. Ernst von Glasersfeld, "An Introduction to Radical Constructivism," in *The Invented Reality*, ed. Paul Watzlawick (New York: W. W. Norton, 1984), pp. 17-40.

43. Merleau-Ponty, *Phenomenology*, p. 54.

44. Maurice Merleau-Ponty, *The Visible and the Invisible*, trans. Alphonso Lingis, ed. Claude Lefort (Evanston, Ill.: Northwestern University Press, 1968), p. 234.

45. Émile Brehier, "Discussion," in Merleau-Ponty, *The Primacy of Perception*, pp. 27-40

46. See Gregory Bateson, *Steps to an Ecology of Mind* (London: Granada, 1978), p. 152.

47. Merleau-Ponty, *Phenomenology*, p. 61.

48. Josiah Royce, *The Religious Aspect of Philosophy: A Critique of the Bases of Conduct and Faith* (New York: Harper and Row, 1958), pp. 309-310.

49. See Edmond Wright, "What It Isn't Like," *American Philosophical Quarterly*, 33 (1996), pp. 23-42 (see pp. 26-27).

50. Edmond Wright, "A Design for a Human Mind," *Conceptus*, 47 (1985), pp. 21-37.

51. Gerald M. Edelman, *The Remembered Present: A Biological Theory of Consciousness* (New York: Basic Books, 1989).

52. Daniel Alroy, "Inner Light," *Synthese*, 104 (1995), pp. 147-160.

53. J. B. Maund, *Colours: Their Nature and Representation* (Cambridge, England: Cambridge University Press, 1995).

54. E. J. Lowe, *Subjects of Experience* (Cambridge, England: Cambridge University Press, 1996).

55. Rosie Mestel, "Hearing Pictures, Seeing Sounds," *New Scientist*, no. 1928 (4 June 1994), pp. 20-23.

56. Edmond Wright, "A Defence of Sellars," *Philosophy and Phenomenological Research*, 46 (1985), pp. 73-90 (see pp. 81-82).

57. Sir Charles Brewster, "On the Knowledge of Distance Given by Binocular Vision," *Transactions of the Royal Society of Edinburgh*, 15 (1884), pp. 663-674.

58. See William Epstein, "The Representational Framework in Perceptual Theory," *Perception and Psychophysics*, 53 (1993), pp. 704-709; Arthur M. Glenberg, "What Memory Is For," *Behavioral and Brain Sciences* (forthcoming).

59. Merleau-Ponty, *Phenomenology*, p. 52.

60. Jean Piaget, *The Development of Thought: Equilibration of Cognitive Structures*, trans. A. Rosin (New York: Viking, 1975); Nicholas Rescher, *A System*

*of Pragmatic Idealism*, vol. 1: *Human Knowledge in an Idealistic Perspective* (Princeton: Princeton University Press, 1992); Clifford Hooker, *Reason, Regulation and Realism: Toward a Regulatory Systems Theory of Evolutionary Epistemology* (Albany, NY: State University of New York Press, 1995).

61. Hans-Georg Gadamer, *Truth and Method*, eds. Garrett Barden and John Cumming (London: Sheed and Ward, 1975), p. 273.

62. Paul Ricoeur, *Fallible Man*, trans. Charles Kelbey (Chicago: Regnery, 1965), p. 41.

63. For the term "update" in this context I have to thank Karl Hammarling (personal communication).

64. Edelman, *Remembered Present*, p. 92ff.

65. William James, *Writings*, p. 524.

66. Maurice Merleau-Ponty, *The Prose of the World*, trans. John O'Neill, ed. Claude Lefort (London: Heinemann, 1969), p. 142.

67. William James, *Writings*, p. 433.

68. Richard Woodfield, "Introduction," in *Gombrich on Art and Psychology*, ed. Richard Woodfield (Manchester: Manchester University Press, 1996), p. 11.

69. Richard L. Gregory, "Hypothesis and Illusion: Explorations in Perception and Science," in *New Representationalisms: Essays in the Philosophy of Perception*, ed. Edmond Wright (Aldershot: Avebury, 1993), pp. 232-262.

70. Jean-Paul Sartre, *Nausea*, trans. L. Alexander (London: Hamish Hamilton, 1962), p. 171.

71. Hermann von Helmholtz, *Epistemological Writings*, eds. Robert S. Cohen and Yehuda Elkana (Dordrecht: D. Reidel, 1977).

72. Lewes, *Problems of Life and Mind*.

73. Sellars, *The Philosophy of Physical Realism*.

74. McClure, "Seeing," p. 92.

75. Edmund Husserl, *Ideas: A General Introduction to Pure Phenomenology*, trans. W. R. Boyce Gibson (London: Collier Macmillan, 1968).

76. Merleau-Ponty, *Phenomenology*, p. 52.

77. James, *The Writings of William James*, p. 524.

78. Emmanuel Levinas, *The Levinas Reader*, ed. Sean Hand (Oxford: Basil Blackwell, 1989), p. 66.

79. Jacques Lacan, "Television," trans. Denis Hollier, Rosalind Kraus, and Annette Michelson, *October*, 40 (1987), pp. 5-50 (see p. 31).

80. Sartre, *Being and Nothingness: An Essay in Phenomenological Ontology*, trans. Hazel E. Barnes (London: Methuen, 1969), pp. 259-268.

81. Merleau-Ponty, *Structure of Behaviour*, p. 221.

82. Roy Wood Sellars, "The Epistemology of Evolutionary Naturalism," *Mind*, 27 (1919), pp. 407-426 (see p. 407).

83. Davidson, "Idea of a Conceptual Scheme," p. 189.

84. Hilary Putnam, *Representation and Reality* (Cambridge, Mass.: MIT Press, 1988), p. 3.

# Three

# FRENCH EXISTENTIAL ETHICS AND THE CREATION OF VALUE

## Matthew Kieran

### 1. Introduction

We now come to the second theme in our discussion of French existentialism: the theme of ethics. However, in doing so we immediately come upon a peculiar problem. For from the perspective of French existentialism, the very idea of ethics can easily strike us as almost contradictory. For, according to this school of thought, any contrast between subjective and objective value must be a false one. Individuals do not choose from among a competing range of values. Instead, as Sartre claims, the act of choice itself confers value: "Whenever a man chooses his purpose and commitment in all clearness and sincerity, whatever that purpose may be, it is impossible to prefer another for him."[1] This view of ethics, as is well known, has received much criticism. Recently, however, existentialist scholars have tried to reply to these criticisms. In this chapter I shall explore both the traditional criticisms of the ethics of the French existentialists and the recent attempts to defend their ethics. In doing so I hope to show where the difficulties with this view still remain.

The idea that human beings create value is taken to follow from the fact that we are self-conscious beings. The intentionality of human consciousness means we must employ our own categories in order to apprehend the world. These categories are not antecedently given but depend upon the desires, interests, and purposes we have for apprehending the world. This is the basis of the belief, fundamental to French existential thinking, that the significance of the world is itself constructed by us. Consider the opening chapter of Simone de Beauvoir's *She Came To Stay* :

> She went out of the office....When she was not there, the smell of dust, the half-light, and their forlorn solitude did not exist for anyone; they did not exist at all. And now she was there. The red of the carpet gleamed through the darkness like a timid nightlight. She exercised that power: her presence snatched things from their unconsciousness; she gave them their colour, their smell....It was as if she had been entrusted with a mission: she had to bring to life this forsaken theatre now in semi-darkness....She alone evoked the significance of these abandoned places, of these slumbering things. She was there and they belonged to her. The world belonged to her.[2]

The idea is that without our human presence the world's brute existence is nothing but a void of unformed stuff. Only the human presence brings into being smells, sensations, significance, and values. In effect, this is merely a development of the Kantian insight that only through the application of categories which constructively mediate our perception can we come to understand the world. When Françoise returns to the office, "she turned back with a qualm of conscience. This was desertion, an act of treason. The night would once more swallow the small provincial square; the rose-coloured window would gleam in vain; it would no longer shine for anyone."[3]

But given that the context to which questions of value are relative is, at best, the human one, in a significant sense we are creators of value. It is only by virtue of a certain human interest that we distinguish weeds from flowers, that coffee beans, gold, or rubies have a definite value or that sex is prized as a covenant of love or vehicle of pleasure. The idea that values transcend human interests and desires is held to be nonsensical. This is not to deny that objects in the world have properties independently of the human mind. But the way those properties are picked out and their significance depends upon our freely chosen purposes and projects. The value of objects, activities, and ways of behaving in the world is not antecedently given but depends upon the purposes we choose to put them to. The point of shaking hands, opening doors, pursuing philosophy, or having sex depends upon the purposes for which they are chosen. Once we have chosen to use or value something in a particular way, value flows into it. But, prior to our choice, the object or activity can only be valueless for us.

In Albert Camus's *The Myth of Sisyphus*, we see how even under the most coercive of conditions persons remain free to make of their lot what they will. Sisyphus was a legendary king of the ancient Greek city of Corinth renowned for his cunning. He offended the gods by chaining Death up when it was his turn to be led to Hades, so no one died until Aries managed to release Death. For his offense against the gods, Sisyphus was eternally condemned to rolling a huge boulder to the top of a hill, watching it roll back down, and repeating the same process over again. The vicious nature of the punishment inheres not merely in the exertions involved, its tediousness, or eternality but its utter pointlessness. Sisyphus' labors achieve nothing of note or worth and contribute to nothing. Indeed, any little achievement Sisyphus might take satisfaction in is undermined since the cycle of activity is unbreakable. The achievement of pushing the boulder to the top is undermined the very next instant when it rolls back down the hill.

The activity of endlessly rolling a stone up a hill may well have no objective point or meaning. Sisyphus is condemned to a fate he otherwise would not choose. Even so, he remains free to meekly accept or mock his punishment. The very fact that Sisyphus is self-conscious and thus aware of the absurdity of his fate is what enables him to transcend it. Objectively speaking, the activity remains pointless. But Sisyphus is free to take up his individual attitude toward his fate. He is free to face it in in joy, sorrow, scorn, or hope. For Camus:

> It is during that return, that pause, that Sisyphus interests me...that hour like a breathing space which returns surely as his suffering, that is the hour of consciousness. At each of these moments when he leaves the heights and gradually sinks toward the lair of the gods, he is superior to his fate. He is stronger than his rock....The lucidity that was to constitute his torture at the same time crowns his victory. There is no fate that cannot be surmounted by scorn.[4]

Camus seeks to bring out the idea that the attitude taken up is what that confers whatever significance the world and our activities within it have. To take a trivial case, consider football. In the average school playground, although some children might love football, others couldn't care less about it. Thus, a compulsory school trip to the Football Association's Cup Final or Super Bowl might be bliss for one child and yet hell for another. But even among those interested in football many different football teams will be supported. Does it make sense to ask, objectively speaking, just which football team all these boys ought to support? If the school is in Leeds do we think that non-Leeds supporters have made some kind of objective mistake? No. For, objectively speaking, no more reason exists to support one team rather than another. I might support Leeds because they win a lot, because I admire their captain, because I like their kit, because my family comes from Leeds, because I now live in Leeds, and so forth. Prior to my decision to support Leeds, I care not a jot for their position in the League. But once I choose to support them, it matters desperately to me that Leeds wins, and I follow their trials, tribulations, and triumphs with all my heart. It is the act of commitment I made to Leeds, and not any reason which explains the teams supported by others, that makes their progress significant to me.

Consider, in a similar light, questions we think of as moral matters. The significance of sex varies if we compare someone who chooses to link sex closely with romantic love and someone for whom sex is merely a vehicle of pleasure. For the first, sex should only be directed toward the object of one's love, whereas for the second there need be no such constraint at all (Beauvoir, for example, claimed that, even though Sartre discussed his many sexual conquests with her he only really loved her, and because they understood sex in this way she should not have felt betrayed in the way someone in a traditional marriage obviously would). Indeed, though enforced celibacy might impoverish the lives of some, for others, such as Roman Catholic priests, celibacy may constitute a positive boon. What matters in conferring significance and value is the attitude I freely choose to take up toward the object, activity, project or commitment concerned. The significance of the flowers a husband brings home to his wife depends upon his motivation: whether it is to express love, soften her up because he wants to watch the football, or to assuage his guilty conscience because he has been carrying on an adulterous affair. On this view, the significance of marriage itself depends upon the motivating spirit with which it is undertaken. Its nature, and the significance of infidelity, differ according to whether it is conceived of as embodying claims of ownership, a legal contract of cohabitation, or a covenant of love.

Human freedom is thus not merely the capacity to choose what to value from some preexistent societally ordered set. Here choice is conceived of as heteronemous and something we can get right or wrong. Instead, for the existentialist, human freedom is strongly autonomous: we choose what to make valuable. This is the basis of Sartre's claim that action presupposes a plurality of values and that, therefore, it is the act of choice itself which confers value. Sartre here compares the individual's anguished choice to that of military leaders who know they will send a number of men to their death by ordering the attack: "All leaders know that anguish. It does not prevent their acting, on the contrary it is the very condition of their action, for the action presupposes that there is a plurality of possibilities, and in choosing one of these, they realize that it has value only because it is chosen."[5] For there are a multifarious number of different possible objects, activities, ends, goals, and values we may choose to pursue and thus render valuable in many different ways. The significance we confer upon objects is an open matter. So what is important is not so much what is chosen as the mode of choice. That is, we must choose to confer value in full consciousness of the fact that we are free to do so. No external authority, tradition, normative conception of human nature, or coercive force can truly compel my assent. Even at gun-point, I can nonetheless choose what attitude to take up toward what I am "asked" or ordered to do: I may condone or be scornful of the order I am given and act accordingly. This is why Beauvoir, Camus, and Sartre, who all fought for the Free French in the Second World War, could be fierce critics of collaborators and soldiers who attempted to excuse or justify their actions on the grounds that they were ordered to do so and therefore had no choice but to comply. One can always refuse even if the alternative is death. What matters in the moment of choice is whether I freely choose to confer the object or activity with significance with regard to my life.

The existentialist answer to the question "How should I live my life?" does not concern the content of our choices. Instead, it focuses upon how we so choose. To speak of right or wrong *per se* is nonsensical. What is valuable, good, or right depends upon my freely chosen ends. Radical freedom does not entail merely that each person can do as he or she pleases. True, for the existentialist, the fundamental constraint upon a good human life is not constituted by what is chosen. But this does not mean there are no constraints. According to the existentialist, what matters is the manner in which a particular choice is made: the mode of choice. The truly human life, one that is authentic, is possible only for those who properly recognize the inescapability of freedom and responsibility.[6] It is because of this that we have the deep anguish and feelings of responsibility associated with existential freedom. The only cardinal moral vice, according to the French existentialists, is bad faith. For bad faith is the futile attempt to deny our human freedom and responsibility.

The anguish and responsibility we feel in the realization that we are radically free provides a strong motive for trying to deny our human condition. For, confronted with terrifying freedom, individuals may seek to escape by subsuming or ordering their lives according to some social role or external value. Thus rather than embrace their own subjectivity and freedom they seek to objectify themselves through roles and values they act out. Sartre's well-known example here is that of the waiter in the café who identifies himself solely in terms of the social function he is employed to perform. He mechanically moves about in an affected waiter-like fashion and "plays with his condition in order to realize it."[7] People in the state of bad faith thus merely pretend to themselves that they cannot but follow the role or orders they have been given by others.

Ultimately, only we can determine, and are thus responsible for, the values we choose to create. The individual bears the sole responsibility for the decisions she makes and the ends she pursues. To defer to external authorities, whether it be one's family, society, or religion, is to abdicate one's freedom. Because of this there exists the need to cultivate the demanding independence of thought and action required to act authentically. As radically free agents, we are in a continuous process of self-creation, and there is always room for us to reinterpret past events in the light of newly chosen fundamental aims and values. What matters is that we should strive for authenticity and thus responsibility for what we make of ourselves.

## 2. Authenticity and Evil

However, though the existentialist emphasis upon individual freedom and responsibility is attractive, there are standardly held to be severe problems with it. First, we might wonder whether this constitutes an ethics at all. The point of ethics is to articulate and thereby guide our actions toward what should be chosen. But the existentialism of those like Sartre, Beauvoir, and Camus hardly guides our actions at all. We are provided with a formal side-constraint: choose authentically. But that is certainly no help in enabling us to understand what we should be choosing or striving for. If everything is permissible, given authenticity, then what guidance do I have regarding how I ought to live my life? At the pragmatic level, existentialism affords an unhelpful contextualism which cannot guide us toward what we should or should not do. The notion of an existentialist ethics seems misplaced, since the idea that we could have more reason to do one thing rather than another is considered a mistake.

But existentialism's silence over the nature of our choices is taken to reveal a much deeper inadequacy. The problem is not merely that existentialism is unhelpful in guiding our particular choices. Rather, as presented here, it inevitably leads to a simplistic, wholly implausible, and vicious subjectivism. If free choice creates value, then there can be no substantive constraints upon any of our possible choices. That is, what I authentically choose to value and deem to be moral is thus valuable and moral for me. So, unless the mode of choice is contaminated, the existentialist can only embrace any free choice made by someone in good faith. But one might authentically choose to be a vicious criminal like the Kray brothers or Al Capone, just as one might authentically choose to be like St. Vincent de Paul and devote one's life to society's poor and neglected. In both cases, we may consciously express our freedom in good faith to the same degree. Yet surely such commitments are not equally morally admirable.

At the funeral of one of the Kray brothers, a family of long-time gangsters who ran the East End of London, various criminal associates were present who were happy to reminisce about the good old days. One of them, called something like Frankie Knuckles, lamented the passing of an era. What he really valued about the Krays and the old criminal fraternities, Frankie said, was that they had "efficks." They chose not to intimidate more people than was required to get enough money, they chose never to hit children, mothers, or old grannies, and they never ever killed more people than was necessary to protect themselves. Certainly, they were not like the criminal delinquents around today.

The ridiculousness of such claims does not depend upon whether the Krays made their choices in a state of good or bad faith. We need not deny that the Krays acted according to their own freely chosen norms and values. We might even recognize and perhaps admire in their criminality the strength of character required to resist what would otherwise have been their allotted fate in a deprived area of the East End of London. Nonetheless, even if their decisions were made in good faith we are inclined to judge them to be evil: by virtue of the vicious malice and callous disregard for human life displayed in their pursuit of profits and power.

Consider, in a similar vein, the well-known problem of the sincere Nazi. Here we have the case of someone who presents a fundamental problem for French existential ethics.[8] For the sincere Nazi freely chooses to devote his life to the persecution and obliteration of Jews. Not only does existentialism remain silent regarding the nature of the ends he has devoted his life to, but it is condemned to praise the Nazi's life as virtuous. Far from condemning evil, it looks as if existentialism ends up condoning it. Indeed, on this picture, the sincere Nazi is certainly more morally admirable than, say, someone who gives to charity because the church tells the person to and yet tries to deny his or her mixed motives. The mode of choice in the charity case seems to constitute bad faith. The action is motivated by one thing, religious authority and instruction, and yet the charity giver tries to persuade himself or herself that the real reason concerns his or her interests in the welfare of the poor.

Yet this is to get the relationship entirely the wrong way around. Normally we would recognize that though not the actions of a moral saint, because of his or her mixed motives, the charity-giver is performing a morally admirable action. It is better to do a good act from mixed motives than an evil act from pure ones. The compliment hypocrisy pays to virtue is the very recognition that particular acts or ends are right and good in themselves. Hence, we can make sense of the notion that the road to hell is paved with good intentions. We might freely and authentically choose with good will to pursue a particular act or activity which, as it turns out, is intrinsically immoral. Certain colonial imperialists, slave owners, and aristocratic landlords may well have freely chosen to act in what they believed the best interests of others. Yet, we are inclined to think, they may remain open to moral censure and blame.

Conversely, despite the authenticity of his choice, the Nazi is deeply evil. Authenticity is insufficient for virtue. Indeed, it is symptomatic of true evil that the person knows exactly the nature of his or her choice and freely chooses it. Because of this we distinguish someone who is truly evil from the ignorant or the mentally ill. The ignorant or mentally ill may perform evil actions but do not or perhaps can not grasp their nature. Conversely the truly evil person knows the vicious nature of certain ends and freely chooses to pursue them knowing he or she could have chosen otherwise.

French existentialism's incapacity to recognize that our choices can be mistaken would suggest a deep flaw not only in the ethical sphere but in its phenomenological analysis of value quite generally. Consider the following case. At one time a British breakfast TV program, *The Big Breakfast*, had a section entitled something like "keep it up or give it up." Viewers wrote in, their hobby was aired, and a loosely assembled panel got to vote on whether they should carry on or give it up. One middle-aged professional man's hobby was playing Subbuteo (miniature soccer) by himself at least twice every night, keeping league tables of all the match scores, and even sometimes playing the F. A. Cup and League Cup games on top of the regular League games.

Such activities, in moderation at least, are not quite as bizarre as we might presume. Many people collect useless glass objects, all things cat-like, stamps, old books, or go trainspotting. But we might meaningfully ask, what is the point? Anyone who pursues such activities might reply in various ways: because I like the look of cut glass, the weight, feel, and smell of old books, or I enjoy simulating football matches. But whatever the particular reason given as an explanation, it constitutes an attempt to account for why the activity is valued. We might not understand why someone enjoys or derives pleasure from such things. But we may at least find the explanation intelligible in the sense that, so far as the activity gives someone pleasure, he or she has a reason to value it.

But on the existentialist account, the response as to why something is valuable does not refer back to something the activity itself gives rise to. Instead, value is deemed to be conferred by free and authentic choice. Hence, the existentialist would reply, "it is valuable because I freely chose to do it." But this is wholly uninformative. The mere fact that an activity has been chosen does not straightforwardly bestow meaning or confer value upon it. Indeed, no one is disputing that the activity in question has been chosen. The whole point of the question is to ask why on earth you or anyone else would so choose. Unless we can give a story about why someone might so choose, then the activity looks unintelligible. My fundamental commitment to pursue a particular activity does not yet make it valuable. Hence, we can be mistaken about what we choose to do and value: something French existentialism allows no room for.

Moreover, even when we consider activities that afford us pleasure we quite happily recognize that some are more valuable than others. If we ask why anyone should bother pursuing philosophy, it is inadequate merely to refer to the pleasure it affords. Reading Kant's *Third Critique* is hardly the fastest or surest way to any kind of pleasure at all. But we do think that philosophical activity cultivates something of great intrinsic value: knowledge and understanding. Though watching soap operas such as *Dallas* or *D.I.Y.* may give us greater pleasure, we are naturally inclined to value philosophy much more. One affords us insight into the human world in a way in which the innocent pleasures of bad soap operas never could.

The pleasure afforded through pursuing philosophy is not constitutive of its value but a mark of its value. Whereas if watching *Dallas* gave no pleasure at all there would be no clear reason as to why anyone would watch it. Thus, if someone devoted his entire life to philosophy we would certainly find this more intelligible and perhaps admirable than if he freely decided to devote his entire life to watching *Dallas*. For we think that valuing soap operas to such an extent is misplaced. In claiming this we do not merely state that we happen to so value philosophy relative to soap operas. We appeal to inter-subjective intuitions, reasons, and values which we can reasonably expect others to share. Thus, we point to the nature of the activities concerned and try to show others how they might come to be seen as possessing the relevant kinds of values and thereby contribute or not to human life.

No one can recognize and assent to the relevant values and activities for me. But this is quite trivial. The important point to grasp is that choice is normally a matter of following reasons for a particular evaluation rather than choice itself conferring value. We strive to recognize what is valuable; hence, we can fail and be mistaken. This is not to deny that the value of particular things may be culturally relative. Nonetheless, we normally recognize that certain activities are valuable to all humanity, such as philosophy, art, and science. Moreover, whether an individual or society chooses to be so or not, we are inclined to demand that they should always be just, fair, and tolerant. It is only because we can and do recognize what is often termed categorical morality that we can and rightly do condemn those who sincerely and freely choose to break with it. Although the existentialist emphasis upon individual freedom and responsibility is admirable, ultimately it can only prove to be seriously mistaken. Human free choice, of itself, can not create all aspects of value.

## 3. The Existentialist Response

The standard existentialist response to such criticisms is to claim that the problem posed is an artificial one. The very idea that the Third Reich was populated by hundreds of thousands of sincere Nazis seems a little too glib. After all, many "committed" Nazi Party members merely used the party for their own personal ends. Many Jewish shops were burned down, people were turned in or persecuted simply because fellow businessmen or businesswomen saw an excuse to get rid of competitors, acquire some property, or neighbors saw an opportunity to get rid of people they did not like in favor of friends or family. Many officials even sought to innovate or enforce various policies with zeal because of the gain in social and institutional prestige such actions brought with them. Albert Speer, for example, used the Nazi Party to further his architectural dreams.[9] So the furtherance of Nazi Party goals were often pursued so far as they helped to realize more fundamental ends. Many ordinary Germans and collaborators chose to do what they did in a state of bad faith, disguising from themselves the truth about the regime they were serving or pleading the necessity of following orders. Thus what really explains Nazism and its evil, so the existentialist may be tempted to claim, is bad faith.

Consider the reaction of the townsfolk of Belsen when they were forced by Allied soldiers to file past the concentration camp at the end of the war. The overwhelming reaction was one of both horror and denial: for they could not understand why this was supposed to concern them. For they had not pulled the trigger, manned the fences, or opened the gas chambers. Yet, even if they had not actively persecuted Jews themselves, they had all supported or colluded in a regime which did persecute Jews for their own individual ends. To deny responsibility for the end state of affairs is thus a futile and misguided attempt to avoid responsibility by denying one's free choices or capacity to act freely.

It is important to recognize that such instances of bad faith are not peculiar but are, in fact, a widespread phenomenon. Consider the psychology of many who get drawn into the causes of extremism, racism, and vicious forms of nationalism, ranging from the former Yugoslavia, Palestine, South Africa under apartheid, and Northern Ireland, to groups such as the Klu Klux Klan, British National Party, and Combat 18. Ostensibly, what is involved is the commitment to bring about a certain end, such as the protection of a particular ethnic group. But when one examines the reasoning and actions involved, the underlying motivation is often revealed as an excuse to exclude or exterminate a particular group of people. The plight, failings, disappointments, and self-hate of one group are effectively projected on to the external group, who are then identified as the cause for all the failings and problems.[10] Rather than face up to the actual state of affairs, such people find it easier to turn outward and blame others. Bad faith is to be avoided because it constitutes a fundamentally inauthentic mode of existence. Evil actions result because people either falsely presume that there are objective values, in the name of which individuals can be sacrificed, or act in a state of bad faith. According to Sartre, to believe that there are objective values is to fall into the trap of being too serious-minded but it is not yet to be in a state of bad faith. Both are problematic because they involve acting in the world upon a false basis, but only bad faith involves self-deception.[11]

Yet though no doubt many Nazis were in a state of bad faith, as Gordon Graham points out, this is not true of all.[12] For some people at least, Nazism appeared to embody aims, goals, and values they freely chose to serve. People like Himmler accepted full responsibility for their actions. They willingly sought to shape the world in such a way as to cultivate and embody Nazi values. Thus, where those values implied persecution, genocide, and eugenics they were to be embraced. Nor are such episodes in human history as unique as we might like to think. Consider, for example, the brief but particularly cruel history of the Aztec Empire of Mexico in the fifteenth century. It's estimated that around the 1480s there were 20,000 human sacrifices annually in various forms, including cutting out the hearts of prisoners of war while they were alive.[13] Throughout history, some people and cultures have chosen freely to devote their lives to what we consider to be fundamentally evil.

The problem is that, as a matter of principle, existentialism remains silent about such people when we would expect any decent moral theory to condemn them. In fact, existentialism suggests that they are good by virtue of their authentic choice. But normally we think that if someone freely chooses to perpetrate evil that is a damning rather than a redeeming feature of his or her action. Ignorance mitigates guilt only because sincere, clear-sighted evil compounds a person's guilt. Hence, Hitler is thus worse than a youth brought up in Nazi Germany who could not be expected to have known the nature of the commitments, values, and policies involved. Moreover, to be in a state of bad faith under certain conditions may itself be partly redemptive. The Belsen townsfolk wished not to know what was going on precisely because they hoped that things weren't in fact as they turned out to be. At least such people possess the right moral sentiments, even if they lack the courage and commitment to act upon them. Conversely, figures such as Himmler, who accepted full responsibility for his part in the Holocaust, clearly do not possess the right moral sentiments at all. Such people are evil precisely because they know the nature of what they do and are indifferent to or positively rejoice in what is fundamentally inhumane and immoral.

A further move open to the existentialist is to claim that cases of sincere evil may involve not just bad faith but also ignorance. Thus a sincere Nazi may not be in a state of bad faith but might just be straightforwardly ignorant. Morally speaking, it is important to distinguish between someone who is genuinely mistaken and one who recognizes the relevant belief is false but attempts to deny it and is thus in a state of bad faith. But bad faith is bad not just because it involves self-deception, it is bad because it leads us to act within the world on a false basis. Ignorance too, though not involving self-deception, may lead us to confront the world on an illusory basis. Indeed, in *Truth and Existence* Sartre's exploration of ignorance suggests that it can be an intentional state constituted by the goal of aiming to avert oneself from recognizing the truth. Thus, evasive and willful ignorance itself may be akin to a form of bad faith.[14]

To draw the point out a little, consider the following non-moral case. We do not say that because someone has freely and sincerely signed up for the Flat Earth Society that therefore the earth is flat for that person. We rather say that the society-member believes the earth to be flat and is mistaken in that belief. What underlies the person's belief is either ignorance, perhaps the person remains within the walls of a flat earth cult, or bad faith, because despite the evidence he or she prefers to remain with friends and the cult. This is not to presuppose the objectivity of value which existentialism denies. But it is to claim that the values chosen and thus created must engage with the way the world is rather than an illusory fantastical one. The ignorance in such cases is willful precisely because were these fundamental beliefs to be subjected to reason and verification they would be shown to be false. In the case of Nazism, for example, the belief that Jews are essentially sub-human and pose a poisonous racial threat would be revealed as incoherent, inconsistent, and thus illusory. Those who were prey to such beliefs are guilty of willful ignorance.

For the belief can only be retained by actively avoiding the relevant evidence and a refusal to test the relevant claims against reason. Such a refusal is an abrogation of reason and thus human freedom. Therefore, Sartre says, "to want to not know (*ignorer*) is, ultimately, to want to place ourselves in the hands of chance."[15]

Just as the paralytic cannot choose to walk but is free to make of his or her condition what he or she will, so too we cannot alter the truth or falsity of certain propositions but remain free to make of them what we will. Like the flat earther, the Nazi can not deny the relevant evidence without putting himself in a state of bad faith. Nazism, Aztec sacrifices, trial by ordeal, slavery, satanic sacrifices, and many other practices we would condemn as evil all clearly rested upon false beliefs. So evil is the product of willful ignorance or bad faith. This does suggest that, as Maurice Merleau-Ponty recognized, it is only in the light of certain cultures and beliefs that we can come to see whether we are mistaken in what we have chosen to commit ourselves to.[16] Therefore, existentialists can recognize that those such as apparently sincere Nazis are morally corrupt.

Such a response may seem convincing in relation to cases obviously involving false beliefs and ideologies. But it remains inadequate precisely because it does not entirely get us around the motivating worry. Imagine a man who is an expert torturer and killer. He does not kill because he believes he is furthering some great cause or promoting the purity of humanity. Rather, he just enjoys inflicting intense pain and subsequently taking the lives of the weak and innocent. This is the basis of the dedication and commitment to his art. None of his actions depends upon false beliefs. Indeed, he is very careful to pay close attention to how much pain particular methods of killing cause. He knows just when to stop to keep life going so he can extend the pain inflicted and, as a very sensitive torturer, knows just when to apply the most excruciating techniques to maximize the pain felt by his victim. Such a man is paradigmatically evil. For he recognizes and strives for the infliction of suffering, pain, and death for no other reason than that he chooses to derive pleasure from it. Even if most of the historical cases cited involve mistaken beliefs it is at least conceivable that, as a matter of principle, some people might freely choose to devote their lives to inflicting pain and suffering upon others. Given that such a commitment and activity need not depend upon false beliefs, the existentialist cannot say anything negative about such a person. Indeed, given there are no false beliefs and the choice is made authentically, the existentialist is condemned to say that here is a good person. So the basic objection remains.

French existentialism suggests that the good life—how we ought to live—is governed by the ideal of authenticity. That is, what matters ethically is the mode of choice. But one may authentically choose to do evil. Any plausible moral theory had, at the very least, better rule out paradigmatic instances of evil. But if I choose, authentically and under conditions of full knowledge, to devote my life to torturing the weak, then existentialism is committed to the claim that this constitutes a good life. Yet we want to say that such a life is manifestly evil. This is not to deny that the torturer's life is good for him: the time and energy he has invested in satisfying certain desires affords his life an apparent meaning. Nonetheless, objectively speaking, it is a bad life. As Aristotle might put it, a genuinely fulfilling human life does not aim at the act of torture because, for the most part, such activities undermine rather than promote true happiness.[17] Although the torturer's life embodied those things which were values for him, values he freely and sincerely chose, nonetheless we want to say his life was evil.

## 4. Universal Freedom and Moral Particularism

However, in defense of French existentialism, it is worth focusing more closely upon the intuition that sincere Nazis and torturers are evil. Presumably, we think the perpetrators immoral because they inflict upon others what they would not concede in relation to themselves. Obviously, this suggests the Kantian thought that an act is only morally permissible if it survives the test of universalizability.[18] This is often expressed, somewhat crudely, by the golden rule: do unto others only as you would be done by. An action is thus permissible only if we would consent to others performing the same action in similar circumstances or if our roles were reversed. The evil of the sincere Nazi and the sensitive torturer inheres in their infliction of suffering upon others they would never be prepared to accept themselves.

Now, as articulated, such a move might seem unhelpful. For if the test of universalizability holds good, then we can generate legitimate moral principles which are objectively true independently of a particular individual's assent. That is, we have a content to morality which prescribes certain actions. But the notion that there are objective moral principles seemed to be precisely what the French existentialists denied. Thus, existentialism's answer to what the moral life consists in is either false or collapses back into nothing more than a rather trendy form of Kantianism.

But this would be too quick and is to miss what is truly distinctive of French existentialist thought. The core thought remains that in annihilating or oppressing the existence of another the oppressor seeks to deny the fundamental humanity of others. Killing involves the annihilation of exactly what the killer takes to warrant, in himself, the pursuit of his own ends and goals. Taking the life of another thus involves a fundamental contradiction. As Terry Keefe points out in the next chapter, Sartre's requirement that we "assume" our being-for-others should be seen as an implicit recognition of the fundamental freedom of others just as we are required to recognize that freedom in ourselves. This is why we find Sartre in his *Notebooks for an Ethics* arguing that the recognition of my own freedom is what grounds the recognition of the autonomy of the other. But the appropriate attitude to take up toward others is neither to see them as impinging upon my fundamental freedom nor, conversely, to assume their goals as one's own, but to engage with them and the world so that they may act in order to realize their goals.[19]

Given that the killer's freedom to pursue authentically chosen ends applies by virtue of the killer's self-consciousness, then the same reasoning must apply to all who are self-conscious, including the killer's victims. As Beauvoir puts it, "to will oneself free is also to will others free."[20] Thus implicit in the killer's action is a fundamental contradiction: self-consciousness both does and does not warrant the exercise of the capacity to choose. The basic existentialist assumption is that all self-conscious beings should choose freely what to pursue or value. This is a fundamentally different matter from merely choosing to pursue particular activities or goals. My achievements might preclude others from attaining their goal. Only one person can hold the 100 meters world-record at any given time. But this is merely to frustrate the successful pursuit of a particular choice. My achievement of itself does not preclude others, as a matter of principle, from trying to outdo me or pursue other activities they may freely choose. The claim that we should be free to choose does not entail the claim that we should have every choice available to us. The first is a claim about exercising the capacity which enables us to choose certain things. The second claim concerns how many and what kind of choices there should be open to us in the exercise of this capacity. Killing or enslaving another does not merely prevent someone from realizing a particular choice. In killing someone, the killer denies others the existence required to choose or pursue anything at all. Existence, after all, is a precondition of choice.

The self-contradiction argument allows the existentialist to condemn killers and oppressors as evil even where the victims may welcome their oppression. Hence, Beauvoir claims, for example, that "the existentialist doctrine permits the elaboration of an ethics, but it even appears to us as the only philosophy in which an ethics has its place. For, in a metaphysics of transcendence...evil is reduced to evil....Existentialism alone gives—like religions—a real role to evil, and it is this, perhaps, which makes its judgments so gloomy."[21] One might imagine a world full of evil killers who wish to persecute the weak, and, moreover, the weak consider their lives will be rendered meaningful by such a fate. Now it may seem that the capacity for choice is not being denied because the euthanasia or sadomasochism involved is voluntary. Such actions may be done from a state of ignorance or in bad faith. A killer may not have realized that it is by virtue of our self-consciousness that we are free to choose how to pursue our lives: in which case he or she is deeply and reprehensibly mistaken. Alternatively a killer may have realized the link between self-consciousness and freedom but attempts to deny it: thus attaining a state of bad faith. There is, I think, good reason to suppose that those who kill on grounds of weakness or inferiority are self-deceived at some fundamental level. Hence, Nazis, racists, vicious nationalists, and other extremists tend to believe themselves to be splendidly meritorious in ways others are not. But the action's fundamental evil inheres in the self-contradiction made manifest through the act of asserting one's own will by annihilating or oppressing that of another.

One might have some residual worries about whether such an account of existentialism allows for the possibility of self-defense, something the French existentialists would obviously not want to deny given their support for the Free French. But, as Beauvoir states, "the ill-will of the oppressor imposes upon each one the alternative of being the enemy of the oppressed if he is not that of their tyrant; evidently, it is necessary to choose to sacrifice the one who is an enemy of man; but the fact is that one finds himself forced to treat certain men as things in order to win the freedom of all."[22]

It is necessary, given that various people attempt to oppress others, to fight and defend the freedom of all to choose how to lead their lives. Unfortunately, certain people are involved in oppression due to ignorance rather than through the wish to subjugate the freedom of others. Nonetheless, unless we are to remain in complicity with oppression, we have a duty to revolt against it. After all, the oppressor remains free to renounce his or her self-contradiction. It is only because the oppressor insists upon attempting to subjugate the freedom of others that we are forced into a position of asserting our freedom against him or her.

Thus, French existentialism holds to the Kantian assumption that what explains the wrongness of acts such as murder is that they invoke an inherent self-contradiction. But, as Beauvoir distinguishes existentialism from Kant and Hegel, "for existentialism, it is not impersonal universal man who is the source of all values, but the plurality of concrete particular man projecting themselves toward their ends on the basis of situations whose particularity is as radical and as irreducible as subjectivity itself."[23] One precondition of living a genuinely authentic life is: always respect the capacity to choose freely which values to live by. But, given that, no substantive universal and general moral principles exist which can determine what we can and should do. For our freely chosen normative commitments are worked out in and through our particular engagement with the world. To the extent any principle can be formulated from our actions thus far, it will either be useless, as it can only tell us what we already know, or distorting, since it attempts to set in stone what our future normative commitments and projects should be. Yet moral principles cannot determinately capture all the ethical possibilities open to us.

Given that the values of our human projects and activities are multiply ambiguous, and thus determined by the significance we confer upon them, the possibilities can only remain under-specified and thus inherently open. For we are forever free to revise our past commitments in the light of newly chosen values and projects. Our moral commitments cannot be comprehensively captured by any one set of moral principles no matter how infinitely complex they may be. Thus, when deliberating about what we should do in a given situation, far from appealing to the test of universalizabilty, the existentialist appeals only to particular features of the case, its context, and the normative commitments I choose to adhere to then and there.[24]

The plausibility of existentialism rests upon the multifarious differences between us as to what to value and pursue. Divergences over what our good consists in, within the constraints of authenticity, appear blameless and justifiable. Such a position seems closer to commonsense morality than the Kantian preoccupation with regulative moral principles. For the moral ideals we choose to pursue, like the friendships we choose to develop, may vary immensely. After all, we do not typically blame our friends for liking people we ourselves are not particularly interested in or would not choose to be friends with. We do not think we all ought to have the same friends with the same qualities. Similarly the lives of the ascetic, the pragmatic, the intellectual, the philanthropist, the devout, the family man, the housewife, or the public servant are all moral ideals which we are prepared to allow involve various normative commitments and the pursuing of certain goals. In Beauvoir's words, "it is not impersonal universal man who is the source of values, but the plurality of concrete, particular men projecting themselves toward their end on the basis of situations whose particularity is as radical and irreducible as subjectivity itself."[25] But we are far from inclined to think that there is some lexical or rank ordering we can or should give to these different ideals. Instead, they are all valuable in their own way, and what makes them such is the authentic choice of one prepared to commit themselves to such an ideal. That we chose the life of an intellectual over and above that of the pragmatic is not open to blame as such; it is only a reflection of what I choose to give value and meaning to my particular life. What others choose is a matter for them alone.

The same point comes through if we consider the nature of moral dilemmas. We are confronted by a number of different possible constraints which pull us in different directions. Consider a simple dilemma of the following form: your best friend confesses she cheated in her logic exam. If one chooses to recognize the constraints of justice, one will inform the lecturer. Cheating falsifies the mark awarded and undermines the achievements of others. Conversely, if one chooses to value friendship, then one will be committed to resolving not to let her guilty secret slip out. Which way one ought to go is not straightforwardly given by some lexically-ordered set of moral principles but depends upon individual judgment. It is a question of which value one chooses to adhere to in the given case, something even one's prior choices cannot determine since one can always revise previous commitments. Our decision is not so much open to considerations of praise, blame, or opprobrium but rather reflects the person we have chosen to be.

The ethical ideals we choose to uphold need not be arbitrary on the existentialist picture. We can point to features of the activities and characteristics of the ideal we choose to pursue in a way which helps to explain our choice. Yet we do not, or should not, demand that everyone else should pursue and thus confer upon our ideal exactly the same value. There are many great works of art, but we do not demand that everyone esteem them all to the same degree or, more perniciously, lexically order them as if art were a game with one winner and many losers. Similarly, there are a great many ethical ideals, and we should not demand some kind of lexical ordering of priority. Instead, we are free to choose which values to pursue as long as we are clear that the responsibility is ours alone. Our universal freedom, that which is the precondition of free choice, is realized through the creation and pursuit of our own particular set of ideals and values. We create and must take ultimate responsibility for our own ethical world.

The particularity of each individual's ethical world explains why, as was mentioned in the introduction to this volume, much of French existentialism's moral philosophy is found in novelistic form. Many of Sartre's philosophical writings are riven with moralistic descriptions and analysis. But given that the answer to how I should lead my life is not properly guided by universal moral rules, what is needed is a phenomenological analysis of the kinds of commitments our choices might entail. This is a matter properly explored through works of art and, in particular, the novel. Indeed, according to existentialism, the normative goal of works of art is to explore the conditions of authentic choice and what the implications of particular choices might be. This is the reason for Sartre's condemnation of poetry such as symbolism, which he takes to obscure and mystify rather than deepen our understanding of what possible worlds might be like.[26] For the point of art is to show us the kind of commitments involved in living particular kinds of lives, and how certain self-understandings guide particular people through their moral perplexity. What we glimpse through the artwork is certainly not reducible to general moral maxims, nor should it be taken to prescribe how we ought to choose or act. Instead, works of art offer to show us how particular individuals understand themselves and attempt to negotiate and resolve their problems in confronting others and the world. Thus, through affording us a deeper understanding of the possibilities open to us, we can understand better the choices and values we are free to create. Moral understanding is thereby a matter of self-knowledge conjoined with a grasp of the possibilities and commitments to which we may freely choose to commit ourselves.

## 5. The Problematic Nature of French Existentialism

Although many thinkers find the arguments from self-contradiction and ignorance plausible, underlying worries remain. It seems odd that I should not kill someone for fear of self-contradiction or that the wrong inheres in my ignorance. The fundamental moral wrong of murdering another is apparently reduced to the kind of rational error or inconsistency one may be guilty of in getting a maths equation wrong. Still, for the sake of argument, let us grant that this way of putting the worry is just too glib. The moral error is held to be of a fundamentally different order given it concerns the very basis of our mentality. Thus, it looks as if the arguments from self-contradiction and ignorance enable existentialism to fend off the objection concerning sincere evil. Moreover, Beauvoir's emphasis upon the particularity of moral choices, dilemmas, and ideals allows us to distinguish existentialist ethics from the more familiar Kantian variety.

One standard worry about existentialism concerns the fact that normally we think it a good thing that principles govern our choices. But, the objection goes, existentialism holds no truck with general moral principles, only authentic particular choices. Yet if no governing principles really existed and everything was a matter of authentic choice, then society would be impossible. We would end up in a Hobbesian state of nature where, for fear of what others might choose to do, we would be unable to drive our cars, go shopping, or trust in the society of others. Without the idea that principles should govern our conduct, we are left with few choices which make it worthwhile being an authentic individual. Moreover, we cannot in each case seek to examine the choices open to us. The very attempt to do so would lead to a form of existential paralysis as manifested in Hamlet. Such critical questioning tends to corrode the bonds to which we have authentically chosen to commit ourselves.

Yet, as expressed, such a worry is far too crude to trouble the existentialist. Our actions should originate spontaneously and my authentic self is created by my freely chosen actions. But to presume that therefore I must ponder on which action to perform in each and every case and that there cannot be general principles we should appropriately take to guide our actions is to betray a shallow misconception of existentialism. Sartre's and Beauvoir's emphasis upon the particular context of actual choices does not preclude appeal to general principles at all. Rather, the point is that our commitment to general principles arises out of and is created by the particular choices we make. Thus, general principles are operative, but they are a function of the fundamental interests we have chosen to pursue as made manifest in our particular choices. What is fundamental is that such principles are the upshot of our freedom to take risks and to be open to experience both of others and the world. They are the result of our authentically encountering the world, and thereby are an attempt to remake it in our own image.[27] As Jacob Golomb puts it,

> Sartre claims that there is rarely a single significant act which is not part of some 'original projection of myself which stands as my choice of myself in the world' (*Being and Nothingness*, p. 39). Authenticity is not one notable action, as it is not the self or a predicate; rather, it is from this fundamental project of self-choice that all other predicates of authenticity and authentic actions derive their meaning.[28]

The crucial point to grasp here is that what matters for existentialism is the fundamental animating spirit underlying the creation of the self in action. But this is perfectly consistent with the recognition that we take general principles to guide our actions. The general principles themselves are taken to be an upshot of whatever fundamental spirit we have chosen to lead our lives in. For example, if the fundamental spirit in which I have chosen to lead my life is one of beneficence, then this naturally underwrites such general principles as always give to charity, always help people in difficulties, and so on. What these principles amount to, and how they are to be reconciled when they clash, depends upon the precise nature of my underlying beneficence. Nonetheless, I can authentically take such principles, where they are consistent and cohere with my fundamental animating spirit, to guide my life. I need not be forever questioning Hamlet-like what it is I should do in each case and why. Only from time to time need I examine whether the fundamental spirit in which I have lived my life thus far is one I wish to reaffirm or revolt against, as in the case of a radical conversion. But it is not the principles that I question here, it is the fundamental spirit in which I freely choose to lead my life. Thus, as Joseph S. Catalano puts it, "Sartre's point...is that glimpses of the possibility of a radical change surface now and then from beneath our everyday choices. The professor of philosophy, who is deliberating about what textbook to use, will at times realize that this everyday choice is also a way of choosing to continue his life-style as a college professor, and this choice to continue his role is interesting and significant."[29]

Given this conception of how general principles relate to one's fundamental authentic choices, the existentialist will point out that worries about a society full of existentialists being reduced to a Hobbesian state of nature are ill-founded. For existentialists can authentically subscribe to legal principles, laws, and regulations which all would ideally agree to as long as they enshrine and protect the individual freedom of all and do not seek to proscribe any particular substantive conceptions of the spirit in which people should seek to live their lives. French existentialism is thus, as a matter of principle, consistent with the early kind of Rawlsian contractualism regarding sociopolitical governance.[30]

Nonetheless, despite the adequacy of the existentialist's reply, something more fundamental remains to the objection which can be articulated in a more sophisticated and pressing manner. It is not so much that existentialism cannot account for the governing role we take principles to have in our moral lives. As we have seen, existentialism clearly allows both that we should deliberate at times about whether we should authentically renew our commitment to a particular project, activity, or value, and that, as a product of our authentic commitment, we take principles to guide how we fulfill or adhere to those commitments. But, the worry goes, the guiding principles themselves are not and cannot be taken by existentialists to have any inherent justificatory force. To be sure, given a fundamental commitment certain general principles can be taken as appropriate. But the basic problem remains that whichever fundamental commitment, and thus principles, I take as given is held to be a wholly contingent and arbitrary matter. Thus, the motivating spirit of my life and the subsequent principles taken to govern it are not open to any kind of rational criticism.

True, as we have seen, the French existentialist can preclude various commitments on the grounds of self-contradiction or ignorance. As Golomb argues, this very ideal does entail commitment with respect to certain notions such as reciprocity and respect, since we are constrained to recognize others as autonomous persons and far from seeking to dominate or oppress them we should allow them to create and express their own authentic selves.[31] But all this having been said, within these constraints many options remain of which we would want to say they are more or less open to moral praise or censure, and this is something existentialism cannot do. Compare, for example, the life of one who has chosen to devote herself to helping the poor, one who devotes her life to her farm, and one who devotes herself to creating increasingly elaborate and obscene fantasies. The first case, other things being equal, is akin to that of a moral saint. The second case is, with respect to self-interestedly tending one's own farm, neither particularly morally praiseworthy nor blameworthy. The last case, at least to the extent delight is taken in the imagined obscenities, is morally dubious to say the least. But French existentialism, given that all three cases do not abrogate the proscriptions against self-contradiction or inconsistency, can only remain blind to any moral differences in the characters of these lives. For each of the fundamental commitments is regarded as arbitrary and contingent as the other and thus only valuable to the extent they have been chosen authentically.

Although this appears to be a natural damning consequence of French existentialism, William L. McBride and Catalano, among others, have claimed that this is only so given a misunderstanding, albeit a rife one, of Sartre's conception of existentialism.[32] Such a view is only a consequence of existentialism if we understand it as an entirely individualistic doctrine concentrating solely upon the isolated subject's authentic choice. But, following McBride and Catalano, we might deny this to be the case. True, the emphasis in Sartre's earlier works does seem to be almost entirely preoccupied with the individual. And yet, if we take into account the ways in which his earlier work may be considered of a piece with, rather than distinct from, his later work, such as his *Critique of Dialectical Reason*, then McBride and Catalano argue that this emphasis is perfectly consistent with a view of existentialism distinct from the one thus far articulated. Namely, the human being, *qua* self-conscious being, must strive to live freely and authentically. Nonetheless such an aim is rendered difficult, if not impossible, by virtue of the socio-economic conditions and structures prevailing in contemporary society. My relationships with others are endemically contaminated by the fact that how we interact and on what basis are an upshot of iniquitous historical conditions under which various groups or classes are oppressed, relations mediated, and thus freedom inhibited. For example, it may seem as if my employing someone for $2.50 an hour constitutes an authentic relationship since they have freely consented to the job and conditions I freely offered them. Nonetheless, that they freely consent is not enough to make the relationship an authentic one. For the unequal historical socio-economic conditions framing the agreement constrain how those involved construe themselves and what they consider themselves to be realistically free to choose to do. The very possibility of authentic self-creation is undermined by the social structures which themselves both manifest and give rise to bad faith.

As Catalano characterizes this reading of Sartre, we must be careful to recognize Sartre's distinction here between simple social relations and historical ones. According to Catalano:

> In a simple social relation, for example, a mother loving her child, there can be one-to-one reciprocity. Even here we must add that the reciprocity is constituted by the actions of the mother and child and is not a priori. But as a historical relation, the mother faces the child through the mediation of a third. For example, the mother, as a woman, has a historically determined role in society. In the concrete, her love for her child is affected by the mediation of the way society sees her womanhood. If the mother is poor or rich, the love for her child will also be affected by this mediation.[33]

Thus, given that the historical socio-economic relations themselves render social relations *de facto* inauthentic, presumably we ought to devote our lives to political action in order to get rid of the structures which hinder the realization of both our freedom and that of others. This is possible once we recognize that the nature of human society is not given but historically contingent. We should work for radical social change, perhaps encompassing revolution, so that we can create a society in which truly authentic relations are possible. Thus, on this reading, presumably the life of one who identifies with the oppressed, working for social change and thereby the freedom of all, is much more admirable and authentic than the life of a self-interested farmer who ignores others and merely tends to the farm for personal material benefit.

Although such a move definitely goes a long way to meeting criticisms often made about French existentialism's extreme individualism, and though insightful as a reading of Sartre's philosophical development, such a move does not dispose of the fundamental worry. An implicit tension remains between the claim that authenticity is possible, even under the most hostile of conditions, and the claim that authenticity requires the right kind of socio-economic structures and relations. But let us merely note this and move on. The basic point is that either, first, the worry has just been moved one stage further back or, second, we are left with a doctrine that is no longer readily recognizable as existentialism at all.

First, presuming we could and did achieve a state where socio-economic relations were not endemically inauthentic in this manner, we are still held to aim for the freedom to lead our lives authentically. Prior to the realization of socio-economic conditions which enable all to live authentically, we can characterize lives as better or worse by virtue of how much or how little they are devoted to it. Yet the fundamental values we could authentically choose in such a utopian society were it achieved would remain, according to the French existentialist, wholly arbitrary and contingent. In other words, it is all well and good to cultivate an ideal of self-creation, and encompass the social conditions relevant to attaining this ideal, but we still have no non-arbitrary standards by which to help us evaluate what kind of moral self we should and should not aim for under ideal conditions.

Second, we could attempt to avoid the charge of arbitrariness by taking up a suggestion made by Catalano. Given the emphasis on Sartre's recognition of the social as well as individual aspects of authenticity, perhaps it is not so much an arbitrary matter as to what kind of life we should authentically strive to live but our authentic life is defined by where we happen to be in the socio-economic structure. As Catalano himself says in summing up his gloss on Sartrean authenticity:

> The task of being authentic is different, depending upon where one is in the social strata. Sartre implies that the authentic person always aligns oneself as much as possible with the most disadvantaged members of a

community. For the disadvantaged, the task of being authentic is precisely their challenge to the image of themselves as being naturally disadvantaged; and they challenge this image not so much by trying to succeed, but by denying the justification of the image. For the advantaged members of the community their task is to see that their position is not merited....In the concrete, this historical picture must be balanced by the conditions of the immediate environment, particularly the family environment. Also the type of work that an individual is doing has to be taken into consideration....In the concrete, the self to be realized exists differently in each family environment and on each social level.[34]

Such a move avoids the charge of arbitrariness by rendering how the authentic life is defined as a matter determined by the complex socio-economic situations and roles I find myself occupying. But, for any argument claiming to support the doctrine of existentialism, this cannot be right. As Eric Matthews says,

To deny that we choose our own values, after all, is to contradict the basic doctrine of existentialism, that, because we are ultimately nothingnesses, because we have no being-in-ourselves, what our situation is can only be what we freely choose it to be. The exploited worker's situation cannot, for the existentialist, determine that he regard it as one of oppression, to be overcome by revolution: how he regards it must be his free choice.[35]

Thus, despite Catalano's suggestive reading the dilemma persists for any true existentialist. Either the value of the kind of self we authentically aim to create remains an arbitrary matter, which is deeply problematic since we need to allow that there are better or worse selves we can aim to create, or if it is not arbitrary then it is defined for us by our complex social roles and situations, but to allow this is to contradict the fundamental basis of existentialism.

To emphasize why being committed to the claim that moral values are an arbitrary matter is problematic, we need only consider how we explain to others why we pursue or value what we do. We give reasons which attempt to show that there is a link between the particular object or activity chosen and why people generally might have reason to pursue or value something. According to the existentialist analysis, it is merely because they have been created by my particular choices in the light of the fundamental values I have freely chosen. But we tend to think that particular moral commitments, such as justice, are required, as opposed to particular moral ideals, precisely because they pick out salient features about cases to which we all ought to attend and should take as determining our judgment. Particuliar kinds of moral reasons, those that tend to be bound up with matters of duty and obligation, for example, are taken to have a general, universal force by virtue of their concern with what is inherently right or wrong *qua* self-conscious human being quite independently of what my particular further moral ideals, personal values, and aesthetic idiosyncrasies may be. Yet even in Sartre's *Notebooks for an Ethics*, where he moves toward privileging certain values, such as love and generosity, the idea remains that obligations, to the extent they are conceived of as external and related to general constraints concerning what is right or good for us *qua* human beings, are fundamentally alienating.

Emphasizing the nature of various kinds of moral reasons might not persuade everyone that the existential analysis of value is mistaken. But it is crucial that the description under which we make our judgment is the appropriate one. Coming to see the significance of certain facts and the appropriate shading between terms such as devious, hypocritical, two-faced, tactless, unscrupulous, callous, indifferent, and fickle depends upon picking upon salient features of the way things are. Such judgments require an appropriate description of what the motivation and intention in action really was, coupled with a judgment that is amenable to rational justification that what was said was unwarranted or slanderous. Other things being equal we recognize that such behavior is intrinsically unfair and unjust. As Iris Murdoch claims, in any given situation "if I attend properly I will have no choices and this is the ultimate condition to be aimed at."[36]

Murdoch's moral particularism places the primary emphasis upon moral perception and judgment in a way which stands in direct contrast to existentialism. For the presumption is that there is an appropriate way to see things: one's perceptions may be aright or awry. Hence, we can see or discover how things really are and thus what ought to be done. Generalists think that this is the job moral principles perform: they enable us to track across cases what we have, ethically speaking, reason to do. But the objection does not rely on one being either a particularist or generalist about moral principles. Instead, the point is that we seek to judge appropriately, under the right description, what we have reason to do which may, *contra* existentialism, come apart from what we authentically choose to do.

This is not to deny an element of subjectivity to our ethical ideals and values generally. We do value different projects, goals, activities, and ideals differently. Moreover, given our different tastes, temperaments, and skills this can be quite blameless. Even so, in order to see why someone actually values something we must be able to see why he or she pursues it. Apart from noticing that someone has committed himself or herself to a given project, we must have some understanding of why he or she had reason to choose it and what he or she could expect to achieve. The person's choice will, in part, depend upon reasons for choosing that way arising from the nature of the object or activity concerned. Furthermore, for such choices to be appropriate, the values implicit in them, and ethical values in particular, must ultimately rest upon certain basic inter-subjective values constrained by our nature as human beings.[37] But if that is all existentialism claims, then it is thereby rendered trivial.

It is fundamentally revealing to consider that all the ethical perplexities, choices, and dilemmas upon which existentialism typically concentrates are deeply personal ones. Sartre's novels, for example, are full of characters such as Mathieu who deliberates and procrastinates over whether to commit himself to his lovers, to looking after his mother, or joining the Free French. Now the existentialist picture looks plausible when considered in relation to such matters. Some people naturally tend to think that such private matters as sexuality, friendship, the importance of family, and the significance of resistance depend for their value upon the way particular individuals conceive of and understand them. But think how such a conception might apply to morality wholesale, including what we think of as essentially public matters such as justice.

Consider the following case. A woman has been sexually harassed by her boss. Her boss chooses to think of it as merely a pleasant distraction from his office work and confers no more significance on his activities than that. The woman, on the other hand, finds her privacy intruded upon in a manner she finds offensive and highly distressing, and that prevents her from performing her office duties. Obviously, the significance and morality of what is going on is not reducible to how the individuals concerned consider it. We naturally recognize that one or other of the individuals concerned is mistaken: either the woman has taken mere flirtation, falsely, to constitute sexual harassment, or the man has, quite wrongly, sought to use his power to force an office junior to submit to his sexual advances. Thus, we are concerned with the unjust nature of the action, which inheres in the coercive imposition of one person's will upon another, rather than just what the individuals themselves choose to make of it. Furthermore, imagine the case comes before a tribunal. The only witness to the affair is called up and faces a stark choice: she can either tell what she saw and lose her job or deny seeing anything and keep her job. The existentialist response to such a dilemma is to state that, given good faith, one may choose to take up either option. Yet our response to such a situation is quite different. There is a dilemma, but the clash seems to be between the demands of prudence—for the self-interest of the witness lies in keeping her job—and the demands of morality: she has a moral duty to disclose what went on. Thus, it may well be rational for her to keep quiet and retain the job. But, with all due regards to the French existentialists, we would hardly describe that choice as a moral one merely because it was chosen in good faith.

The point is that only by recognizing individually transcendent principles, which are constitutive of categorical morality, can we make sense of some of our deepest ethical intuitions. Only then are we in a position to explain why we often aim to bring about changes, in the name of justice, to practices, traditions, or conventions that others may accept and participate within in good faith. After all, we think it constitutive of what it is to be just that we treat people impartially in a significant sense, and this requirement trumps whatever personal concerns, prejudices, and significance we might choose to project on to the world and others. We are thus inclined to say that even in a society where everyone gets along in a state of good faith there may still be endemically unjust or dubious practices. Yet this is precisely the kind of claim that the French existentialists deny we can make. They presents us with a flawed phenomenology of value, as if value, moral or otherwise, were merely conferred by authentic choice. Such an inadequate analysis is driven by their implausibly strong conception of freedom and being. We naturally talk not of conferring but recognizing value: whether we have reason to value something depends upon the nature of the object or activity concerned. Our authentic choices and evaluations can be mistaken.

The same point might be put more narrowly. Ethics cannot be, as the French existentialists conceive it to be, purely a matter of self-knowledge. As Plato recognized, in conditions of full self-knowledge, one might authentically choose to pursue evil. Existentialism thus parallels Socrates' assumption that evil arises due only to ignorance since human beings seek to bring something about only if they conceive of it as good. But, as Plato makes clear, one's appetites might be directed toward something which is inherently evil, one may recognize it as such and still pursue it because one's reason and conscience are not ordering but subordinate to one's non-rational passions.[38] Rather what makes someone good is both that he or she has full self-knowledge and that his or her authentic desires, goals, and projects are directed toward the right sort of thing. It is precisely this possibility, the idea of a right sort of thing toward which one's motivations and actions should be directed, that French existentialism is at great lengths to deny.[39]

## Notes

1. Jean-Paul Sartre, *Existentialism and Humanism*, trans. Philip Mairet (London: Methuen, 1948), p. 50.
2. Simone de Beauvoir, *She Came to Stay*, trans. Yvonne Moyse and Roger Senhouse (London: Flamingo, 1989), pp. 1–2.
3. *Ibid.*, p. 3.
4. Albert Camus, *The Myth of Sisyphus*, trans. Justin O'Brien (London: Penguin, 1975), pp. 108-109.

5. Sartre, *Existentialism and Humanism*, p. 32.

6. Jean-Paul Sartre, *Being and Nothingness: An Essay in Phenomenological Ontology*, trans. Hazel Barnes (London: Methuen, 1956), pp. 553-554.

7. *Ibid.*, p. 59.

8. See Gordon Graham, *Living The Good Life* (New York: Paragon, 1990), pp. 78-80.

9. See Gitta Sereny, *Albert Speer: His Battle with Truth* (London: Macmillan, 1995).

10. See Miles Hewstone, Wolfgang Stroebe, Jean-Paul Codol, and Geoffrey M. Stephenson, *Social Psychology* (Oxford: Basil Blackwell, 1988) on group attribution theory.

11. See Sartre, *Being and Nothingness*, p. 626.

12. Graham, *Living The Good Life*, pp. 78-80.

13. See Oliver Thomson, *A History of Sin* (Edinburgh: Canongate, 1993), pp. 168-169.

14. Jean-Paul Sartre, *Truth and Existence*, trans. Adrian van den Hoven (Chicago: University of Chicago Press, 1992), especially pp. 30-34.

15. *Ibid.*, p. 32.

16. Maurice Merleau-Ponty, *Phenomenology of Perception*, trans. Colin Smith (London: Routledge and Kegan Paul, 1970), p. 452.

17. See Aristotle, *Nichomachean Ethics*, Bk 2, trans. David Ross (Oxford: Oxford University Press, 1925).

18. See Immanuel Kant, *Foundations of the Metaphysics of Morals*, trans. Lewis White Beck (Indianapolis: Bobbs Merrill, 1959).

19. See Jean-Paul Sartre, *Notebooks for an Ethics*, trans. David Pellauer (Chicago: University of Chicago Press, 1992), pp. 288-295.

20. Simone de Beauvoir, *The Ethics of Ambiguity*, trans. Bernard Frechtman (New York: Citadel, 1994), p. 73.

21. *Ibid.*, p. 34.

22. *Ibid.*, p. 97.

23. *Ibid.*, pp. 17-18.

24. See *Ibid.*, pp. 78-81; Jean-Paul Sartre, *Existentialism and Human Emotions* (New York: Philosophical Library, 1985), p. 26.

25. Beauvoir, *The Ethics of Ambiguity*, pp. 17-18.

26. Jean-Paul Sartre, *What is Literature?*, trans. Bernard Frechtman (New York: Philosophical Library, 1949).

27. See Juliette Simont, "Sartrean Ethics," in *The Cambridge Companion to Sartre*, ed. Christina Howells (Cambridge, England: Cambridge University Press), pp. 178-210.

28. Jacob Golomb, *In Search of Authenticity* (London: Routledge, 1995) p. 151.

29. Joseph S. Catalano, "Good and Bad Faith," in his *Good Faith and Other Essays* (Lanham: Rowman and Littlefield, 1996), p. 107.

30. See John Rawls, *A Theory of Justice* (Oxford: Oxford University Press, 1972).

31. Golomb, *In Search of Authenticity*, pp. 152-167.

32. See William L. McBride, *Sartre's Political Theory* (Bloomington: Indiana University Press, 1991), and Catalano, "On Action and Value" and "Authenticity: A Sartrean Perspective," in his *Good Faith and Other Essays*, pp. 113-125, 151-175.

33. Catalano, "Authenticity: A Sartrean Perspective," p. 165.

34. *Ibid.*, p. 170.

35. Eric Matthews, *Twentieth Century French Philosophy* (Oxford: Oxford University Press, 1996), pp. 76-77.

36. Iris Murdoch, *The Sovereignty of Good* (London: Routledge, 1991), p. 40.

37. See Sartre, *Existentialism and Humanism*, p. 29.

38. See Plato, *The Republic*, trans. H. D. P. Lee (Harmondsworth: Penguin, 1974).

39. I thank the participants at the conference of the British Society for the History of Philosophy, University of Cambridge, and in particular Philip Stratton-Lake, for helpful comments, and also James Giles for both his helpful comments and patience.

## Four

# THE ETHICAL CONCEPT OF "ASSUMING" IN THE EXISTENTIAL PHILOSOPHY OF SARTRE AND BEAUVOIR

## Terry Keefe

What might reasonably be understood by the "existential" philosophy of Jean-Paul Sartre and Simone de Beauvoir is the early philosophy associated with the period up to the end of the 1940s; that is, before it begins to be reasonable to call them in some sense Marxists. This is part of the period that has recently come to be seen as that of Sartre's *first* ethics, for French and American commentators now commonly refer to Sartre's *two* ethics, and in many cases to a *third* that was emerging at the end of his life. His second ethics, however, is seen as dating from the early to mid 1960s, whereas his "existential philosophy" refers to positions adopted much earlier in his career—positions, essentially, that either lead up to *Being and Nothingness* in 1943, or develop more or less directly out of it.

Many aspects of, and questions about, Sartre's first ethics—not least the way in which it is complemented, completed, or modified by the writings of Beauvoir—are by now familiar, some of them having been extensively and almost continuously discussed, in one form or another, from the mid-1940s onwards. But the concept of "assuming" has been badly neglected, although it plays an extremely important, even crucial, role in the moral thinking of both Sartre and Beauvoir from late in the 1930s until at least the end of the 1940s. In a general way, "assuming" might, in any case, be thought to be a key existentialist concept, linked with the injunction to assume responsibility for ourselves rather than handing it over to others, or to fate. Or, again, expressing the idea of facing up to reality rather than escaping from it into some kind of *mauvaise foi* or bad faith. The crucial terms in French—the verb "*assumer*" and the noun "*assomption*"—are obviously just two of a whole cluster of expressions used by Sartre and Beauvoir in this area, some of which do the same and related work, and others of which serve as points of contrast. These expressions include "*bonne foi*" and "*mauvaise foi*," "*sincérité*," "*authenticité*" and "*inauthenticité*," and so on.

Two specific preliminary points about the terms "*assumer*" and "*assomption*" themselves are worth making. First, the noun "*assomption*" has little currency in non-technical French (except in its religious sense), yet Sartre uses it fairly commonly in his particular way. Second, dictionaries commonly give the verb "*assumer*" as having the basic meaning of "taking on," or "taking up"—as in taking on responsibilities or a particular role or office—then go on to refer to a second sense categorized as a neologism, and one that they often associate with Sartre himself. In other words, there is already a kind of prima-facie case for believing that Sartre and Beauvoir may be doing something special and distinctive with the terms as such, something that involves forging for themselves what I call a "concept of assuming."

A schematic account of the history of the concept of assuming in the period we are concerned with would be as follows:

(1) it is scarcely used at all in the earliest writings of Sartre and Beauvoir;
(2) it emerges quite strongly in Sartre's *War Diaries* of 1939-1940;[1]
(3) it comes to be used at critical junctures of his philosophical argument in *Being and Nothingness*;[2]
(4) it becomes a pivotal concept in the moral writings of both Sartre and Beauvoir in the middle and late 1940s.

Beauvoir's writings come strongly into play in the last phase because of Sartre's failure to publish the volume on ethics announced at the end of *Being and Nothingness*. Some of her statements about the nature of ethics in this period make "assuming" one of the cornerstones of existentialist morality and, as we shall see, in works like *The Second Sex*, when she is effectively applying that morality to particular issues, it continues to play a key role (the term "*assumer*" and its associated forms, for instance, are used some 20 times in the last 50 pages of that text).

It seems that the first use of the concept of assuming in Sartre's writings—Beauvoir published nothing at all before 1943—is in *Sketch for a Theory of the Emotions*, which was probably completed in 1938 and was published in late 1939.[3] When he is paraphrasing Heidegger in the Introduction, he uses the term "*assumer*" four times and the term "*assomption*" once. The fact that he italicizes the first use of "*assumer*" and puts scare-quotes around "*assomption*" suggests that the terms are important, and that he is aware of doing something new with them. It might be taken that the terms derive in some sense from Heidegger, but when one looks at the German text of Chapter One, Section Nine of *Sein und Zeit* (as well as the English and French translations), it no longer seems that that is the case, so that for the moment some slight mystery surrounds the origins of these terms in Sartre's works. What he actually *says* in *Sketch for a Theory of the Emotions*, presumably on behalf of Heidegger, is that "to exist is always to *assume* one's being"; that the "*assumption*" of self that characterizes *Dasein* implies an understanding of *Dasein* by *Dasein* itself; that "the *Dasein* that is *me* assumes its own being by understanding it"; that "to *exist* for *Dasein* is, according to Heidegger, to assume its own being in an existential mode of understanding"; and that "emotion is *Dasein* assuming itself and 'directing-itself-in-a-state-of-emotion' at the world."[4]

Turning to the *War Diaries*, we find that the term "*assumer*" itself is little used in the first of the diaries, which was only recently discovered and first published in French in early 1995.[5] However, the first diary indicates Sartre's preoccupations and introduces the cluster of moral ideas with which he will later associate the concept of assuming in the third (the second diary is lost).

The concept comes strongly into prominence in the context of a number of major sequences specifically devoted to morality or ethics. On 1 and 2 December 1939 Sartre tries to formulate "certain moral constants" that he has discovered in his own attitudes between 1923 and the late 1930s. This leads him, on 7 December, to begin "putting my ideas on ethics in order." And in between these two important sequences, on 4 December, we find a significant series of short entries where he focuses on, and explains, the notion of assuming. These have all the appearance of recording the first time that he has given much explicit thought to the concept, and they offer a kind of definition. Clearly, Sartre regarded himself as having developed some new moral ideas during this critical period. He dismisses Stoicism and a Kantian-type ethics of duty, concluding: "In the end I can scarcely see anything other than an ethics of authenticity that escapes the charge of self-satisfaction. (Of authenticity and not of purity.)"[6] A letter to Beauvoir shows that his new ethics came to him rather suddenly in the course of the evening of 3 December: "All of a sudden, when I got back I *saw* the ethics that I have been practicing for three months without theorizing it—which is strictly contrary to my usual habits."[7] And he has already written in his diary: "I think that I now understand and *feel* what true morality is."[8] This, then, is the context of his first specific comments on the concept of "assuming" on 4 December:

> Don't *accept* what happens to you. That is too much and not enough. *Assume* it (when you have understood that nothing can happen to you other than by your agency); that is, take responsibility for it exactly *as if* you had decreed that it should happen to you and, shouldering that responsibility, use it as an opportunity to make new progress *as if* it were for that purpose that you had decreed it should happen.
>
> This "as if" is not lying. It arises out of the intolerable human condition whereby men are at one and the same time their own cause and without fundamental justification, so that they are not the judge of what happens to them, but all that happens to them can only happen *by their agency* and can only be their responsibility.[9]

The ideas here can clearly be seen as deriving directly from those that we have seen him, a year or so earlier, describing Heidegger as having, although there the emphasis fell on the notion of humans *understanding* their own being, rather than on their taking responsibility for it. But Sartre has now moved on from his central interest in phenomenological psychology, and the passage in the *War Diaries* seems to mark the moment when "*assumer*" becomes an important *ethical* concept for him. Certainly, some of the other separate and self-contained remarks that he goes on to make at around this time sound much like what we normally take to be his existentialist ethics of the 1940s. Consider, for example: "We are totally responsible for our lives"[10]; "We never have an excuse, because an event can only affect us if it is assumed by our own possibilities"[11]; "The metaphysical value of the person who assumes his life or authenticity. It is the only absolute"[12]; and so on.

When Sartre comes to "put my ideas on ethics in order" on 7 December, he is concerned with the nature of ethics at the most fundamental level and once more goes back to ontological considerations. He suggests that ethics is a system of ends, and that the only end for human reality is human reality itself; that is, some vision of itself projected into the future and demanding to be realized through freedom. The world is that which it has to overcome in striving for its end; without such resistance, there would be no ethics. A number of sequences are clear forerunners of *Being and Nothingness* (thus making obvious nonsense of recent claims by Kate and Edward Fullbrook that Beauvoir invented all of the major ideas of *Being and Nothingness*) and Sartre goes on not only to adumbrate his distinctive view of human freedom, and how nothing can happen to it *from the outside*, but also to argue that human reality is first and foremost consciousness; that is, it is nothing at all without being conscious of it. We are conscious of being responsible for what we are, but also of not being responsible for our facticity, for the fact *that* we are; conscious of not having the complete independence of the *ens causa sui* or God. According to Sartre, consciousness throws itself forward into the world, in order to escape its gratuitousness, and to become its own foundation in the future. But he makes it clear that he regards this as an illusion.[13] He calls it a "transcendental" illusion and says that the goal of being one's own cause is the transcendental structure of human reality. It is what makes human reality moral. The project of being one's own foundation constitutes the supreme value, and is the source of all other values. Nevertheless, this quest for the absolute is a kind of evasion or flight—a flight from gratuitousness; an unavailing flight from unjustifiable facticity.

Sartre sees inauthenticity as involving an attempt to free oneself of the burden of freedom by using facticity as an excuse, seeing oneself as a thing, subject to external forces. And he talks of a view of human reality as "tossed about" or "buffeted" ("*ballottée*"), as if on the waves. He uses as a typical example one of his fellow-soldiers, who says: "Me, a soldier? I consider myself a civilian dressed up as a soldier." That would be fine, says Sartre, if the person did not simultaneously *make* himself a soldier, by obeying orders, perceiving things as a soldier, and so on. Sartre says that the individual refuses to "assume" a particular event on the pretext that he or she has rejected the principle behind it.[14]

This kind of self-contradiction makes the person wretched, and Sartre goes on to argue that his wretchedness *could* be something that leads him back to the correct view of himself ("*la vue exacte de soi-même*"). It is, however, rather uncharacteristic of Sartre to use such a phrase. Furthermore, the fact that he uses "*revenir à*" cannot be taken as carrying the implication that the correct view comes first, comes before the project to be God, since he has already talked of an "original fall" and an "effort at redemption," these two together constituting human reality.[15] This arriving at the "correct view of himself" involves a "conversion," whereby the "buffeted consciousness" freely comes to carry out authentically the effort to be its own cause, ridding itself of all elements of *evasion*. Thus, in the case of war, I assume it or take responsibility for it *in order* subsequently to adopt a particular attitude toward it.

The first assumption that human reality can and must carry out when it turns back on itself, Sartre says, is the assumption of its freedom. We never have any excuse. It is part of my facticity to be plunged into a war, but what war will be for me, what aspects of itself it will disclose to me, what I myself will be in the war and for the war—all that I shall be *freely*, and I am responsible for it. It is not just a matter of *recognizing* that we have no excuses, but of *wanting* to have none. Hence my freedom becomes my own; I assume for ever that terrible responsibility. The assumption of my freedom must obviously be accompanied by the assumption of my facticity. That is, I must will it. And doubtless will it *in order to give it a foundation*. Everything that happens to me is *given*, by virtue of my facticity and gratuitousness, but on the other hand I am responsible for it because I have given myself reasons for discovering it.

We must suppose that the concept of assuming would have figured prominently in the rest of Sartre's thoughts on ethics, but unfortunately the sequence just summarized runs to the end of a particular notebook that he was using and breaks off in the middle of his meditation. The next one is lost, and the published diaries resume only on 16 December, some ten days later. In the rest of the diaries as we have them the concept of assuming is not especially prominent. The uses that there are of it, however, are all much in line with the explanation already given. They all involve taking responsibility for something that we have not ourselves brought into being—the war itself but, more broadly, our facticity as such. However, Sartre also talks, for instance, about our assuming our historicity in general; or assuming our epoque.

In short, then, having, understandably, been preoccupied by the question of what attitude to adopt toward the war—should he resist it or in some way go along with it? In what sense was it *his* war?—Sartre was struck by the contradictions of those around him, by the ways in which they were seeking in one way or another to deny, refuse, disown, or evade the war, and realized after three months or so that his own attitude, what was for him the *right* attitude and one that he was prepared in some measure to prescribe, consisted in "assuming" the war; that is, taking responsibility for it, thinking and acting as if he were himself directly responsible for it, as if he himself had *willed* it and brought it about. His revelation on 3 December consisted in a full awareness that this was, and had been, his own attitude, and he developed this awareness, as he clearly indicates, into a kind of morality or ethics. He generalized on the basis of the particular case and formulated the view that we should "assume" our facticity. Moreover, what is extremely important for a broad understanding of Sartrean ethics is that he already went on to make crucial use of this idea in his talk of a "conversion."

Leaving the last point aside for a moment, there are obviously many things to say about these ideas in the *War Diaries*. But because of what is already familiar about Sartre's position, it is important to emphasize the much less well-known point that Sartre here appears as a proponent of the philosophy of the "as if," not something that one readily associates with his name. The pedigree of this philosophy is a good one, since its importance in Kant is undisputed. Sartre knew his Kant but he was probably also familiar with the book by Hans Vaihinger, *The Philosophy of "As If"* (of 1911). It is worth making two points about this aspect of Sartre's views at this stage. First, for all the different aspects of Kantian philosophy that are capable of being construed in terms of "as if," it is not clear that any are the same as Sartre's particular use of this method of analogy, or regulative principles, or heuristic fictions, which seems precise. If Kant says, "You should act as if you were making universal legislation, or as if God exists," Sartre says, "You should act as if you were responsible for things that you are not responsible for." Secondly, in the light of all of this, we should be rather less inclined to see Sartre's use of the idea of universalizability in *Existentialism and Humanism* as an unexpected aberration, or as something that comes entirely out of the blue, since it seems to contain a kind of "as if" appeal.

This is unmistakably a *prescriptive* position in the *War Diaries*; that it has to be construed in some way in terms of moral recommendations or injunctions. Yet these do not seem to me to be any less vulnerable to the question "Why?" than any other basic prescriptions. *Why* should I act as if I were responsible for things that I am not responsible for? But, even more obviously and importantly, it remains obscure *which* things I should act as if I am responsible for, and what exactly such action entails. In this respect, Simone de Beauvoir's reactions to Sartre's new ethics on 14 December are interesting:

I've finished your diaries. I'd have liked to write you the big letter you ask for—about your ideas—but it all makes the same impression on me as Bergson (forgive me) when I was young: so absolutely true and definitive that I can find nothing to say. It's extraordinarily interesting, and so true that one thinks: "Well, yes, of course!," though it's devilishly ingenious. All that part about human will and ethics is convincing—I can't find any fault with it and am dazzled by its self-evidence. What a good head you have, my sweet little one. Only I'm greedy for the rest; I can't see at all how you will manage the transition to practical ethics. So far it remains formal, just like Kant's good will, which is defined by the will to be a good will. I've just read it through again, but really I can't comment without having read the rest. I find everything right line by line; I only wonder how you'll resolve it; what I must assume; and, when I assume my freedom, what I do with that assumed freedom. Send me the rest as soon as you can—it's really, really interesting.[16]

These are apposite questions, and we can go on to show how some of the subsequent history of "*assumer*" in Beauvoir's own writings as well as Sartre's bears out this fact.

But first it is appropriate to jump more or less to the end of the period under consideration; that is, to Sartre's *Notebooks for an Ethics*, written in 1947-1948 and published for the first time in French in 1983 (English translation 1992).[17] The three vital points to make about the *Notebooks* for present purposes are: (1) that the concept of assuming has a crucial part to play in the book's arguments; (2) that in general Sartre understands by the concept what he came to understand by it in the *War Diaries* in December 1940; and (3) that, since the *Notebooks* dwell at considerable length on the "conversion" to authenticity that Sartre flagged up as possible in a footnote on page 484 of the French edition of *Being and Nothingness* (and, probably, also in a footnote on page 111), saying that he could not describe this conversion in the book, then what we have in the concept of assuming is one of the key notions of the ethics that Sartre was envisaging at the end of *Being and Nothingness*. Hence it is a notion that we are now in a position to say straddles that major work in an interesting way.

The *Notebooks* clearly take up where *Being and Nothingness* left off, and—although this is not yet widely understood outside the circle of specialist Sartre scholars—from the first pages they begin tackling the "conversion" that Sartre had enigmatically alluded to in *Being and Nothingness*. More generally, fragmentary and disjointed though they are, the *Notebooks* in a sense build up to a final 100-page section under the heading "The Conversion." Without undertaking to explain systematically what the conversion amounts to, we need briefly to emphasize some of those aspects of it that Sartre explains in terms of assuming.

The continuity with the relevant entries in the *War Diaries* is striking. But there is a new element, the key to the conversion, and that is "pure" or "purifying" or "non-collusive" reflection, as opposed to the "impure" or "collusive" reflection that was predominantly or even exclusively associated with the state of humankind and the state of human relations described in *Being and Nothingness*. By means of pure reflection, Sartre now says, human beings can can achieve the conversion to authenticity and leave behind them the over-arching project to be being-in-itself-for-itself (*en-soi-pour-soi*), or God. At the level of the self, this involves *assuming*—exactly as Sartre was already saying in the *War Diaries*—one's facticity, one's contingency, one's freedom. He even comes back at one point to the example of the war, saying that I must live it as if it was I myself who had brought it about:

> I may do everything I can practically so that the war can be avoided, but if it does break out I *have to live it through*. I do not change my point of view on it; I persist in condemning it. Perhaps I even decide in the midst of the war to carry out an antimilitary propaganda campaign. But, even so, I have to live it out as if it were I who had decided it should happen. I reject it and assume it exactly as in the case of my own moods. It is an opportunity for unveiling the world. At the very moment when I condemn it, or reject it, I must make it yield the maximum unveiling of being.[18]

Reference to Simone de Beauvoir is useful at this point, since, in the absence of the published work on ethics that Sartre promised at the end of *Being and Nothingness*, Beauvoir felt able to publish a number of essays on ethics herself in the mid-1940s. It is clear from all of these that she considered herself as, in some sense, saying what Sartre *would* have said if he had published such a treatise. She insists that she is working within the framework of the ontology of *Being and Nothingness*, and in her memoirs she gives the following explanation of how she came to write her most substantial moral essay, *The Ethics of Ambiguity*.[19] In conversation with a student friend, after she had given a talk at the home of Gabriel Marcel, she says: "I told him that in my opinion one could base an ethics upon *Being and Nothingness*, if one converted the impossible desire to *be* into an assumption of *existence*."[20] Her moral essays at the time, then, duly make crucial use of the concept of assuming: we must assume the ambiguity of the human condition; we must assume the failure of our desire to be God; we must assume our freedom; we must assume our finitude and death; and so on.

Beauvoir's essays also make some use of the idea of "unveiling" or "disclosing" the world ("*dévoiler*"), and this is, in fact, the second important new element that one needs to draw attention to in Sartre's *Notebooks*. There were traces of it in the *War Diaries*, but it is especially important now, because, broadly speaking, it forms the over-arching project that replaces that of seeking to be God. Once we have chosen to unveil the world, Sartre says, we consider everything that happens to us as a stroke of good fortune, in that whatever happens to us allows us to unveil more. We assume, as part of our contingency, the date when we are born, and thereby take the historical perspective in which we are placed as *our own*. In general, then, the conversion consists in my freedom assuming my contingency: "I assume these eyes, these senses, this head, this body, because through them I am free; I assume the ignorance that makes me free."[21] He develops the example of someone who is ill, arguing that he must come to *want* the illness, must assume his illness in order to change it. He must take responsibility for what he is not responsible for. This, in addition to the more predictable but no less important point that we must all, all of the time, take responsibility for the consequences of our actions, even those that we did not intend or wish to come about.

It has been worthwhile to stress the continuity between the *War Diaries* and the *Notebooks*, especially with regard to the concept of assuming, for two main reasons. The first is that this does not appear to have been much recognized or noted. And the second is that a great deal happens to the concept *between* these two works. What happens, one might say, actually pulls our attention away from the continuities just outlined, and it is this that now needs to be explained. There is, however, still a great deal of scholarly work to be done on Sartre's discussion of "conversion" in the *Notebooks*, and it cannot even be taken for granted that the continuity we have found in relation to "assuming" is there with other key concepts. It is possible that marked *dis*continuities and inconsistencies over the concepts of conversion, reflection, authenticity, bad faith, and so on, may be found, even just by means of careful comparison of the *War Diaries* and the *Notebooks*. And when one also brings into the equation *Being and Nothingness*, as well as some other texts in between, the issues become a great deal more complicated. There have been major books on Sartre's ethics in the past few years and gradually some of these complex matters are being brought into focus as his vast posthumously-published writings come to be better understood.

What, then, happens to the concept of assuming between the *War Diaries* and the *Notebooks*? If it can be argued that, to quote Iris Murdoch, "Human relationship is no doubt the most important, as well as the first, training and testing-ground of morality,"[22] then the viability of the "*morale*" that Sartre arrived at on 3 December 1939 is, as Beauvoir suggested, rather dubious, since it tells us next to nothing about how to behave toward others. Beauvoir's point that Sartre's position in the *War Diaries* is a general one and does not issue in any obvious specific moral advice should really cause us to look more closely into the question of what "ethics" or having an ethics was for Sartre. We would need, in any case, to think whether the French term "*morale*" is the strict equivalent of "ethics" or "morality," or both; and, indeed, what exactly is the difference between the two English terms. At least in his early period, Sartre seems to have understood something quite personal by the term "*morale*." Yet he had thought a great deal about human relations by the time he completed *Being and Nothingness*, which was his first published work of philosophical significance after his release from captivity.

It is fascinating to see him, therefore, in a letter of 6 January 1940, apparently waking up for the first time to the fact that there are some problems about "assuming" in the broad area of human or social relations. He has had what he describes as "some curious reflections" on reading a biography of Heine:

> Indeed, as I was praising him to myself for having managed to assume his Jewish condition, and as I understood with great clarity that rationalist Jews like Pieter or Brunschvick [*sic*] were inauthentic in that they thought themselves to be men first and foremost and not Jews, the idea came to me that, as a rigorous consequence, I had to assume myself as a Frenchman; I had no enthusiasm for the idea and, above all, it had no meaning for me. Just an inevitable and obvious conclusion. I don't know where it leads and I'm going to think about all that tomorrow.[23]

An exchange of comments between Sartre and Beauvoir subsequently ensues in their correspondence. Beauvoir says he needs to define his position on assuming; to limit it and see what it commits him to. Sartre discusses it in other letters to a woman with whom they were both having an affair—and who, incidentally, has recently brought out a book arguing that their ill-treatment of her was to do with the fact that she is Jewish![24]—and then he develops for Beauvoir the alternative ways in which one might assume oneself as a Jew. He asks, for example, "Does one assume oneself as Jewish in order to aim at the later suppression of the race and of the collective representation 'Jew?'...Or isn't it also possible that in assuming himself as a Jew the Jew is acknowledging that Judaism has cultural and human value?"[25] Beauvoir says one of these ways is "foolish"; Sartre comes back at her arguing that both are sustainable. The point about all of this is that it constitutes the first signs of some significant difficulties and confusions related to the concept of "assuming" itself, particularly with regard to its application to the matter of our "being-for-others."

In Part III of *Being and Nothingness*, Sartre first engages with the matter of our being-for-others. In the section on "The Look," focusing on the question of the qualities that others ascribe to us—"wicked," "jealous," "likable," and so forth—he says that when others describe my character to me, I do not "recognize" myself in the descriptions and yet I know that "it's me": "I immediately *assume* the stranger that is presented to me, without its ceasing to be a stranger."[26] His reasons for saying that I immediately assume the being-for-others that I become aware of are based on his ontological analysis as such, since he goes on to argue: "I can neither grasp nor conceive of a consciousness that does not grasp me."[27] In short, he is saying at this point that our *original* way of seeing others has to involve seeing them as subjects. They differentiate themselves from me and see me as an object, and in rejecting this I break away from others and define myself. In doing so, I am recognizing and affirming not only others, but also the existence of myself-for-others. But there is also a second moment or stage in my relations with others, and this involves the *objectification* of others. In fact, the instability in both states is such that each is periodically replaced by the other. This notion is picked up in the third chapter of Part III, when Sartre goes on to talk of our "concrete relations with others" and to analyze, in its first two sections, the two basic "attitudes" towards others between which we constantly oscillate.

All of this constitutes the background to the second and third sections of Part IV, Chapter One, where Sartre makes even more crucial use of the concept of "assuming." In the course of discussing "Freedom and Facticity: Situation," he has a long sequence in which he examines the role of the other in our situation in the world.[28] But when he refers back to his earlier point that freely recognizing the transcendence of others involves assuming my being-for-others, it comes to look much more puzzling and problematic than before. It is appropriate to focus on his assertion that we cannot *not* assume our being-for-others, taking the following quotation as the key one:

> Although I have available an infinite number of ways of assuming my being-for-others, I *cannot not assume it*: we come back here to our being sentenced to being free, which we defined earlier as *facticity*; I can neither abstain altogether in relation to what I am (for others)—since to *refuse* is not to abstain; it is still to assume—nor undergo it passively (which, in a sense, amounts to the same). Whether it be in anger, hatred, pride, shame, disgusted rejection, or joyful acknowledgement I must choose to be what I am.[29]

An interest in the concept of assuming might well start from this particular passage, since there seems to be something badly wrong with it.

The first clarification, however, is that Sartre himself leaves permanently open the possibility of treating the other as an object, so that in one sense there *is* an alternative to assuming our being-for-others. But since he claims that when we do this our being-for-others disappears altogether (at least for a time), we should perhaps revise the formulation of his point and see him as arguing that *when I regard others as subjects*, I have no alternative but to assume my being-for-others. This use of the others-as-subjects/others-as-object distinction raises some interesting questions in its own right. One can understand what he means by it: it seems to be just a particular application of his general point that we can only be anything at all via the point of view of others, or his claim that assuming my being-for-others is the only way in which I can affirm that I am not the other. Yet we find that many of Sartre's references to the permanent possibility of seeing the other as object clearly imply that this involves *some* kind of refusal or rejection of our being-for-others (he sometimes says that we are thereby "liberated" from it). And when he is looking back on "My Fellow-Man" in the following sub-section, "My Death," he reemphasizes that all of the alienations of our being that he has considered can be negated (*"néantisé"*) if we transform the other into a transcended-transcendence: "As long as I am alive, I can contradict what others reveal of me by projecting myself toward other ends and, in any case, by revealing that the dimension of my being-for-myself is incommensurable with the dimension of my being-for-others."[30] The question, then, of whether the assertion that we cannot *not* "assume" our being-for-others still applies when we see others as objects is not one that receives an entirely unambiguous answer in this section of Sartre's text. Even so, the problematic aspect of the suggestion that when I regard others as subjects, I have no alternative but to assume my being-for-others, is that it seems that we are somehow logically or conceptually obliged to assume anything that others think of us, any category that they put us into, any judgment that they make about us. And this is not the end of it, for there is actually a much deeper problem than this, since some kind of initial rejection of the other, which is something quite different from an assumption, is absolutely indispensable to Sartre's own view of our awareness of others.

That we might be conceptually obliged to assume anything that others think of us is problematic, in the first place, because we are inclined to want to distinguish between true and false attributions. It seems a great weakness of this section of *Being and Nothingness* that it makes no mention of mistaken attributions. In fact, Sartre often talks of our being-for-others as "objective," in a way that implies that its *content* is in some sense accurate, correct, unquestionable. It is noticeable, too, that this is unobtrusively built into the formulation of a major example to which he constantly returns: "To acknowledge the existence of others and, *if I am a Jew*, to assume my Jewish-being are one and the same thing."[31] In other words a judgment of truth about our being-for-others, which Sartre is not always careful enough to bring out explicitly, somehow seems to be one of the foundations of his argument. Hence it may be necessary to reformulate his argument again and say: "if someone attributes a characteristic to me *and they are right to do so*, I am—as long as I regard them as a subject and not an object—in some sense obliged to 'assume' that characteristic." (Interestingly, in the *Notebooks* he claims that it is not true that I only learn about myself via the other: I also have a kind of direct knowledge of myself.[32])

In any case, what has happened by now is that we have moved from the general to the particular, at least to the extent of beginning to discriminate between different beings-for-others that we might have. It is clear that the level of generality at which *Being and Nothingness* operates is itself one of the sources of the problem. Even if accepting others as subjects is tantamount to acknowledging that I have a being-for-others *of some kind*, this is a long way from arguing that I must assume any particular characterizations or categorizations that are attributed to me. But Sartre gives no indication of awareness of this point. Nor does he seem concerned that he is taking the key term "being-for-others" to cover wholly different things, like profession, social position, race, nationality, physique, character, and so forth. Yet the question of whether we can *ignore* our being-for-others or not may have to be answered in different ways in different types of case. This becomes obvious when we consider the list he gives: "Jew, Aryan, ugly, beautiful, king, civil servant, untouchable."[33] (Another list he gives is being a teacher or a café waiter, being beautiful or ugly, Jewish or Aryan, witty, vulgar, or distinguished.) There seems to me to be no reason to suppose that what applies to one of these categories necessarily applies to the others. He often talks of *discovering* our being-for-others, but while it makes sense to think of discovering that one is ugly, the idea of discovering that one is a coal miner or a university professor is odd to say the least. Again, if we take Sartre to be insisting that I can't *ignore* my being-for-others, then our attitude to his view may depend upon what sort of examples we have in mind. There seem to be all kinds of circumstances in which I *can* simply ignore what others think of me, how they see me, what they take me to be. Sartre may have been over-influenced by his own major examples. Doubtless, in Nazi Germany there was no way, in practical terms, of ignoring the fact that one was taken for a Jew, whether or not it was true. But there appear to be all manner of situations where I am under no obligation to react in any way whatever if someone takes me to be, say, Belgian, or tone-deaf, or somewhat on the mean side.

In short, what appears to be offered as some kind of conceptual or analytic truth produces paradoxical and problematic consequences when we try to understand it in a concrete rather than an abstract way. Let us return, then, to Sartre's own principal example of Jewishness. If I consider Anti-Semites as objects, he says, then my Jewish being disappears altogether. My being Jewish only appears as an objective external limit upon my situation if I recognize the freedom of the Anti-Semite and assume the Jewishness that he ascribes to me. But even if we are somehow sympathetic to this position, what begins to press in on us now is the basic question of what "assuming my

Jewish-being" means, or amounts to. One of Sartre's major points is that it does not necessarily mean *accepting* it: even to refuse or reject our being-for-others, he says, is still to assume it.

Now, one might certainly try to defend this position by taking "*assumer*" to mean something like "acknowledging that my being-for-others is indeed a being attributed by others to *me*, and not to someone else" (this is not as tautologous or trivial as it might seem; one thinks of Sartre's point in *Existentialism and Humanism* about the anguish of Abraham: that Abraham himself must decide, among other things, whether God's message is really addressed to him). Words like "recognition" and "acknowledgement" come to mind here, and it does periodically look as if Sartre means something like this in *Being and Nothingness*. Some sense exists in the idea that to reject an attribution of a particular being-for-others to me, I have first to accept that it is targeted at me (or, to put the matter the other way around, once I have decided that some characteristic is attributed to me, then even if I flee from it or reject it, my reaction still implies that I have accepted that it is attributed to me). But the trouble with this is that the sense of the term "*assumer*" has by now been weakened immeasurably. It seems to amount to little more than the equivalent of saying that in order to go anywhere, I have to start from where I am.

This minimalist reading of "*assumer*" is quite distinct from the much stronger sense of the term in the *War Diaries*. In fact, once we go back to the meaning from the *War Diaries*, all kinds of problems ensue for the stance in *Being and Nothingness*. Sartre would have to be saying something like the following: "by virtue of the very meaning of the terms, and/or the ontological situation, I must 'assume' or take responsibility for the Jewish-being that others ascribe to me, as if I had deliberately brought it into being." We would also have to qualify this by adding, "if, indeed, I am a Jew." But one of the obvious major problems with this is that it is impossible to decide whether it is some kind of analytic proposition, as *Being and Nothingness* implies, or whether it is a straightforward moral prescription or recommendation. In either case, it is dependent upon various empirical matters in ways that are left obscure.

It is hardly surprising if, in what is meant to be the exclusively ontological context of *Being and Nothingness*, Sartre has retreated from the *moral* sense of "*assumer*" established in the *War Diaries* and is using the term ostensibly in a morally neutral sense. But this leads to substantial confusion over the concept itself and certain related ideas. There is, moreover, another significant twist to the issue. Coming back to the matter of treating others as subjects or objects, it is easy to see that, whatever the main thrust of his argument in *Being and Nothingness*, Sartre is hardly likely to be wholly neutral in relation to these two possibilities. When he talks of my accepting the freedom of others and assuming my being-for-others as being my link with, as well as my separation from, others, it is hard to believe that he has no preference. Chapter One of Part IV stops short of explicitly giving any kind of precedence or priority to the attitude of seeing others as subjects over that of seeing them as objects, but the fact that Sartre, having argued in Part III that conflict is the basic meaning of our being-for-others[34] and having stressed that conflict is the basis of all human relations, should now entitle the major sub-section of the chapter "My Fellow-Man" ("*Mon prochain*") is already extremely revealing, as is the way in which, in practice, the idea of treating others as objects virtually disappears from sight.

In short, these may be seen as signals within *Being and Nothingness* itself — albeit feeble ones — that Sartre either wishes to, or has always intended to, go beyond the restrictions imposed by the pattern of human relations established in Part III; that his utterly pessimistic view of human relations is not one that we should take as in any way complete or final. A more obvious signal was the well-known earlier footnote foreseeing the possibility of a "radical conversion" and "an ethics of deliverance and salvation."[35] It looks, then, as if many commentators need to make a significant paradigm shift and to see not the note promising an ethics, but the conflictual theory of human relations itself as the aberration. As a matter of fact, it is far from certain that anyone has ever taken that theory seriously in its entirety, and indeed, as James Giles shows in Chapter Eight of this volume, the theory is beset with numerous inconsistencies. In any case, when it comes, in Part IV, to focusing on doing and emphasizing that freedom overcomes facticity, Sartre needs to find at least the beginnings of a way out of the vicious circle of other as subject — other as object — other as subject — other as object...It was presumably unthinkable for him that that route should involve a systematic effort to objectify and oppress others, so that one is inclined to see his insistence on the necessity of "assuming" our being-for-others as an initial, tentative, somewhat disguised move toward recognizing the freedom of others, toward a proper ethics taking account of other people. But the problem is that this is, as it were, forcing its way through his argument rather than arising out of it. The result is the kind of theoretical confusions that we have been examining, and I think that this whole picture can be confirmed by brief reference to one or two other works by Sartre and Beauvoir from the 1940s.

Sartre's essay, *Anti-Semite and Jew*,[36] written in October 1944, little more than a year after the publication of *Being and Nothingness*, is particularly appropriate in this connection because of the way in which Sartre has regularly used Jewishness as an example of our being-for-others. On the basis of *Being and Nothingness*, one would expect a major element here to be the insistence that Jews have no alternative but to "assume" their Jewish being-for-others. Yet none of the four uses of the term in the text is of any relevance to this issue. And there is an obvious reason for this. A major structural feature of *Anti-Semite and Jew* is the distinction between inauthentic and authentic Jews. By "inauthentic" Sartre means, roughly, denying or fleeing from the Jew's (objective) situation in society—he describes at length *"chemins de fuite"* or "escape routes." However, having argued in *Being and Nothingness* that even to reject or flee from an identity is to "assume" it, he cannot now say that what marks off the authentic Jew from the inauthentic is that he "assumes" his Jewish being-for-others.

In *Anti-Semite and Jew*, Sartre is plainly in ethical rather than ontological territory, but he is still saddled with the difficulties or confusions attached to "assuming" in *Being and Nothingness*. In spite of actually acknowledging here the case of people *mistakenly* taken as Jewish, Sartre still fails to integrate this possibility into his theory, and has nothing significant to say about such cases. Since the matter of what exactly constitutes being Jewish can be a difficult and contentious one, and was such a vital issue in the Second World War, the omission is serious and remarkable. A further point is that the question of which of our beings-for-others we must assume arises, as it were, practically in this text, since there is obvious vagueness or ambiguity about *whose* ascription the Jew needs to react to. The essay claims, most prominently, that the Anti-Semite has made the Jew, but equally it sometimes suggests that it is Christians who have done so, or, again, that it is society, or "other men," or "all of us" who have made the Jew. Exactly where, then, is the Jew supposed to locate the being-for-others which *Being and Nothingness* would claim that he *must* assume? Because of these difficulties, *Anti-Semite and Jew* is a work that may be seen as marking a kind of transitional stage. But by the time of the *Notebooks*, as we have seen, he is explicitly leaving *Being and Nothingness* behind and trying to elaborate a post-conversion ethics. Thus, on the Jewish question in the *Notebooks* we find him not only openly using "assuming" in this connection, but also coming back to positions that have a clear basis in the views expressed in the *War Diaries*: "I can only rid myself of my situation as a bourgeois or a Jew, and so on, by assuming it *in order to change it*."[37]

Intriguingly, the period when Sartre was writing his *Notebooks* is exactly the time when Simone de Beauvoir was writing *The Second Sex*.[38] The framework and the difficulties that we have just examined are very much part of that text, as Beauvoir, too, is struggling to find a well-founded ethical position from which to deal with her particular social issue. Just as, in *Anti-Semite and Jew*, Sartre replaced the idea of a Jewish soul or intrinsic Jewishness with the notion of a Jewish *situation*, so in *The Second Sex*, the basic premise of Beauvoir's argument is that there is no female nature, no pre-existing femininity or womanhood: there is just a women's *situation*. Beauvoir has no reason to have inhibitions about using the concept of assuming, and it is, in fact, quite central to her thinking on the subject of women. She says they must give up trying to be, and *assume* their existence; that they must assume their situation; that they must assume their bodies, their desire, their sexuality, their facticity, and so on.

Yet, in the end, "assuming" is no less a problematic notion for Beauvoir than for Sartre. The difficulties go right back to Sartre's early recognition of a difficulty over whether the Jew should assume himself or herself as a Jew or as a person. And the relevance of that to the question of whether women should defend the universal aspects of their lives or assert the allegedly distinctive qualities of their sex is obvious. As is the whole matter of acceptance and revolt: like Sartre, Beauvoir actually argues at some points here that the way of assuming oppression is to revolt against it—thereby raising again the whole question of the fundamental meaning of "assuming." But also, to confuse matters still further, she sometimes talks as if inauthentic assumptions are possible, and even mentions contradictory assumptions.

Thus, the precise problems over assuming that Sartre himself located as soon as our being-for-others came into the picture, as well as the precise problems that we found in his treatment of this in *Being and Nothingness*, are still coming home to roost as we draw to the end of the early period of the philosophy of Sartre and Beauvoir. The only way forward seems to reside in the possibility of a radical conversion, envisaged by Sartre but barely elaborated by Beauvoir. In one way it might be thought that none of this is surprising; that it was precisely problems of this general kind that led Sartre, and slightly later Beauvoir, to either abandon or significantly modify their early existential philosophy of freedom and adopt a broadly Marxist stance

One final cluster of points is worth mentioning. The Conclusion to *The Second Sex* contains a call for a kind of co-operation and reciprocity between men and women that is not always acknowledged by commentators. And this corresponds in some way to a second level or dimension to the "conversion" that is such an important feature of Sartre's *Notebooks for an Ethics*. So far we have mentioned just the narrowly personal level at which pure reflection brings the individual to leave behind the project of being God and to assume his existence, facticity, and freedom. But on a second level, another thing that Sartre says in his *Notebooks* is overcome by "pure" reflection and the conversion is the Hell of conflictual relations with others that was dominant—and thought by many to be presented as comprehensive and permanent—in *Being and Nothingness*. The conversion is deliberately shown as going beyond the vicious circle described in "The Look," and as providing a framework for co-operation between human beings. The dilemma of the two attitudes spelled out in *Being and Nothingness*—either transcend the other's transcendence or be transcended by it—and even the subsequent dichotomy of seeking either to objectify the other or to *assimilate* his freedom without destroying it, is here overcome by a *third* attitude, whereby we recognize the other's freedom, situation, and projects, and seek to act or work with the other to bring about *his* ends. This third possible attitude toward others is said to be—entirely contrary to what is claimed in *Being and Nothingness*—the only authentic attitude. Sartre also talks of my "giving myself" to the other as an object that I create in order that the other can give the objectivity back to me.[39] Sartre now makes a crucial distinction between others' look and others' ends. It seems that only in seeing others as freedoms, as subjects, can I be aware of their ends, for they could have no ends if I saw them as objects. Here he argues that I should will that others' ends be realized by them and actually engage in the activity involved: "Here the only authentic form of willing consists in willing that the end be realized by the other person."[40]

All of this is again expressed partly through the concept of assuming. He says, for instance, near the beginning of the *Notebooks*:

Sadism and masochism are the revelation of the other. They only make sense—as, moreover, does the struggle between consciousnesses—before the conversion. If we have assumed the fact of being free and an object for other people (for example, the authentic Jew) there is no longer any ontological reason to stay on the level of struggle. *I accept* my being-as-an-object and I surpass it.[41]

The vital point now, brought out strongly in a section of the text centering on the concept of the "appeal," is that the authentic attitude that he now envisages involves *reciprocity*.[42] While I seek to help the other achieve his or her ends, I simultaneously appeal to him or her to help me attain mine, thereby bringing into being a certain intermingling of freedoms that may well constitute "the human realm" ("*le règne humain*").[43] This last term is particularly significant in the light of Sartre's insistence in the early 1940s that morality is nothing to do with God, is "the business of men"; and especially of his idea in *Being and Nothingness* that we unavailingly strive to be *ens causa sui*, or God.

In the outline plan for his ethics set out in the *Notebooks*, Sartre has a heading: "New Relationship between my For-itself and my For-others: through Work."[44] (Sartre's final term "*l'oeuvre*" might be better rendered as "activity," or even perhaps "action"). And elsewhere he acknowledges that the dimension of reciprocal recognition of freedoms was missing from *Being and Nothingness*.[45] This may not exactly confirm our earlier suggestion that in that text Sartre was already sensing the need to break out of a particular dichotomy or dilemma, but it certainly increases its plausibility. One of the major questions now, as I have already suggested, is whether the moral positions in the *Notebooks* are, in fact, wholly compatible with the views in *Being and Nothingness*, or whether there is serious discontinuity of some kind—perhaps a discontinuity that might explain why Sartre did not publish the *Notebooks* and seems to have considered that that particular attempt at an ethics had failed.

## Notes

1. Jean-Paul Sartre, *Les Carnets de la drôle de guerre. Novembre 1939—mars 1940* (Paris: Gallimard, 1983). Trans. Quintin Hoare as *The War Diaries* (New York: Pantheon Books, 1984). I will give page numbers for the French edition only. Translations here follow Hoare, with some amendments.

2. Jean-Paul Sartre, *L'Etre et le Néant* (Paris: Gallimard, 1943). Trans. Hazel E. Barnes (London: Methuen, 1958) as *Being and Nothingness: An Essay n Phenomenological Ontology*. Translations here are largely my own.

3. Jean-Paul Sartre, *Esquisse d'une théorie des émotions* (Paris: Hermann, 1939), ("*Actualités scientifiques et industrielles*," no. 838), pp. 16-17. Trans. Bernard Fretchman as *The Emotions: Outline of a Theory* (New York: Carol Publishing, 1993). Also translated as *Sketch For a Theory of the Emotions*. Translations here are my own.

4. *Ibid.*, pp. 14-15.

5. See the new French edition, *Carnets de la drôle de guerre. Septembre 1939—mars 1940* (Paris: Gallimard, 1995).

6. *Ibid.*, p. 121.

7. Jean-Paul Sartre, *Lettres au Castor et à quelques autres* (Paris: Gallimard, 1983), I, p. 455. Trans. Lee Fahnestock and Norman MacAfee as *Witness to my Life* (Oxford: Macmillan, 1992). Translations are my own.

8. Sartre, *Les Carnets*, p. 121.

9. *Ibid.*, p. 121.

10. *Ibid.*, p. 122.

11. *Ibid.*, p. 123.

12. *Ibid.*, p. 123.

13. *Ibid.*, p. 140.

14. *Ibid.*, p. 142.

15. *Ibid.*, p. 140.

16. Simone de Beauvoir, *Lettres à Sartre* (Paris: Gallimard, 1990), 2 vols. Trans. Quintin Hoare as *Letters to Sartre* (New York: Arcade, 1992). Translations here follow Hoare, with some amendments.

17. Jean-Paul Sartre, *Cahiers pour une morale* (Paris: Gallimard, 1983). Trans. David Pellauer as *Notebooks for an Ethics* (Chicago: University of Chicago Press, 1992). Translations here follow Pellauer closely.

18. *Ibid.*, pp. 504-505.

19. Simone de Beauvoir, *Pour une Morale de l'ambiguité* (Paris: Gallimard, 1947). Trans. Bernard Frechtman as *The Ethics of Ambiguity* (New York: Citadel, 1994).

20. Simone de Beauvoir, *La Force des Choses* (Paris: Gallimard, 1963, "Folio" edit.), p. 98. Trans. Richard Howard as *Force of Circumstance* (London: Deutsch, 1965).
21. Sartre, *Cahiers*, p. 508.
22. Iris Murdoch, *Metaphysics as a Guide to Morals* (London: Penguin Books, 1992), p. 17.
23. Sartre, *Lettres*, II, p. 21.
24. See Bianca Lamblin, *A Disgraceful Affair*, trans. Julie Plovnick (Boston: Northeastern University Press: 1996).
25. Sartre, *Lettres*, II, p. 42.
26. Sartre, *L'Etre et le Néant*, p. 333.
27. *Ibid.*, p. 345.
28. See Terry Keefe, "The Other in Sartre's Early Concept of 'Situation,'" *Sartre Studies International*, 1:1-2, 1995, pp. 95-113.
29. Sartre, *L'Etre et le Néant*, p. 612.
30. *Ibid.*, p. 628.
31. *Ibid.*, p. 610.
32. Sartre, *Cahiers*, p. 466-467.
33. Sartre, *L'Etre et le Néant*, p. 610.
34. *Ibid.*, p. 431.
35. *Ibid.*, p. 612.
36. Jean-Paul Sartre, *Réflexions sur la question juive* (Paris: Morihien, 1946). Since 1954, the essay has been published by Gallimard. Trans. George J. Becker as *Anti-Semite and Jew* (New York: Schocken, 1948).
37. Sartre, *Cahiers*, p. 447.
38. Simone de Beauvoir, *Le Deuxième Sexe* (Paris: Gallimard, 1949), 2 vols. Trans. Howard Parshley as *The Second Sex* (London: Jonathan Cape, 1953).
39. Sartre, *Cahiers*, p. 487.
40. *Ibid.*, p. 290.
41. *Ibid.*, p. 26.
42. *Ibid.*, pp. 295-296.
43. *Ibid.*, p. 302.
44. *Ibid.*, p. 487.
45. *Ibid.*, p. 430.

# Five

# THE ORIGINS OF BEAUVOIR'S EXISTENTIAL PHILOSOPHY

## Margaret A. Simons

In the last two chapters it was seen how Simone de Beauvoir's views on ethics have contributed to the unique philosophical outlook of French existentialism. Here my concern will be with the development of Beauvoir's own distinctive philosophical position, not just concerning ethics, but also concerning her views on consciousness, human relations, and other related concepts which are fundamental to her existential philosophy. The problem, however, is that philosophers have traditionally read Simone de Beauvoir's most important philosophical texts, including *She Came to Stay*, *Ethics of Ambiguity*, and *The Second Sex*, as little more than applications of Sartre's existential phenomenology in *Being and Nothingness*. But scholars are increasingly challenging that reductionist interpretation, beginning the work of tracing Beauvoir's own philosophical development and in the process revealing a much more complicated picture of the Beauvoir/Sartre relationship. Establishing a pre-Sartrean beginning point for an analysis of Beauvoir's philosophy has remained a difficulty, however, without a philosophical manuscript by Beauvoir predating her relationship with Sartre.

That situation changed in 1990 when Beauvoir's handwritten 1927 diary was donated by Sylvie Le Bon de Beauvoir to the manuscript collection of the *Bibliothèque Nationale*. Written while Beauvoir was a philosophy student at the Sorbonne, and predating her meeting with Sartre in 1929, the 1927 diary contains an early formulation of Beauvoir's philosophy. In the diary, Beauvoir records her commitment to doing philosophy, formulates a methodology of doing philosophy through literature, and defines various philosophical themes and problems, including the search for self, the temptation of self-deception, and the opposition of self and other, that remain central to her later existential philosophy. An analysis of the diary, as transcribed by Barbara Klaw and Sylvie Le Bon de Beauvoir, provides the grounds for a new understanding of the origins of Beauvoir's philosophy as well as a critical appraisal of the recent reinterpretations of her philosophy. Before analyzing the diary, it will be helpful to briefly survey three of the most important of these new interpretations of Beauvoir's philosophy which can provide a context for our understanding of the philosophical significance of the 1927 diary.

The most important recent interpretation focusing on Beauvoir's early philosophy has been offered by Kate and Edward Fullbrook, in *Simone de Beauvoir: A Critical Introduction*. In an analysis of Beauvoir's early philosophical novels the Fullbrooks identify several key themes in Beauvoir's early philosophy, which provide a useful context for reading Beauvoir's 1927 diary. They argue that the "first principle" of Beauvoir's thought is the rejection of philosophical universalism, a principle reflected in Beauvoir's method of doing philosophy in literature and in her reliance on personal experience: "Beauvoir is a philosopher of experience."[1] The Fullbrooks see Beauvoir's anti-universalism as a legacy of Kierkegaardian existentialism with its opposition to Kant's universalism and its concern for human freedom and choice. Beauvoir's anti-universalism also makes her an heir to Hume, with whom she shares an appeal to personal experience and a skepticism in regards to the self. Beauvoir's narrative theory of the self in her early philosophy is a solution to this Humean problem.

Also fundamental to Beauvoir's early philosophy, according to the Fullbrooks, is an ontological distinction between conscious beings and nonconscious beings, which she will later use, with the phenomenological concept of intentionality, in defining the two dimensions of human reality, transcendence and immanence. Unlike the traditional Cartesian dualism, consciousness, in Beauvoir's earliest formulation, is embodied and relational in its awareness of other beings. Bad faith, a key element in Beauvoir's early moral philosophy, comes from denying either one's transcendence (consciousness and freedom) or one's immanence (givenness and embodiment).

The Fullbrooks credit Beauvoir with originating the solution to the problem of solipsism usually attributed to Sartre, that is, proving the existence of other minds through one's own experience of being objectified by the gaze of the other. But their Sartrean interpretation of the problem of the other in Beauvoir's early philosophy as the problem of solipsism, is not convincing. In *She Came to Stay*, the philosophical novel on which their analysis is based, Beauvoir's central focus is on a woman's struggle to reclaim a self abandoned in fused relationships with the other. Although Beauvoir provides a solution to the problem of solipsism, it is not her primary focus. For Beauvoir it would not seem to be the existence of other minds that is in doubt, but the existence of the self.

In summary, the Fullbrooks identify the following features of Beauvoir's early existential philosophy: anti-universalism, a literary philosophical method, a reliance on personal experience, a concern for human freedom and choice, a theory of the self as a narrative construct, an ontological distinction between conscious and nonconscious beings, a concept of consciousness as embodied and relational, and, in her moral philosophy, the concept of bad faith, and a concern with the problem of the other, which the Fullbrooks, reading Beauvoir within a Sartrean context, interpret as a primary concern with the problem of solipsism.

Two other recent reinterpretations of Beauvoir's philosophy, both of which influenced the Fullbrooks' interpretation, warrant our attention in establishing a context for an analysis of Beauvoir's 1927 diary. Debra Bergoffen and Karen

Vintges focus on Beauvoir's post-war essays on ethics, rather than on the earlier texts analyzed by the Fullbrooks, but they highlight Beauvoir's overlooked philosophical differences from Sartre. One of Bergoffen's most exciting discoveries is a philosophical difference in Sartre's and Beauvoir's concepts of bad faith. In *Ethics of Ambiguity*, Beauvoir distinguishes between two intentional moments: the first, a desire to disclose being, precedes the second moment of the desire to be being, which in Sartrean ontology grounds bad faith. Bergoffen sees Beauvoir as proposing an existential bracketing of the "will to be" analogous to Husserlean reduction. By focusing on the moment of disclosure, the anguish that fuels bad faith is counteracted by the joys of disclosure.[2] Beauvoir sees bad faith as grounded not ontologically, but historically, in a nostalgia for the lost certainties of childhood. In Beauvoir's ethics of generosity an openness to the other and the world provides an alternative to the inauthentic desire to be being.

But Bergoffen's interpretation of Beauvoir's philosophy is not unproblematic. She assumes a Sartrean beginning point for Beauvoir's philosophy, arguing that Beauvoir writes in two distinct philosophical voices, a dominant Sartrean voice of transcendent subjectivity, characterized by a Cartesian denial of the body, a fundamental hostility and violence towards the other stemming from Sartre's ontology of "the Look," and ethic of the project. Beauvoir's originality, according to Bergoffen, is found in her second, muted, philosophical voice, a voice on the margins of her texts. In this muted voice, according to Bergoffen, Beauvoir affirms an ambiguous, fleshed subjectivity, more influenced by Merleau-Ponty than by Sartre; open to disclosure of the world, of self and others; valuing spontaneity and freedom; and marked by an ethic of erotic generosity. But, if, as the Fullbrooks claim, Beauvoir's early philosophy does not begin with Sartre, how are we to understand Bergoffen's evidence of Beauvoir's divided philosophical voice? Does the muted voice reflect Merleau-Ponty's later influence, as Bergoffen implies, or are both voices together an authentic reflection of the ambiguity at the heart of Beauvoir's philosophy?

Vintges lends some support to this latter interpretation. Vintges agrees with Bergoffen in attributing Beauvoir's recognition of the separation and conflict in human relations to Sartre's influence, but instead of disparaging this element in Beauvoir's philosophy as inauthentic, argues that it is a crucial element in Beauvoir's ethics of ambiguity. Vintges criticizes readings such as Bergoffen's that see Beauvoir as reflecting a woman's voice of selfless generosity. According to Vintges, Beauvoir's advance over Sartre, and her solution to the problem of moral solipsism (which Vintges sees as Beauvoir's original philosophical concern), comes not in disavowing his fundamental insight into the negativity of consciousness and our separation from others, but in affirming our embodiment as the grounds for the possibility of connection with the other. Beauvoir establishes the possibility of reciprocal relations with the other and thus the possibility of a genuine existentialist ethics, through her concept of the role of emotions.

But, unlike the Fullbrooks, Vintges does not see Beauvoir's solution to the problem of solipsism as her principal philosophical achievement. Reading Beauvoir's existentialist ethics within the context of Michele Foucault's concept of ethics as art-of-living, Vintges argues that Beauvoir succeeds where both Sartre and Foucault fail in conceiving a morality without foundations and providing answers to the question of how to live.[3] According to Vintges, Beauvoir's autobiographical stylization of herself into an intellectual woman is her most important ethical work, providing practical guidelines to young women on how to reconcile the desires for love and freedom. The interpretative difficulty in Vintges's account lies in tracing the origins of Beauvoir's ethics as art-of-living from Beauvoir's supposed original concern with the problem of solipsism.

As we have seen, an analysis of *She Came to Stay*, which Vintges overlooks, suggests that Beauvoir's original philosophical concern may have been less with the problem of the existence of other minds, than with the problem of the existence of the self. Unlike the problem of solipsism, the solution to this problem of the loss of self, so prominent in the lives of women, if not in the history of philosophy, entails reconciling the desires for love and freedom, and thus points to Vintges's characterization of Beauvoir's ethics as art-of-living. Might Beauvoir's original interest in the problem of the loss of self in love relationships, also provide an interpretive context for understanding Beauvoir's dual concern with transcendent subjectivity and erotic generosity identified by Bergoffen?

Turning to an analysis of Beauvoir's 1927 diary, we can address the question raised by Bergoffen, Vintges, and the Fullbrooks. Could the 1927 diary confirm the Fullbrooks' interpretation of the central themes and problems in Beauvoir's early philosophy? Will the diary allow us to trace the origins of what Bergoffen terms Beauvoir's "muted philosophical voice" with its "ethic of erotic generosity," and the concepts of emotion and embodiment that Vintges agrees spells a philosophical difference from Sartre? Might the diary, which contains an account of Beauvoir's first meeting with Merleau-Ponty, shed light on this question of influence? Finally, will it reveal that Beauvoir's early concern with others was principally a concern with the problem of solipsism, as the Fullbrooks and Vintges maintain, or with the problem of the loss of self, as I have suggested? It is to these questions that we now turn.

1927 was a year of personal crisis and transformation for Beauvoir, as she left behind the Catholic girls' schools of her youth and the secure but stifling confines of family relationships, including an obsessive love for her cynical cousin, Jacques, that had dominated her life the previous winter, to enter the male world of philosophy and the Sorbonne. Central themes of her 1927 diary reflect the turmoil created by a loss of faith and family ties: the search for a justification for her life and the struggle against despair, the search for self, and the desire for love. Beauvoir describes her search for her life's direction in an appeal to a friend, early in the diary:

> I am intellectually very alone and very lost at the entry to my life...looking for a direction. I sense that I have value, that there is something for me to do and to say...but my thought turns in the void: where should it be directed? How to break this solitude? What to achieve with my intelligence?...I am in a great distress at the moment to decide on my life. Can I be satisfied with what one calls happiness? Or ought I walk towards this absolute that attracts me?[4]

Beauvoir, anticipating Sartre, finds a contradiction in human reality between the desire for an absolute justification for one's actions, and the sense of emptiness, of nothingness, in the realization of its absence. In a diary entry dated 16 July, Beauvoir describes herself as "searching for an exigency but finding nothing of value."[5] In another entry, she defines her central philosophical concern with the search for justification and necessity in life: "I know myself that there is only one problem and that it does not have a solution, because perhaps it has no sense; it is the one posed by Pascal, nearer to me Marcel Arland: I would like to believe in something—to encounter total exigency—to justify life; in brief, I would like God."[6] "Basically, I am in a paradoxical situation," she writes, "I sense my intelligence, what positive power it could have; I would love to do something...to have a passion for a philosophical work...I sense also my will, my powers of action....Only, these very qualities that demand to serve show me what an illusion it is to claim to be useful for something."[7]

A central theme of the 1927 diary is one she will share with Sartre: the pursuit of being. "Oh! This perpetual and necessary flow of things and of our selves!...Insane desire for the being that would be at the same time becoming."[8] "These miserable efforts for being!...I possess peace and almost joy, so dear to me are books, conversations and the sweetness of the air. But deep down, masked by these daily diversions, the same void!"[9] Beauvoir's reference in this passage to daily diversions as masking the "void" suggests that an element of Beauvoir's philosophy that both Bergoffen and Vintges attribute to Sartre, the nothingness of consciousness and our separation from others, predates Beauvoir's relationship with Sartre. References to the "void" and "nothingness" run throughout the 1927 diary, as in the entry for 7 July, where her sense of the ultimate futility of human action undermines her celebration of her success on the competitive philosophy exams. "So! A fine success in life, I thought! Ah! void! nothingness, vanity...."[10] With no external absolute to guarantee the rightness of her actions, even her academic success, which had always been a source of pride for Beauvoir, seems empty.

Beauvoir's study of philosophy, which she had undertaken seriously only the previous year, had presented her with the radical implications of her loss of faith: "What has this year brought me intellectually? a serious philosophical formation that has...sharpened my critical spirit, alas!...I have everywhere noted only our powerlessness to establish anything in the realm of knowledge as in that of ethics."[11] Without epistemological and moral foundations, how can we fulfill our desire to be of service, to put our talents and energies to use?

Beauvoir's realization of the impossibility of her desire for an absolute leaves her searching for a philosophical justification for her actions: "There is nothing in which I believe. That is a terrible thing to have to admit. Not even in myself. I can love...and act on my love: that is what permits me to be alive, passionate. But I have no control of love, and as soon as it ceases, I have nothing to cling to. I hate dilettantism, and isn't it in dilettantism that I ought to end up logically? how am I so far from the sceptics that I detest?."[12] Beauvoir, without any absolute standard as a guide, feels herself falling logically into a dilettantism, just as her position would seem to logically lead her to an epistemological relativism, that is, skepticism. Ruled by one's passions, since reason has no grounds on which to rule, one has nothing "to cling to" when these passions dissipate, no reliable grounds for judgment and choice. In this concern we find Beauvoir's initial formulation of a problem at the heart of what Vintges terms Beauvoir's ethics as art-of-living, the struggle to find the grounds for judgment in the absence of moral absolutes.

Throughout the 1927 diary are accounts of Beauvoir's struggle against despair, as in the following excerpt from 4 September: "Again this crushing anguish. The metaphysical anguish of man alone in the unknown. How does one not go crazy? There are days when I cry from fear, when I cry from ignorance; and then I take myself in hand, I say to myself 'get to work'. But alas! I know well that I will die without knowing!"[13] Fear joins ignorance as a source of despair, fear of being alone, cut off for the comfort of friends and family unable to accompany her in abandoning faith in God, but also fear of living a life ultimately bereft of meaning. Given the depth of her despair, it may not come as a surprise that Beauvoir would recognize the temptation to flee despair in self-deception, which would be termed "bad faith," first by Beauvoir, in her *When Things of the Spirit Come First* (written in 1937 but first published in 1982) and then by Sartre, in discussion which comprises the important second half of Part One of *Being and Nothingness* (1943).

But the 1927 diary also confirms Bergoffen's observation of Beauvoir's and Sartre's different understanding of the origins of bad faith, with Beauvoir locating the source of bad faith in a nostalgia for childhood certainties, as the following passage indicates:

> Mademoiselle Mercier is trying to convert me;...and I'm thinking of the remark of Georgette Lévy [Beauvoir's friend and fellow philosophy student]: 'You will be tempted that way.' It's true. This morning...I passionately desired to be the girl who takes communion at morning mass and walks in a serene certainty. Catholicism of Mauriac, of Claudel...how it's marked me and what place there is in me for it! and yet I know that I will know it no longer; I do not desire to believe: an act of faith is the most despairing act there is and I want my despair to at least keep its lucidity, I do not want to lie to myself."[14]

Beauvoir's linking of faith with the temptation of self-deception provides key elements in the concept of bad faith that is central to Sartrean ethics. As Bergoffen points out,[15] by rooting self-deception in a nostalgia for childhood, which can be avoided, Beauvoir opens up the possibility of an ethics of authenticity as an alternative to self-deception, unlike Sartrean bad faith which is ontologically grounded.

The sense of nothingness that figures so prominently in Beauvoir's descriptions of her experiences in the 1927 diary extends, as both Vintges and the Fullbrooks would predict, to her sense of self, fragmenting it: "(28 April) My past is behind me like a thing gone from me; on which I can no longer act and which I regard with the eyes of a stranger, a thing in which I have no part at all."[16] Her self has become a fiction: "I would like to understand how I can isolate myself thus from my dearest memories and my closest desires...they issue from a fiction. I cannot immerse myself in them. They are not my memories" (20 April).[17] Detached from her memories, she must create herself anew. "But me, what am I?" Beauvoir asks in another entry early in the diary. "My unity comes from no principle, not even from any emotion to which I could subordinate everything: it is made only within my self."[18]

In despair, Beauvoir turns to a purified concept of the self at odds with the anti-universalism that the Fullbrooks call the first principle of Beauvoir's philosophy. Her struggle and ambivalence towards a transcendent self is evident in the following entry from late in the diary:

> This evening, it seems to me that these human things are not worth crying over, this self is sufficient, absent from the rest of the earth, absent from what it was, alone...I know that I am not a pure spirit, I remember excesses of mad sensitivity;...but there are hours when I sense how inexistent that all is;...there are hours when my soul alone lives (the passions Descartes says coming from the body)—my egoism affirms itself...I feel myself very detached even from literature...deep down, I don't really know what I

want."[19]

The ambivalence of this diary passage, written during a period of social isolation echoes the following entry written during an earlier period of despair following the departure of a friend:

> Here I am like the ancient sage, so disdainful of human things that neither good nor bad can reach me. I pass, like one who takes no part in it, but regards the spectacle and goes on. I understand the resigned philosophers...and yet I remain profoundly human; I know also how to descend into the *mêlée*. I cried yesterday in leaving him who grasped my hand so nicely....[20]

In both of these diary entries, the attraction of disengagement seems to reflect the despair of isolation and a yearning for reconnection.

Other diary entries show Beauvoir joining in the spectacle rather than watching it from above: "if I see myself as an actor among other actors, I applaud myself as a truly beautiful success. In this moment the passion for this grand game fills my heart. As my creation, how beautiful life is! so painful when it is a given to which one must submit. Live, act, be fully!"[21] Arguing for an "irreducible given that constitutes the individuality" of each one, Beauvoir defends individual differences and rejects the argument that persons can ever be identical and with it the Kantian transcendental ego: "There is always a give which excludes identity. That's why I feel myself to be not phenomenon but noumenon, the quality is a reflection of the noumena on the level of experience."[22]

She vows to "never detach" herself from "these human things": "Never will I cease to passionately love others and myself because the infinite is in us."[23] The threatened loss of the joys of particular, concrete experiences counteracts the desire for God: "I would like God and yet gods frighten me because then this pain, this love, this flowing minute would be little passing things and would no longer contain the infinite."[24] She does not want to believe in God, she writes in another passage because: "this infinite God saves me only as a person; and it is my entire individual that I want to save." She then vows to rework her philosophical ideas and perhaps begin "writing this narrative that I would love to write."[25] Beauvoir observes her changing sense of self and rejects the purified ascetic ideal: "today already I no longer have Wednesday's fervor for the solemn image of my self," and asserts her determination to "neglect nothing of that which gives charm to life, but without being its slave," refusing to be limited by "a rigid ideal" and rejecting an "artificial unity."[26] Beauvoir's narrative theory of the self described by the Fullbrooks and, earlier, by Vintges,[27] takes shape in the diary, where writing the diary becomes a way of unifying apparently fragmentary experiences:

> I well know that under this apparent dispersion there is this strong unity of my self! if I judge myself from outside alone I am frightened to see myself ardent with the social welfare group, intellectual here, crying and worn down at home, joyous and foolish elsewhere. All of that is me. My faiths as well as my confusions. It's only necessary to establish a hierarchy in order for me to find my way, to have a permanent home base from which I will then be able to move away. Here is what I am going to do: in this diary I will recount my varied and even absurd experiences that I accept.[28]

Paired with a "work of thought" marked by a contrasting "strong, detached and disdainful judgment,"[29] Beauvoir will use the diary to write her self into existence. Another passage affirms the success of this strategy: "Rereading the first pages of this diary, I marvel at all of the lucidity, of the precision in the analysis and of the gift for describing the states that I traverse. I am moved by it as before pages that another would have written. Could I also, me, do something?."[30] This passage anticipates Beauvoir's depiction of the main character in the two unpublished chapters of *She Came to Stay* gaining a sense of self in writing a diary.

In 1927 Beauvoir writes of creating herself by telling her story: "I create myself, I create my story."[31] Beauvoir's reflects further on how the self "is made only within my self," in an important, but lengthy diary entry dated 6 May. In this passage, which illustrates Beauvoir's use of a descriptive philosophical methodology, Beauvoir describes an experience of falling in love with Barbier, a fellow philosophy student:

> This morning I experienced a strange moment the echo of which has not yet died away in me. I had just seen Barbier again....He spoke to me of myself, of philosophy and literature....And then...one instant I held in my hands an entirely new life...I saw myself between his love and that of Jacques. Well! the past did not enchain me, a new passion blossomed in me, splendid, I loved him....How to render that? It was not at all speculation, reasoning; nor dream, imagination...my life is no longer a ready-made path on which already from the point where I have arrived I can discover everything and on which I need only place one foot after the other. It is a path not yet opened up, which my walk alone will create. I think again of Baruzi's course and of Schopenhauer: empirical character, intelligible character. Yes, it is only by a free decision, and thanks to the play of circumstances that the true self is revealed. I told Mlle Mercier, that, for me, a choice is never made, it is always being made; it's repeated each time that I'm conscious of it...Well: this morning I chose Barbier.

The horror of the definitive choice is that it engages not only the self (*moi*) of today, but that of tomorrow, and it's why marriage is basically immoral....Naturally, I did not ask myself the question of this definitive choice, but for the self (*moi*) of today, it is Barbier and not Jacques who suits me. One instant I was free and I lived (*vécu*) that: me, abandoning the friend to whom I'm attached by so many tender memories, for the unknown who knew how to conquer me....It's very complicated...it's thus that I see life: a thousand possibles in childhood, which fall little by little until on the last day there is no longer more than one reality, one has lived one life; but it is the *élan vital* of Bergson that I'm thinking of here, which divides, allowing tendency after tendency to fall away until only one is realized.[32]

This passage is interesting for several reasons, including Beauvoir's reference to Jean Baruzi, whose interests in Henri Bergson, Leibniz, William James, and Husserl may have influenced Beauvoir's descriptive methodology in this diary entry ("How to render that? It was not at all speculation, reasoning; nor dream, imagination"). Beauvoir's early use of this methodology confirms the interpretations of Beauvoir's philosophical reliance on personal experience and anticipates her description of women's "lived experience," in *The Second Sex*. It also links her both with Husserlean phenomenology and with Bergson's focus on the "immediate givens (*donnés*) of consciousness."

In this passage Beauvoir describes the self as constructed by choice and action. Marking an early philosophical difference from Sartre is Beauvoir's sense of the interconnection of self and other implied in her linking of freedom and choice with the experience of falling in love and being "conquered" by an other. Beauvoir's phrase, "our changing self," and her contrast of the "self of today" and "that of tomorrow," may reflect the influence of Bergson's concept of "becoming," an important figure in the history of French philosophy ignored by the Fullbrooks in their account of Beauvoir's narrative theory of the self. Beauvoir's reflection, at the end of the passage, on the experience of choosing one's self from among "possibles," and her earlier reference to the "play of circumstances" suggest Beauvoir's early view of the compatibility of freedom and determinism, a position aligning her with both Leibniz, and, through the concept of the "given," with Bergson.

Beauvoir's valuing of particular, concrete experience which we have seen in the above discussions, has relevance not only to the Fullbrooks' interpretation of Beauvoir's philosophy, but to that of Bergoffen. Beauvoir's 1927 diary suggests that what Bergoffen describes as Beauvoir's muted philosophical voice is actually dominant in her early philosophy where Beauvoir converts the failed desire of being into a desire for the joys of disclosure of the phenomenal world. "I would like to believe in something—to encounter total exigency—to justify life; in brief, I would like God. Once this is said, I will not forget it.

But knowing that this unattainable noumenal world exists where alone could be explained to me why I live, in the phenomenal world (which is not for all that so negligible), I will construct my life. I will take myself as an end."[33]

Turning to description of the phenomenal world and vowing to construct a philosophy from her own experience, Beauvoir rejects a sterile rationalism for a philosophy of passion that defies Cartesian dualism and defines a very unSartrean philosophical beginning point:

> Oh! I see my life clearly now:...a passionate, frantic search...I didn't know that one could dream of death by metaphysical despair; sacrifice everything to the desire to know; live only to be saved. I didn't know that every system is an ardent, tormented thing, an effort of life, of being, a drama in the full sense of the word, and that it does not engage only the abstract intelligence. But I know it now, and that I can no longer do anything else.[34]

This passage (28 July) confirms Beauvoir's early commitment to philosophy as well as Vintges's interpretation of the central importance of emotion in Beauvoirean existentialism.

Characteristics of what Bergoffen describes as Beauvoir's muted philosophical voice are also found in Beauvoir's project of combining literature and philosophy, in a methodology that integrates passion into philosophy itself: "I must ...write 'essays on life' which would not be a novel, but philosophy, linking them together vaguely with a fiction. But the thought would be the essential thing, and I would be searching to find the truth, not to express it, to describe the search for truth."[35] Using a fictional narrative to link together philosophical meditations defines a methodology that Beauvoir defends in her 1946 essay, "Literature and Metaphysics," as uniquely suited to the situated, ambiguous subjectivity identified by Bergoffen as Beauvoir's muted philosophical voice, and by Vintges in her analysis of Beauvoir's contextual ethics of ambiguity.

But rather than bifurcated into a muted, authentic philosophical voice and a dominant, but inauthentic voice, as Bergoffen suggests, Beauvoir's 1927 diary reveals a philosophy of ambiguity, with features of both voices, combining reason and emotion, philosophy and literature, as the Fullbrooks argue. The concept of transcendent subjectivity, characterized by choice and project as well as negativity and separation, seems in its earliest formulation in Beauvoir's 1927 diary to incorporate elements of immanence, disclosure, spontaneity, and erotic generosity. It also points to the early influence on Beauvoir of Bergson, a French philosopher who both anticipates Husserlean phenomenological description and challenges Cartesian dualism. The diary also reveals the influence of Beauvoir's philosophical mentor, Baruzi, in encouraging

Beauvoir's early methodological use of phenomenological description.

What of Bergoffen's suggestion that Beauvoir's notion of fleshed, ambiguous subjectivity might be traced to the influence of Merleau-Ponty? The diary suggests that the influence might have proceeded initially in the opposite direction, as Beauvoir defends herself (arguing in the style of Aquinas) against the cold rationalism and Catholicism of her new friend:

> Well, Ponti is right. I do not have the right to despair. I accepted that despair was justified, but it needs to be demonstrated...But: if, trying to think without passion, I say: 'I have no reason for choosing to despair,' I also say, 'I have no reason to move towards Catholicism rather than in any other direction'....And, on the contrary, it's because Catholicism appeals too much to my heart that my reason defies it: tradition, heritage, memories lead me to adhere to it....Raised otherwise, Merleau-Ponti [*sic*], would your reason, stripped of all passion, attract you to Catholicism? [36]

Beauvoir welcomes Merleau-Ponty's enthusiasm for philosophy, without sharing his fondness for metaphysical absolutes: "Ponti says 'better to sacrifice becoming rather than being'; I say that seeing a flaw in a system, I want to sacrifice to the entire system."[37]

Meeting Merleau-Ponty exacerbates Beauvoir's problem of trying to accommodate herself to the cold rationality of philosophy: "Oh! tired, irritated, sure of arriving at nothing through this desperate appeal to philosophy—and yet I want it, I owe it to myself to do it—who will help me do it? myself...Reason coldly. Ah! there's a lot to do to make myself a philosopher!"[38] Exploring the value of emotions in her experience and differentiating her position from that of Merleau-Ponty, Beauvoir defends a notion of embodiment that anticipates both her own mature philosophy and that of Merleau-Ponty:

> I envy this straightforward, strong young man who lives a tranquil life with a tenderly beloved mother and who searches calmly for a truth that he hopes to find....'Aristocrat' he calls me? it's true. I can't get rid of this idea that I am alone, in a world apart, being present at the other as at a spectacle....Dreams are forbidden him. Ah! me, I have riches there that I do not want to get rid of. Drama of my affections, pathos of life...Certainly, I have a more complicated, more nuanced sensibility than his and a more exhausting power of love. These problems that he lives with his brain, I live them with my arms and my legs...I don't want to lose all of that. [39]

Beauvoir's argument, in the context of a 1927 debate with Merleau-Ponty, for "living" a philosophical problem not only with one's brain, but with one's arms and legs, suggests Beauvoir's influence on Merleau-Ponty's later concept of the lived body, a concept which Beauvoir refers to in *The Second Sex*, where she contrasts it with a woman's experience of bodily alienation. Thus the 1927 diary, in recording the development of Beauvoir's philosophy, her rejection of Catholicism, and her affirmation of the value of emotion and embodiment, challenges the view that Merleau-Ponty originated the philosophical concepts shared with Beauvoir.

The 1927 diary also challenges the traditional interpretation, maintained by Bergoffen and Vintges, that Sartre originated the theory of the self-other relations found in *Being and Nothingness*, *She Came to Stay*, and *The Second Sex*. In the 1927 diary (10 July) Beauvoir turns to a description of her own experience as her philosophical subject, and defines as her central philosophical concern, "the opposition of self and other": "I must rework my philosophical ideas...go deeper into the problems that have appealed to me...The theme is almost always this opposition of self and other that I felt at beginning to live. Now has come the time to do a synthesis of it."[40] Beauvoir's early interest in the phenomenon of "the Look," as providing evidence of the existence of the consciousness of the other, is also evident in the diary, although in contrast to Sartre's description in *Being and Nothingness*, Beauvoir's description reveals that the experience can be a source of consolation: "I'm lonely to the point of anguish today...To console myself, I must glance at this 'me' of multiple faces that is reflected in the eyes of my friends."[41] In this passage (18 April) from one of the first pages of her diary, Beauvoir calls on her experience of being seen by others to overcome the experience of isolation from others, and the loneliness it entails.

Beauvoir's description of the anguish of loneliness and the comfort in being seen by others, contrasts with the anguish of being seen by others and the comfort in solitude, that is more characteristic of Sartrean existentialism. Instead of a Sartrean ontology in which interpersonal relationships are frequently defined in terms of encounters with hostile strangers (see Chapter Eight), epitomized by the threatening look of the sniper, the opposition of self and other that concerns Beauvoir seems to arise primarily within intimate relationships of love and generosity. Beauvoir's interest, in the 1927 diary, is in the problem of love and the temptation to abdicate one's self and evade one's freedom in fusion with the other: "Once again, this necessity to be strong! to be always alone if I do not abdicate."[42] In the following passage (3 June) describing her love for her cousin, Jacques, the diary highlights the idea of one's emotional connection with the other: "we cling to one another so tightly that we can support the great vertiginous void; we will not fall into the abyss."[43] Beauvoir values relations with the other for opening up the world to her, and for the opportunity to serve, to find a sense of utility on a human level, as is evident in one of the final entries of the 1927 diary: "I dream of immense sacrifices; but I have nothing large enough for...a gift."⁴⁴ This passage with its references to "sacrifices" and a "gift" points to the origins of what Bergoffen terms Beauvoir's ethic of generosity.

Already in the 1927 diary, the desire for love, the desire to abdicate oneself for the other and "to feel oneself dominated," is a problem of philosophical interest for Beauvoir. She discusses the problem of setting limits on love as a possible thesis topic: "even for the most beloved there is a measure [of love] since it is not God. In fact, perhaps not...I'll deepen this for my *diplôme*."⁴⁵ That Beauvoir struggled with the problem of limiting generosity and love is evident in the following passage where Beauvoir writes of her love for Jacques: "I will sacrifice my exams for him; but not my work if I can produce one, nor my self...Refuse to submit to any slavery. And deep down I don't know...maybe I will sacrifice everything for him, everything and it will not be a sacrifice."⁴⁶ Beauvoir knows that the desire for total fusion with the other is an impossible desire. Either the self rebels against its annihilation, or the other rejects the attempt of fusion; love is "the only great human thing where I sense the nothingness of everything human," Beauvoir writes in one of the final diary entries.⁴⁷ But she finds the temptation to self-abdication in love an almost irresistible desire. In the 1927 diary, she describes her obsessive love for Jacques as a betrayal of herself, as "the supreme defeat": "My self does not want to let itself be devoured by his."⁴⁸ The temptation to self-deception in love, is the temptation of "idolatry," making the other an absolute: "But love is a fact to which one must submit; the only sin is idolatry. Don't think too much about that! Alas! life is less and less simple for those who want to feel and think their feelings."⁴⁹

Beauvoir's struggle with the temptation to abdicate the self in love marks an origin of what Vintges has described as Beauvoir's most important contribution to ethics, her practical guidelines to young women on reconciling the desire for love and freedom. Beauvoir, in 1927, was well aware of breaking away from the confines and comforts of women's traditional role. Denied the possibility of an arranged marriage by her family's impoverishment, she faced her unknown future with a mixture of pride and dread. "Yesterday, how I envied M. de Wendel so pretty and simple! without pride as without envy, I cried in thinking of the lot which was reserved for me, and of all the force, and the tension required so that I could find it preferable to any other."⁵⁰ Actively planning her writing projects, she experiences a joyous discovery of her individual power in a future defined by her own action: "Friday I established with force a life's program; in such instants my solitude is an intoxication: I am, I dominate, I love myself and despise the rest."

But there is an underlying ambiguity to the experience, the loneliness that accompanies an independent life, that leaves Beauvoir yearning, in despair, for woman's traditional feminine role: "But I would so like to have the right, me as well, of being simple and very weak, of being a woman; in what a 'desert world' I walk, so arid, with the only oases my intermittent esteem for myself...I count on myself; I know that I can count on myself. But I would prefer to have no need to count on myself." In this passage we find the source of Beauvoir's description in *The Second Sex* of woman's traditional role as a temptation to flee one's freedom in loneliness and dread. The depth of her despair as she faces her unknown future is indicated by a marginal annotation in the diary dating from 18 May 1929: "Could I again bear to suffer as I suffered in writing these lines?"[51]

Beauvoir's description anticipates the analysis of women's moral development offered by the feminist psychologist, Carol Gilligan, whose work, disparaged by Vintges, can illuminate Beauvoir's ethical project. According to Gilligan, the desire for abdication of the self in fusion with the other sets the stage for a "conflict of self and other" that Gilligan terms "the central moral problem for women, posing a dilemma whose resolution requires a reconciliation between femininity and adulthood."[52] Beauvoir's definition of the philosophical theme of the opposition of self and other, and her concern with the temptations of self-abdication in love, thus provide the grounds for her later contribution to young women in providing practical guidelines for reconciling the desires for love and freedom. Rather than egocentrism, the potential error inherent in women's moral development, according to Gilligan, is selflessness. Beauvoir's 1927 diary suggests that Beauvoir's original philosophical concern is not the problem of solipsism (only self), but, to coin a new term, the philosophical problem of "solaltrism" (only other).

Ten years later, in writing *She Came to Stay*, Beauvoir makes this problem of solaltrism, the problem of love and selfless generosity, her subject. But her conclusion is not, as Bergoffen maintains, to simply espouse an ethic of generosity. When the main character, Françoise, murders her young rival, Xavière, in the novel's dramatic conclusion, Beauvoir is exposing what she will term in *The Second Sex*, the "ordinary dialectic of devotion," when "the gift becomes a demand" and "love takes itself for a gift when it's a tyranny."[53] When, at the end of the Second World War—an experience more reflective of Sartrean ontology of hostile encounters with strangers—Beauvoir returns to the problem of love in *The Second Sex*, she emphasizes that authentic love must be "founded on reciprocal recognition of two freedoms... neither [lover] would abdicate his transcendence, neither would mutilate themselves...For one and the other love would be revelation of self by the gift of self and enrichment of the universe."[54] This critique of the ethic of selfless generosity supports Beauvoir's own naming of her ethics an ethics of ambiguity, and it points to the value of beginning with Beauvoir's earliest texts, rather than in *Being and Nothingness*, to locate the origins of Beauvoir's existential philosophy.[59]

## Notes

1. Kate and Edward Fullbrook, *Simone de Beauvoir: A Critical Introduction* (Cambridge, England: Polity Press, 1998), p. 37.
2. Debra B. Bergoffen, *The Philosophy of Simone de Beauvoir: Gendered Phenomenologies, Erotic Generosities* (Albany, NY: State University of New York Press, 1997), pp. 76-77.
3. Karen Vintges, *Philosophy as Passion: The Thinking of Simone de Beauvoir*, trans. A. Lavelle (Bloomington, Ind.: Indiana University Press, 1996), pp. 7-8, 99-102.
4. Simone de Beauvoir, Unpublished Diary (1927), Holograph manuscript, transcription by Barbara Klaw, Margaret A. Simons, and Sylvie Le Bon de Beauvoir (Paris: Manuscript Collection, *Bibliothèque Nationale*), pp. 41-42.
5. *Ibid.*, pp. 101, 47, 56.
6. *Ibid.*, p. 62
7. *Ibid.*, p. 24.
8. *Ibid.*, p. 143
9. *Ibid.*, p. 55.
10. *Ibid.*, pp. 5, 72, 79, 80, 144, 155, 87.
11. *Ibid.*, pp. 11-12.
12. *Ibid.*, p. 27.
13. *Ibid.*, p. 157.
14. *Ibid.*, p. 94.
15. Bergoffen, *The Philosophy of Simone de Beauvoir*, p. 182.
16. Beauvoir, Diary, p. 18.
17. *Ibid.*, p. 11
18. *Ibid.*, p. 26.
19. *Ibid.*, p. 122.
20. *Ibid.*, p. 68.
21. *Ibid.*, p. 88.
22. *Ibid.*, p. 96.
23. *Ibid.*, p. 119.
24. *Ibid.*, pp. 120-121.
25. *Ibid.*, p. 95.
26. *Ibid.*, p. 52.
27. Vintges, *Philosophy as Passion*, p. 86.
28. Beauvoir, Diary, pp. 52-53.
29. *Ibid.*, p. 53.
30. *Ibid.*, p. 54.
31. *Ibid.*, p. 90.
32. *Ibid.*, pp. 34-35, 37.
33. *Ibid.*, p. 62.
34. *Ibid.*, pp. 133, 134.
35. *Ibid.*, p. 54.
36. *Ibid.*, p. 36.
37. *Ibid.*, p. 37.

38. *Ibid.*, p. 116.
39. *Ibid.*, p. 126.
40. *Ibid.*, p. 95.
41. *Ibid.*, p. 5.
42. *Ibid.*, p. 138.
43. *Ibid.*, p. 74.
44. *Ibid.*, p. 165.
45. *Ibid.*, p. 68.
46. *Ibid.*, p. 90.
47. *Ibid.*, p. 160.
48. *Ibid.*, p. 38.
49. *Ibid.*, pp. 154-155.
50. *Ibid.*, p. 57.
51. *Ibid.*
52. Carol Gilligan, *In a Different Voice: Psychological Theory and Women's Development* (Cambridge, Mass.: Harvard University Press, 1982), p. 71.
53. Simone de Beauvoir, *Le Deuxième Sexe* (Paris: Gallimard, 1949), vol. 2, pp. 495, 492. Trans. Howard Parshley as *The Second Sex* (London: Jonathan Cape, 1953). The translation here is mine.
54. *Ibid.*, p. 505.
55. This research was made possible by the generous support of the Graduate School and the College of Arts and Sciences at Southern Illinois University at Edwardsville. I gratefully acknowledge the following persons for their helpful comments: Hazel Barnes, Bill McBride, Kristana Arp, James Giles, and audiences at the University of Southern Colorado at Pueblo, Illinois State University, Illinois Wesleyan University, the Society for Phenomenology and Existential Philosophy, and the Eastern Division of the American Philosophical Association. I owe special thanks to Barbara Klaw for generously sharing with me her transcription of the 1927 diary, and to Sylvie Le Bon de Beauvoir, whose warm encouragement and steadfast support have been invaluable, for kindly granting me permission to quote from the diaries.

# Six

# SARTRE'S CRITIQUE OF HUMANISM

## Juliette Simont

*Translated from French by Linda Chusid and Terry Keefe*

To think is to think against oneself: this is well known as a Sartrean attitude *par excellence*. I want to try to illustrate it by bringing out a few of the twists and turns which mark out Sartre's thoughts on a concept which is basic to French existentialist thinking; namely, humanism. Here I shall to try to show how these changes are not signs of indecision, but how, on the contrary, in spite of the tensions involved, they can be brought together coherently.

### 1. The Rejection of Human Dignity

In *Nausea*, things seemed clear, and humanism in all its forms detestable. A paradigmatic passage is the one where Roquentin dines with the Autodidact, when, along with dishes in a brownish sauce, the Autodidact tries to get his guest to swallow his delectable secret: he loves men. Roquentin is revolted and launches into a violent diatribe (kept to himself in large measure), in which, as if in a shooting gallery, he knocks down one by one the "radical" humanist (the champion of civil servants), the Catholic humanist (who excels at turning the wretched life of the docker into a fairy tale), the communist humanist (who emerged with the second five-year plan), the humanist of the Left (who loves all people, but nevertheless prefers the humble), the philosophical humanist (a big brother who carries the responsibility for humanity on his shoulders). Roquentin is the loner who goes so far as to believe that he may belong to "another species,"[1] and not to the human race which, as one person, is occupied—without knowing what it is doing—in warding off any possible resurgence of Otherness, and forever reinforcing the citadel of Sameness: "I am alone among these joyful, reasonable voices. All these fellows who spend their time justifying themselves to one another, and happily recognizing that they have the same opinions. Goodness, how important it is to them that they should all think the same things!"[2] Roquentin feels a kinship only with those down-and-outs who occasionally stand out from the smooth crowd of right-thinking people (the strange fellow on a bench who, one sensed, was forming crab-like thoughts or lobster-like thoughts in his head,[3] or Mr. Achille, the "old loony" waiting in the café for his attack of Nausea[4]). Roquentin himself becomes a crab after his meal spiced with humanism: "All of a sudden I stopped looking like a man and they saw a crab backing out of that room which was so strongly human."[5] Roquentin is the guardian of the miserable drama of contingency, the only one to recognize the collapse that is common to human beings and objects, in which everything is distorted, and which destroys meaning and common sense, the categories that enable us to interpret the world theoretically, the ways in which we arrange things for pragmatic, utilitarian purposes. Roquentin is resistant to all human collectivities, "simply an individual," according to the epigraph of *Nausea*.

Sartre's *War Diaries*, written shortly after *Nausea*, retain something of the biting quality of Roquentin's comments—something that could be called the rejection of human dignity. After one of his apocalyptic visions (Bouville deformed by a "sort of frightful meaning weighing heavily on things"), Roquentin found himself shouting jubilantly to the good people panicking in their unrecognizable town: "What have you done with your humanism? What have you done with your dignity of a 'thinking reed'?"[6] And Sartre echoes this in his *War Diaries*, noting that at least what is good about war is that it deprives you of human dignity. The "world of war" yields "*the complete loss of all human dignity*; and, in principle, this is not such a bad thing."[7]

## 2. Pride in Human Action

But, however steadfast he is in his rejection of "human dignity," because of the war something has already turned around in Sartre's thought. It was by taking a kind of distant overview and being angelically detached from human ends that Roquentin discovered, beneath worthy bourgeois appearances, the effusions of contingent-being (for instance, beneath the official face of Jean Parrottin—the "phoney bastard" of Idealism, the mummy of pure Rights, Legitimacy itself, an incorporeal creature, as pitiless as a knife-blade—he discovered soft, pale cheeks, "vulnerable flesh, puffy, oozing, vaguely obscene"[8]). Sartre also speaks in his *War Diaries* of a "nakedness-weakness, oozing and obscene,"[9] and this similarly signifies the loss of human dignity. But he no longer experiences it by withdrawing from human contact (as Roquentin does), but, on the contrary, through immersion in the military community. Now, if the loss of human dignity is a good thing in itself, one imagines that being thrust into intimate situations with people, which is what brings about that loss here, is also a good thing. Consequently, we must take it that if it is a good thing to lose human dignity, that is because it was only a deviant face of humanity. In other words, humanity does not disappear with it, as Roquentin and his strange world might lead us to believe—constantly oscillating between something like the Nietzschean superhuman and the amorphous disintegration of matter. There is a pride in being human, which is no way to be confounded with dignity, and which yields a possible humanism:

> *Simone de Beauvoir*: It is very clear from our conversations as a whole that you are proud. But how would you define your pride?

> *Sartre*: I don't think it's a pride that centers on myself, the private individual Jean-Paul Sartre, but rather on those characteristics that are common to all men. I am proud to perform acts that have a beginning and an end, to change a certain part of the world to the extent that I act....It's the fact of being man, a being condemned to be born and to die, but, between the two, acting and distinguishing himself from the rest of the world by his action, by his thoughts—which are also a form of action—and by his feelings, which are an opening on to the world of action. To tell you the truth, I don't understand why all men are not as proud as I am, considering that all of that seems to me to be a structural characteristic of conscious life and life in society.[10]

We can see that, with his reference to "all men," Sartre is already in the process of passing from the loner, "simply an individual" in the epigraph of *Nausea*, to the person "made up of all men and who is worth as much as any of them and whom anyone is worth as much as," at the end of *Words*.

In *The Roads to Freedom*, which Sartre started writing at the same time as *Nausea*, Mathieu seems to be unable to manage to rid himself of this "dignity" as easily as Sartre. Before the war, in a museum with Ivich, and jealous of her admiration for a Gauguin self-portrait, he understands, by contrast, his own inadequacy in the eyes of this stubborn and spiteful young mind that he cannot manage to control; he is a pusillanimous civil servant forever tied down by that human dignity, that application, that self-restraint that Gauguin succeeded in abandoning: "The heavy face with its enormous chin came back to Mathieu. Gaugin had lost his human dignity, he had accepted its loss."[11] But during the war, it is still forever that same inexcusable dignity that will stop him losing himself with his army comrades by getting drunk from the basin of wine and "draining the cup of defeat."[12] "He found this basin full of wine and filth revolting, but at the same time he blamed himself for feeling revolted: 'Who am I, then, to refuse to drink when my mates are drunk?'"[13] Still in connection with Gauguin, Mathieu explicitly distinguishes between dignity and pride:

> Gauguin, stripped to the waist beneath a stormy sky, stared at them with the hard and fraudulent stare of those who are hallucinating. Solitude and pride had devoured his face; his body had become a soft, fleshy tropical fruit with water blisters. He had lost his Dignity—that human Dignity that Mathieu still retained, without knowing what to do with it—but he still had his pride.[14]

It is also by reference to this pride in human action, or in person as action, that Sartre replies, in *Existentialism and Humanism*, to the objection that he reckons might be raised against him on the basis of *Nausea*: "You were briskly dismissing all forms of humanism, and now here you are going into reverse and becoming your own Autodidact to yourself." Sartre says it is nothing of the sort, since there are two different meanings of "humanism" at stake in the two cases. The humanism that Roquentin rejected, and which Sartre, seven years later, continues to reject, consists in taking the person as an end in himself or herself, or as a value. "That humanism is absurd," for in order legitimately to make the human being the supreme value, one would have had to see humanity from the outside, and to have compared it impartially with the other values;[15] and that is not possible, precisely because we are part of humanity. The fact that we are forms a crack in the global concept that we are claiming to rise above, exactly in the way that, in the paradox of the liar, an undecidable element comes in because of the fact that the liar belongs to the group that he is stigmatizing.[16] But another meaning of "humanism" exists which is entirely compatible with existentialism and even required by it: it is the kind that "will never take man to be an end in himself, since he always *remains to be created*"[17] (italics added); the kind that understands that the human being cannot be circumscribed in a static Value, but is rather, in himself or herself, a constant process of valuing; the kind that no longer says that the human being is the supreme Value, or, equally, that there is an essence or general notion of humanity. Instead, according to the formulation in *Being and Nothingness*, this meaning of "humanism" is that the human being is "the being through whom values exist,"[18] these constantly-invented, multiple values being the way in which the human being sheds light on his or her actions and *creates himself or herself* while acting upon the world: "[existentialism is a] humanism, because we remind man that he is the only legislator...and because we show that it is not by turning back in on himself, but always by seeking beyond himself a goal that takes the form of a particular liberation, a particular achievement that man will, precisely, realize himself as human."[19]

But is there the kind of reconciliation between Roquentin and the existentialist-humanist that Sartre would have us think? Is there a clear complementarity between the cathartic moment constituted by recognition of contingency (which, as far as humanism is concerned, would only bring down the humanism of the "phoney bastards," of humanity in thrall to its own essence), and the constructive moment of activity and project, which is an essential part of legitimate and necessary humanism? One may doubt that there is, and suspect that the passage from "nausea in the face of existence" to "reasons for living"[20] does not take place smoothly. No, Roquentin is not just attacking the humanism of the "phoney bastards," a fixed human Essence, static Value. He is also railing against the kind of optimistic activism which, a little later, Sartre will make his own profession of faith. Here is a statement by the Autodidact, refracted through the sarcastic prism of Roquentin's consciousness: "'Some years ago, I read a book by an American author called *Is Life Worth Living?*...He concluded,' the Autodidact told me consolingly, 'in favor of choosing optimism. Life has a meaning if one really wants to give it one. First of all, one must act, launch into some undertaking...I don't know what you think, sir?'—'Nothing,' I said. 'Or rather, I think that it's just the kind of lie that the commercial traveler, the two young people and the gentleman with white hair tell themselves.'"21 How can we fail to be aware of the discrepancy with the following sentence from *Existentialism and Humanism*, which, this time, is glossed entirely positively by Sartre: "Before you actually live it, life is nothing. But it's up to you to give it a meaning"22 So Roquentin had foreseen and criticized in advance a position that Sartre was to adopt.23

## 3. The Genealogy of Humanism

Yet Sartre does not stop criticizing humanism, or a certain humanism; it is simply that his angle of attack has changed. He will no longer criticize it from a position on high, as Roquentin did from the top of his hill (or Paul Hilbert in "Herostratus," who is fond of upper storeys and looking down from on high). On the contrary, Sartre will explore its underside. And if the superman—a temptation of Sartre's youth—loses his letters of nobility, there is doubtless a dimension of Nietzscheianism that remains relevant in Sartre's eyes: genealogy. The human race does not *exist*: the *Notebooks for an Ethics* and *Existentialism and Humanism* had established that. But the fact remains that, even if only with an illusory status, it *insists*, and that this insistence must be interpreted, in a genealogical framework, as a symptom: as the symptom—to use one of Nietzsche's expressions—of the "forces that take hold of it." It is impossible to stand above or outside the human race, which is the necessary condition of declaring it to be an existing or real totality. But the illusion of the species is formed by a process of internal exclusion, carried out by those who have the strength for it. In other words, it is always those in a dominant position who appropriate for themselves the universality of the species, thereby casting out as non-human those who do not meet the criteria that they have decided upon. Hence, when Roquentin does not distinguish between dignity and pride, when, in the same attacks, he confuses humanity and the "phoney bastards," he is in a sense playing the "phoney bastards" game, considering them, even as he rejects them, as human beings, instead of dismantling the unjustifiable mechanism by which they have taken over humanity.

This mechanism consists in the process whereby freedom both denies as part of itself its own nothingness, rejects the internal split which prevents it from ever being identical with itself, from every ceasing to be in the course of going against itself, and ascribes the nothingness to "others" (delinquents, psychotics, foreigners, prostitutes, and so on). In doing so, it installs itself, at the same time, as the Good, the Law, the Essence, Positivity, in short, as Humanity, making these "others" that it has entirely created itself into subhuman aberrations.

Alienation will reign supreme as long as freedom is split into these two segments, one allegedly all-positive, aggressively normative, erected into the universal law of the species, and another negative, bloody, unmentionable, cast-out scraps. There are numerous concrete examples in Sartre's works of this structure whereby a particular "power," which has no rights other than its strength, monopolizes the universality of the species—whether it be the Christian in relation to Jews, the bosses in relation to the proletariat, the heterosexual in relation to the homosexual, or the mentally "normal" in relation to the insane. Taking the last example, let us remember Mr. Darbédat in "The Room," who will not rest until his son-in-law is locked up: "'As a matter of fact, Pierre would be better looked after in Franchot's home. There's large garden.' And he added, with a little smile: 'I also think that he would get on better with people of his own kind. Creatures like that are like children: you have to let them mix with their own kind. They make up a kind of freemasonry.'"24 A little later Mr. Darbédat, emerging from a visit to his daughter, rediscovers—after the incense and the unhealthy semi-darkness of the couple's apartment—the autumnal light of the street and the unmysterious faces of the passers-by, concluding:

> "I know precisely what it is that I reproach Eva for," he said to himself when turning onto the Boulevard Saint-Germain, "I reproach her for living beyond the bounds of the human. Pierre is no longer a human being. She is rather depriving all these people of the care and attention that she gives to him."25

What is the ontological truth about this nothingness that freedom obstinately tries to cast out from itself, and to embody in the "Other?" Using the terms of *Being and Nothingness*, it is the non-coincidence with itself that characterizes the pre-reflective consciousness. Using the terms of the *Critique of Dialectical Reason*, it is—now that freedom has been given "living" roots—the nihilation ("*néantisation*") that always operates before there is "need." Need is not, as is commonly believed, a passivity being assailed from the outside by a lack of something (just as the for-itself is not affected by stimuli coming from the In-Itself), but always itself a unifying response which explains such lacks (of water, food, and so on), in the light of the unspoken totalizing project of maintaining organic integrity and interiority.

## 4. A Humanism of Need

But only when nothingness is counterbalanced by its "vitalo-corporeal" load, to use Hegelian vocabulary, does it seem to carry, in Sartre's eyes, the possibility of a true humanism, or of a universality that is more than, and different from, an act of strength on the part of those in a dominating position. The *Notebooks for an Ethics* already insist, in connection with the struggle between master and slave, on the liberating capacity of needs:

> *Misery, dependence, hunger*: these are the true liberating elements...hunger is a way of disclosing the world. Through hunger, the slave takes a grip on the world of the master and claims it for himself. Perfumes, rituals, art objects are inaccessible to him, but not the master's food. It is forbidden without being mysterious; it will have the same taste in the master's mouth as in his own. It is common ground, and in a sense, hunger is the positing of equality.[26]

Hence, strung out at intervals in Sartre's work, there are some optimistic, even prophetic pronouncements: "A humanism of need—in the form of a hold taken by every man on all men—is coming into being"[27]; or again, "A humanism is coming into being out of need."[28]

This humanism of need, moreover, is akin to practical humanism, to the pride taken in action mentioned earlier, since need and praxis are intricately related, organic function not being different in its nature from action.[29]

So the question is the following: if, according to one of the opening sentences of the *Critique of Dialectical Reason*, "need reveals everything," if, on the basis of the totalizing view involved in need, "man organizes himself as an active being at grips with the world," if need is the most widely shared thing in the world and thereby the matrix of a true humanism or of a universality that is not reducible to the act of strength of a dominating class, then how is it that there are so many aberrant, alienating and alienated humanisms?

## 5. The Activists: Children of Need

A first answer is that it is only in the abstract situation of the beginning of the *Critique*—a person alone in a world that is still unhistorical—that need is in principle the most widely shared thing in the world. In practice, in the real concrete nooks and crannies of society, not everyone is given the chance to be hungry, and many unfortunate people are deprived of this liberating resource, with its power to disclose. We may remember Frantz, made into a "monarch," that is "someone good for nothing,"[30] by a father who never stops disarming the hostile forces of the world for him; Hugo, who enters the Communist Party, but will never manage to atone for the sin of never having gone hungry, of having left half of his calcium on his plate throughout his childhood ("They made me take cod liver oil. There's luxury for you: a drug to *make you hungry*, while others in the street would have sold their souls for a steak—I could see them going past my window with their banners: 'Give us bread.' And I went and sat down at the table."[31]); Lucien, who *plays* at being an orphan and not having eaten for six days;[32] and Sartre himself, whose slightest desire for food was celebrated as a miracle ("I eat in public, like a king: if I eat *well*, they congratulate me; my grandmother herself cries out: 'What a good boy he is to be hungry!'"[33])

Freedom, then, is born not into an untouched world, but into a world already split. On the one side, there are the children of need; on the other, child-monarchs, who have too good a start, and therefore too bad a start in life. In this Manichean framework, the first group will possibly not hesitate to make a caste privilege out of their deprivation, themselves monopolizing, just as the bourgeoisie does, the right to say "we." Formidable ambiguity can be found in the picture of Brunet pleading with Mathieu about his need to join the Communist Party. Are the solidity, density, and levelheadedness that he brings to his task and opposes to the shapeless and rootless freedom of Mathieu, who is "indecisive, aging badly, in bad shape" amid his ghostly green armchairs, really the expression of his active grip on the world and of his links "with the working classes of all countries?" Are they really the admirable emanations that come from someone who is a human being through and through ("altogether a man, nothing but a man," as Mathieu says), or are they simply one more form of the in-itself-for-itself, the sought-after static embodiment of self that characterizes all "phoney bastards?"[34]

Who is the human being in the end, Brunet or Mathieu? The activist or the loner (who, in Sartrean terminology, is also called the "adventurer")? There is scarcely any doubt about the direction of Sartre's sympathy. The activist "is right in *every* respect....Yet it is the adventurer that I shall follow into his solitude."[35]

Soon the *Critique of Dialectical Reason* will be written, and the main theoretical reason for undermining activism will be deployed. History, in the name of which the activist loses himself or herself, properly speaking *does not exist*. Only the praxises of individuals exist in the full sense of the term. But these are also redefined in the course of Sartre's iconoclastic exposure of the non-existence of History as an "hyperorganism" or a substantial unity. It is true that they are the only things that *exist*, but they give consistence to History by the many ways in which they escape from themselves, form a sediment, stratify, create, together with the other praxises and matter, in which they are inscribed, a monstrous hybrid called the "practico-inert," History doubtless being nothing other than this hybrid.

## 6. The Humanism of the Practico-Inert

Let us return to our question: if it is true that need reveals everything, why are there so many aberrant humanisms? The first answer—not everyone who wants to be a child of need can be—is inadequate. A second answer has to be developed in the light of the notion of the practico-inert. Need reveals everything, need discloses the world; that is what Sartre calls the univocal internal relationship between praxis and its surroundings. "Internal," because, as we have seen, everything comes to light through the totalizing aim of need, which projects the formation of its own unity beyond the present fragmentation of the world; because it is, then, only from inside this unity that lacks and their possible rectification emerge. "Univocal," because this unity subordinates to itself the means of creating itself. Even if it has to use the inert to reproduce its organic interiority, this use is only provisional and, as soon as it is surpassed, is "swallowed up" by life. But the discovery of the practico-inert is the disillusionment that consists in noticing that this "univocal interiority" is not sustainable, that matter and inertia have their own powers, that, in their turn, they subordinate to themselves the praxis which becomes engulfed in them—a reversal of the univocal hierarchy—and irremediably externalize its interiority.

Let us stop for a moment over the terrible ambivalence of the quotation that Sartre notes in his *War Diaries* with an optimism free of any second thoughts: "It is an excellent tenet that J. Romains ascribes to Maykosen...: 'Men are like bees. Their products are worth more than they are'"[36] It is the triumphal chant of intentionality, no longer formulated this time at the structural-ontological level—consciousness has consistency only when it adheres to something that it discloses by making itself not be that thing—but at the pragmatic level: freedom is nothing beyond what it does or makes. It is also "pride," as we defined it earlier. Yes, but it takes almost nothing for this "worth more" that attaches to the product to turn back against its creator, making him or her swing from conquering activism to passivity. which means, in the last analysis—this is another Sartre formula and a much more pessimistic one—that "we are the product of our products?" The human being is the prisoner of worked-upon matter, of the ways of using it, of its injunctions, of its requirements; the prisoner, for example, of machines, those instruments that serve freedom's purposes only so far as it resigns itself to serving them proportionately.

The product makes its creator, molding him or her to its own demands, making of him or her the deformed aborted specimen required for its optimal functioning. And there is worse: it is because the product is a human one that it is unsurpassable. It is because it retains within itself the frozen trace of the freedom that produced it that this freedom can no longer recognize it as an obstacle to be overcome, something inert to be brought to life by being given a meaning, as Being which has to be surpassed. On the contrary, thinking it finds itself in the product, freedom is surpassed *by* it every time. If machines are terrible things, it is because they are not being in-itself, but petrified ideas: "these belligerent ideas holding in their claws a piece of cast iron or steel."[37]

These "belligerent ideas" impose upon us, without our being aware of it, the idea that we must have of ourselves; in other words, they secrete, over and above dark smoke, their harmful versions of humanism. In the *Critique*, Sartre showed, in the most striking way, how much the "pride of the producer"[38] — through which, as we have seen, he himself nevertheless defines the fully human content of humanity — can also be a deceptive enslavement generated by the machine itself. This hides from the worker the only true relationship that he can have with the machine and which would allow him to surpass it and reintegrate into his freedom: that is, "the indignation of the exploited."[39] It is a question of anarcho-syndicalism, which was itself born in the humus of the coal-iron complex and the "universal machine" that goes with it. This non-specialized machine requires specialized servants, who, in return for a long apprenticeship, are qualified to run it in the differentiated operations that it is fit to carry out. Moreover, for the work of these workers to be profitable, they must not waste their skills and must be freed from all simplistic work. Non-qualified workers gravitate around them and support them. Thus, the proletariat is structured by the machine, even down to the details of the intersubjective relations that are generated within it. Sartre says that even if the "pride" of the elite workers, who make their qualifications the supreme human value and the professional the embodiment of the successful person, is "deeply respectable,"[40] it nevertheless cuts them off from the possibility of a real class solidarity. However positively linked with the fate of the laborers, they feel themselves to be, and however sincerely they deplore the laborers' misery, in practice, and irrespective of their intentions, they can only at the same time reinforce their status as sub-humans, even by the paternalistic efforts that they make to lift them out of it — by training them, educating them, as if it were perfectly normal that, as long as they are only laborers, they should be exploited.

One begins to understand the trap, as intangible as it is implacable, that is at the heart of the practico-inert. We should not think that, in the way in which people are formed by the machine, it is a matter of pure and simple determinism. No, far from it being the case that anarcho-syndicalism is the mechanical effect of a cause, it is a "free and full world," which evolves "passionately, ceaselessly."[41] The qualified workers improve their technical skills with all the strength of their freedom. Also freely, the laborers harbor complex and ambiguous feelings about these skills (admiration, envy, suspicion), and work themselves to death. However, this complete freedom is only complete because it is no longer encountering its limits, no longer running up against them—which might possibly allow it to go beyond them, but is entirely confused with them, or *is* those limits, which makes them unsurpassable, for how can one rid oneself *of* oneself, "how could this exploited class have struggled for a proletariat other than itself?" This class has been formed by internalizing the machine, and has thereby externalized itself by condemning itself to a prefabricated future, to the "impossibility of going further, of wanting or understanding anything more."[42] The humanism of work-honor will pass away one of these days, without ever having stopped being unsurpassable, without ever having been freely surpassed. It will sink out of sight as a result of the arrival of another type of machine, the specialized machine, which—this time requiring non-qualified workers—will make possible the restoration of the unity of the working class, on the basis of the interchangeability of workers.

## 7. Conclusion

Basically, Sartre's evolving attitude toward humanism is just a particular case of the evolution of his thought on Value: humanism being the Value accorded to humankind. As early as *Being and Nothingness*, criticism of Value existed. Those who thought it accessible, those who thought they could coincide with themselves in realizing an in-itself-for-itself were the proponents of the spirit of seriousness, or (in the vocabulary of *Nausea*) the "phoney bastards." But a kind of optimism remained concerning Value. This was because for those who, by contrast with the "phoney bastards," know that they are a "useless passion," who know that failure is a constitutive part of all projects, who are conscious that every synthesis must necessarily fail. For such persons it was not impossible that they might be rewarded by grasping a free Value, or freedom taking itself as a Value (see Chapter Nine for a fuller discussion of Sartre on "useless passion"). This was a possibility opened up by the "ethical perspectives" with which the work concluded. But why does freedom alienate itself if it has the possibility of being free? To reply to this question *Being and Nothingness* had recourse to the enigmatic idea of "original choice," a global choice that comes "before" particular choices. It was claimed that freedom has always already chosen for or against itself, and yet expresses itself only through these. This mystery of original choice is removed from the *Critique*. The fact that we project ourselves toward the "synthesis" of the in-itself-for-itself is no longer considered in the *Critique*, as it was in *Being and Nothingness*, as the result of a "prenatal choice,"[43] but just as the result of the material structuring of the relationship between the organism and the environment. The organism is condemned to be able to act only in and on its inert surroundings, or in-itself, with which it consequently synthesizes itself, to make the in-itself-for-itself. But again, it sees its action become petrified, become in-itself, "whether this be a statue, a machine, or a particular interest."[44] The synthesis breaks up, the in-itself-for-itself loses its living qualities by virtue of the fact that it is brought about. It constitutes "failure," exactly as in *Being and Nothingness*. Except for the fact that, if it is because action becomes inscribed in matter that the in-itself-for-itself can only disintegrate into in-itself, thereby alienating freedom, making it a stranger to itself, then there is scarcely a chance that mere lucidity about the failure that is a condition of all undertakings should be enough to rid freedom of its alienation, since such lucidity leaves materiality intact. Correspondingly, no possibility exists of an in-itself-for-itself or of a free and authentic Value which would redeem the "useless passion," or provide the basis of the existential "loser wins." All value is practico-inert; that is, just the falsely ideal formulation of an imperative arising out of worked-upon matter: "Values are linked with the existence of the arena of the practico-inert, in other words of hell...and if a removal of these structures [of the practico-inert] is to be possible, values will disappear with them, to expose the free development of praxis itself as the only ethical relationship between men."[45] In other words, as soon as we make freedom into a value, it is already no longer free.

The same is true of humankind. As soon as we make the human being into a Value, we are already into the territory of the inhuman. The humanism of work-honor is a disguising of the plain demands of the machine, the factory, and profit. What a distance there is between the sublime sentence in *Being and Nothingness*, "Man is a useless passion," and this other sentence, almost literally identical, which this time Sartre sarcastically puts into the mouth of a post-1848 bourgeois: "The essence of humanity can only be a vain Passion"[46]—immediately followed by its crude truth in terms of the practico-inert: "with a little luck, the self-domestication of man in a farmyard guarded by machines."

## Notes

1. Jean-Paul Sartre, *La Nausée* in *Oeuvres romanesques,* eds. Michel Contat and Michel Rybalka (Paris: Gallimard, 1981), p. 186. Trans. Robert Baldick as *Nausea* (Harmondsworth: Penguin, 1965). I will give page numbers for the French edition only.
2. *Ibid.*, p. 13.
3. *Ibid.*, p. 14.
4. *Ibid.*, p. 79.

5. *Ibid.*, p. 146.
6. *Ibid.*, p. 189.
7. Jean-Paul Sartre, *Carnets de la drôle de guerre* (Paris: Gallimard, 1985), p. 28. Trans. Quintin Hoare as *The War Diaries* (New York: Pantheon Books, 1984).
8. Sartre, *La Nausée* , p. 107.
9. Sartre, *Carnets*, p. 29.
10. Simone de Beauvoir, *La Cérémonie des adieux, suivi de Entretiens avec Jean-Paul Sartre, août-septembre 1974* (Paris: Gallimard, 1981), p. 326. Trans. Patrick O'Brian as *Adieux: A Farewell to Sartre* (New York: Pantheon Books, 1984).
11. Jean-Paul Sartre, *Les Chemins de la liberté* in *Oeuvres romanesques*, p. 475. Trans. in three volumes as *The Roads to Freedom*: vol. 1 trans. Eric Sutton as *The Age of Reason* (New York: Vintage Books, 1992), vol. 2 trans. Eric Sutton as *The Reprieve* (New York: Vintage Books, 1992), vol. 3 trans. Gerard Hopkins as *Troubled Sleep* (New York: Vintage Books, 1992).
12. *Ibid.*, p. 1249.
13. *Ibid.*, p. 1253.
14. *Ibid.*, p. 469.
15. Jean-Paul Sartre, *L'Existentialisme est un humanisme* (Paris: Nagel, 1970), p. 91. Trans. Philip Mairet as *Existentialism and Humanism* (London: Methuen, 1948).
16. See Jean-Paul Sartre, *Cahiers pour une morale* (Paris: Gallimard, 1985), p. 73. Trans. David Pellauer as *Notebooks for an Ethics* (Chicago: University of Chicago Press, 1992).
17. Sartre, *L'Existentialisme*, p. 92.
18. Jean-Paul Sartre, *L'Etre et le Néant* (Paris: Gallimard, 1991), p. 691. Trans. Hazel E. Barnes as *Being and Nothingness: An Essay in Phenomenological Ontology* (London: Methuen, 1956).
19. Sartre, *L'Existentialisme*, p. 94.
20. C. Chonez, "Sartre, romancier philosophe," *Marianne*, 23 (novembre 1938), quoted by Michel Contat and Michel Rybalka in *Oeuvres romanesques*, p. 1697.
21. Sartre, *La Nausée* , p. 133.
22. Sartre, *L'Existentialisme*, p. 89.
23. Michel Contat, lecture given at the Maison Française at New York University, 10 October 1994 ("The Florence Gould Lectures"), to appear in *Etudes sartriennes*, 6.
24. Jean-Paul Sartre, "La Chambre," in *Oeuvres romanesques*, p. 237. Trans. Lloyd Alexander as "The Room" in *The Wall (Intimacy) and Other Stories* (New York: New Directions, 1969).
25. *Ibid.*, p. 248.
26. Sartre, *Cahiers*, p. 404.
27. Jean-Paul Sartre, *Critique de la Raison dialectique* (Paris: Gallimard, 1985), vol. 1, p. 351. Trans. Quintin Hoare as *Critique of Dialectical Reason* (London: Verso, 1991).
28. Jean-Paul Sartre, *L'Idiot de la famille: Gustave Flaubert de 1821 à 1857*, 3

vols. (Paris: Gallimard, 1971-1972), p. 433 Trans. Carol Cosman as *The Family Idiot : Gustave Flaubert 1821-1857*, 5 vols. (Chicago: University of Chicago Press, 1981-1993).

29. Sartre, *Critique*, vol. 1, p. 196.

30. Jean-Paul Sartre, *Les Séquestrés d'Altona* (Paris: Gallimard, 1960, "Folio" edit.), p. 362. Trans. Sylvia and George Leeson as *The Condemned of Altona* (New York: Alfred A. Knopf, 1964).

31. Jean-Paul Sartre, *Les Mains sales* (Paris: Gallimard, 1948) ("Livre de Poche"), p. 97. Trans. Stuart Gilbert as *Dirty Hands* in Jean-Paul Sartre, *No Exit and Three Other Plays* (New York: Vintage Books, 1955).

32. Jean-Paul Sartre, "L'Enfance d'un Chef," in *Oeuvres romanesques*, p. 317. Trans. as "The Childhood of a Leader" in *The Wall (Intimacy) and Other Stories*.

33. Jean-Paul Sartre, *Les Mots* (Paris: Gallimard, 1964, "Folio" edit.), p. 29. Trans. Bernard Fretchman as *The Words* (New York: G. Braziller, 1964).

34. Sartre, *Les Chemins*, p. 522ff.

35. Preface to Roger Stéphane, *Portrait de l'aventurier* (Paris: Gallimard, 1981), p. 26.

36. Sartre, *Carnets*, p. 185.

37. Michel Contat and Michel Rybalka, "Légende de la vérité," in *Les Ecrits de Sartre: chronologie, bibliographie commenté* (Paris: Gallimard, 1970), p. 544.

38. Sartre, *Critique*, vol. 1, p. 349.

39. *Ibid.*, p. 349.

40. *Ibid.*, p. 352.

41. *Ibid.*

42. *Ibid.*, p. 353.

43. *Ibid.*, p. 337.

44. *Ibid.*, p. 336.

45. *Ibid.*, p. 357.

46. Sartre, *L'Idiot*, vol. 3, p. 295.

# Seven

# MARCEL, HOPE, AND VIRTUE

## Philip Stratton-Lake

A long Christian tradition exists within which hope is conceived of as a virtue. It is not regarded as an intellectual or moral virtue, but as a theological virtue along with faith and love. But hope is not only valued from within a Christian outlook. One might think that hope against hope—that is, against the odds—expresses a strength of commitment to a loved one, or to some cause which is admirable in its own right. But whether or not one agrees with this positive evaluation of hope, any satisfactory account of what hope is should be able to explain why it is so valued. The problem is that the standard account makes such an evaluation of hope unintelligible. According to this account, hope is defined as a desire plus a belief that there is a possibility of satisfying this desire.[1] This understanding raises two obstacles to a positive evaluation of hope.

First, if we conceive of hope in this way, it will not seem to be the right sort of thing to be a virtue. One may hold that the belief is more or less warranted, and the desire more or less moral. Although the desire may be considered good, it will not be considered a virtue, but instead an expression of a virtue. The virtue will be the quality of character in virtue of which one is disposed to have such desires. The same point can be made in relation to the degree to which the belief is justified. It is not justified beliefs which are virtues, but the rationality of the agent who possesses these beliefs.

Second, this account makes impossible for us to see how the type of hope which is considered admirable is possible. For the type of hope which is apt for such a positive evaluation is usually referred to as "hope against hope." To hope against hope is to hope against the odds—that is, in the face of one's recognition that the facts of the situation point inexorably toward some tragic outcome. According to the standard account of hope, to recognize this type of situation for what it is is to recognize that there is no reason to hope. For to recognize the situation for what it is is to recognize the practical certainty of the tragic outcome. To hope against hope will thus, according to the standard account, turn out to be irrational. For how could one recognize that there is every reason to abandon hope, yet continue to hope, unless one were irrational? If, in these circumstances, one's hope is seen as irrational, it will to this extent be regarded as objectionable. It may be held that, all things considered, it is better if the individual holds on to this illusory hope—it may be the only way in which he can cope with his situation. Nonetheless, if we believe that this hope is irrational, we will tend to take the view that it would be better if one could do without it.

The inability of the standard account to accommodate people's evaluation of hope should make us doubt whether this account is correct, or, if we think it is correct, it should make us consider the possibility that there is another kind of hope which is apt for such an evaluation. Such a possibility has been explored in depth by Gabriel Marcel, the first, but nonetheless least well-known, French existentialist. Marcel's main philosophical concern, in line with other French existentialists, is with giving an account of the human world, and individuals within that world, which does not reduce either to a mere catalog of facts that can be known by a detached spectator. However, central to this account is his distinctive understanding of hope. This alternative to the standard account of hope is worked out in detail in his "Sketch of a Phenomenology and a Metaphysic of Hope." Marcel is not here concerned to reject the standard account of hope, as a description of everyday hopes, such as the hope that the meal is good, or that my friend will arrive early. He is not concerned with such hopes. But although the standard account may be adequate as an account of such hopes, Marcel believes it fails to capture what is distinctive about the experience of hope. The sort of hope in which Marcel is interested—which he describes as absolute, or unconditional hope—cannot, he maintains, be understood in terms of desire and calculation, but is a way of being in the world which is opposed to this.

I think Marcel's account of hope is highly illuminating and informative, and provides a refreshing alternative to the standard account. I also believe it removes the two obstacles to a positive evaluation of hope raised by the standard account. In what follows, however, I shall deal only with the second of these obstacles—that is, with the charge that a clear-sighted hope against the odds is irrational. I will not, therefore, put forward positive reasons for thinking that hope is a virtue, but will simply attempt to remove what I take to be the main reason for thinking that it is not.

## 1. Trial, Captivity, and the Temptation to Despair

Genuine hope is essentially a response to, and part of, a situation, which Marcel describes as a trial.[2] The sort of situation he characterizes as a trial is one that in some way prevents me from living a full life, which can take the form of a disabling illness, separation from a loved one, or even writer's block. What is distinctive of all such situations is that they involve the temptation to despair. Hope is essentially a response to this temptation. It is not merely a means to overcome some particular temptation, but a disposition to overcome all such temptations. Marcel thus approaches the phenomenon of hope by first describing the despair to which it is contrasted. He identifies three characteristics of despair: capitulation to one's fate, an experience of time as closed, and solitude. I will summarize these before considering how hope is contrasted with them.

To despair is, Marcel maintains, primarily to capitulate to a fate we judge inevitable.[3] If I am suffering from some progressive, crippling disease, or am imprisoned in some more literal sense, then capitulation to my fate involves my identifying myself with the useless creature my illness or my captivity may finally make of me. If the situation is one in which my son is reported missing, and in which days go by without any news of his whereabouts, to capitulate involves identifying myself with what this separation, if permanent, will eventually make of me. But to capitulate is not simply to identify oneself with one's fate, but is, he writes, "to go to pieces under this sentence, to disarm before the inevitable. It is at bottom to renounce the idea of remaining oneself, it is to be fascinated by the idea of one's own destruction to the point of anticipating this very destruction itself."[4] The first characteristic of despair is thus capitulation in the sense of identifying oneself with what one judges one's trial will finally make of one.

The second characteristic of despair is the experience of time as closed. In despair time is experienced as a mechanical process, whereby everything which will occur is represented as already determined by what has occurred. Many people believe in a deterministic universe, but do not despair. It is, however, one thing to believe in the theory of universal determinism, and quite another to have a concrete experience of time which might support this belief. Marcel is not saying that those who believe in universal determinism despair. Instead, he is saying that when they despair they actually experience time in a way which corresponds with this belief. When time is experienced in this way, the passing of time is seen as bringing nothing new and is hence experienced as closed. In despair, time is represented as closed not only in the sense that it is seen as lacking possibilities which are not delimited by what has already occurred, but also in the sense that it is conceived of as enclosing or imprisoning us.[5] This brings us to the third characteristic of despair–solitude.

The temptation to despair involves "the temptation of shutting the door which encloses me within myself and at the same time encloses me within time."[6] To despair is to withdraw from the world and from my involvement with others. It is to turn inwards on the self which constitutes the object of my morbid fascination. It is this withdrawal which Marcel has in mind when he characterizes despair as solitude. It is clear that he does not mean that one is alone in the sense that no one is around. One could experience such solitude in the midst of a crowd. The point is that, in solitude, one is not involved with others, or if one is, it is in a distorted and artificial form. Marcel here describes despair as a capitulation before one's fate, as the experience of time as closed and enclosing, and as solitude. Hope is described in contrast to these three characteristics. Marcel thus characterizes hope as a distinctive way of holding on to one's integrity where this integrity is challenged, as involving an experience of time as the place in which a creative process unfolds, and as a form of communion. It is to these positive characterizations of hope that I now turn.

## 2. Integrity

What is the distinctive way of holding on to one's integrity in the face of the temptation to despair which is constitutive of hope? If we think of despair as involving the anticipation of one's fate, we might suppose that hope is simply the refusal to accept it. But although there is an element of refusal in hope, we should be clear about what it is that is refused, and the way in which it is refused. To hope is not to refuse to believe that one's situation is not as grim as it appears. It is not to deny the facts involved in the situation, but is to recognize them without being crushed by them. What one refuses in hope is to anticipate one's fate in advance: "By accepting an inevitable destiny which I refuse with all my strength to anticipate, I will find a way of inward consolation, of proving my reality to myself, and at the same time I shall rise infinitely above this *fatum* to which I have never allowed myself to shut my eyes."[7] The element of refusal in hope is not, therefore, a refusal to recognize the facts, but a refusal to anticipate the conclusion to which the facts point.

But although hope is characterized as the refusal to anticipate one's fate, it should not be understood as a revolt against this. Marcel is at pains to distinguish the mode of non-acceptance implicit in hope, from that of revolt. Revolt is characterized as a self-conscious struggle against one's fate. Such non-acceptance is tinged with an element of anxiety and self-obsession. Thus, so far as one anxiously revolts, or fights against one's fate, one is still under its spell. One does not remove the obstacles to a full life in this way. Rather, such a life is rendered impossible by the contraction involved in such a response in just the way in which the flow of a tennis player's stroke may be distorted if she tries too hard. This form of refusal, Marcel writes, is just another form of fascination with one's own destruction, "a manner of working out one's own defeat."[8]

Marcel attempts to say something about the positive character of the type of refusal involved in hope with reference to relaxation and patience. The type of non-acceptance in hope does not involve an anxious, self-obsessed struggle against one's fate, but involves a kind of relaxation in one's non-acceptance. [9] He suggests that the non-acceptance involved in hope has a kind of grace and suppleness analogous to that of the practiced athlete so far as she does not "tighten up." The notion of relaxation in one's non-acceptance is elucidated with reference to patience.

We can be patient either with ourselves or with others. To be patient with oneself is to take one's time—that is, not to force one's personal rhythm. [10] To be patient with another person involves never hustling or being rough with him or her: more exactly, Marcel writes, it involves "never trying to substitute our own rhythm for his by violence."[11] To state this in more positive terms, to be patient with another is to place our confidence in a certain process of growth, or development, be it our own, or that of another. Such confidence is not the certainty one may have as the result of some argument; it is not, as Marcel puts it, a mere act of theoretical acceptance, but is the embracing of this process so as to promote it from within.

If one loses one's patience with another person, one despairs of him and declares that he is good for nothing. Similarly, to lose all patience with oneself in the face of one's trial is to lose confidence in oneself; it is to proclaim that I am good for nothing. Thus, Marcel writes, "in hoping, I develop in connection with the event, and perhaps above all through what it makes of me, a type of relationship, a kind of intimacy comparable to that which I have with the other person when I am patient with him."[12] Here the analogy with patience may seem to have shifted. It may appear that here the analogy of hope with patience has shifted from being patient with myself, or with another, to being patient with my situation. But no such shift has occurred. The key to this passage is the clause "and perhaps above all through what it makes of me." The trial is that which tempts me to lose patience with myself, for it tempts me give up on myself, to declare that I am good for nothing. It is not the situation with which I am patient in hope, but myself. The trial is that which tempts me to lose my patience.

At this point it may seem as though the analogy with patience has ceased to illuminate the positive character of the non-acceptance involved in hope, for it may seem as though we have ended up where we started. We seem to have ended up with the claim that to refuse to accept what the trial threatens to make of me is to refuse to give up on myself. But, it may be objected, the notion of "refusing to give up" hardly distinguishes different ways of refusing to give up, and hence cannot distinguish the mode of non-acceptance in hope from that of revolt. But I think this objection misses the point of the analogy with patience. The more I am patient with another person, the more I cease to focus on myself, and the more I match my rhythm with his or hers. To the extent that we can conceive of this intersubjective relation as an intrasubjective relation of me to myself, the notion of patience will illuminate the distinctive form of non-acceptance involved in hope. Negative non-acceptance involves a frantic, anxious, self-obsessed struggle against one's fate. Positive non-acceptance involves patiently placing one's confidence in oneself, or in another, in the face of the evidence which tempts one give up on oneself, or another. The trial is thus understood as something which threatens to distort my relation with myself, or with others, by forcing me to become fascinated with myself: a self which is at the same time distorted by this fascination.

In hope, then, one patiently refuses to accept one's fate without becoming obsessed with the possibility of one's destruction, thus allowing it to distort one's normal mode of existence. So far as one can patiently refuse to anticipate one's own destruction in the face of the temptation to do so, one can rise above one's situation without closing one's eyes to it. It is this non-evasive transcending of one's situation which Marcel sees as the distinctive nobility which hope brings with it.

This transcending of one's situation does not depend upon a false belief that one will recover, or that one will be liberated from one's trial. In many cases, such a belief will simply be unwarranted or illusory. But even where there is some chance of recovery, liberation, or reunification, to the extent that one makes the securing of one's integrity conditional on this, one makes this security fragile. For if one pins one's hopes on some specific object, such as the hope for recovery, then one determines the point of disappointment, and lays down a limit beyond which the temptation to despair can no longer be resisted.[13]

Marcel maintains that we can distinguish between hope and the plurality of hopes we have, in just the way that we distinguish between belief and the various beliefs we have. The plurality of different hopes are propositional attitudes, and may be expressed in the form, "I hope that *p*." The hope which is contrasted with these is what Marcel calls "the absolute statement" of hope.[14] This should be expressed in the unconditional form, "I hope." Such hope is not conditioned by any specific object to which hope attaches, but tends to transcend all possible disappointment.[15] This does not mean that hope can exist in the absence of anything hoped for. On the contrary, Marcel thinks that all significant hope is ultimately for salvation. His point is that at its highest point hope is unconditional in the sense that the individual refuses to identify salvation with any particular hoped-for object. So far as we think of hope in this way, Marcel writes, we can conceive "of the inner disposition of one who, setting no condition or limit and abandoning himself in absolute confidence, would thus transcend all possible disappointment and would experience a security of his being, or in his being, which is contrary to the radical insecurity of *Having*."[16] The notion of "Having" to which hope is here contrasted is important. Marcel maintains that one can relate to oneself and the world either as possessor and possessed or in an existential relation of availability. The relation of having is not so much characterized by material possessions, as by a certain self-obsession. Cut off from the other, and the ontological security which the other can bestow by the act of recognition, the subject seeks to give to herself a certain ontological weight by accumulating possessions, and by attempting to identify with these. But this possessive relation is a dialectical one in which the subject becomes the victim of her possessions.[17] She is always in fear of losing what she has, and since she identifies with these, she is always in fear of losing herself. Just as the master becomes subordinated to the slave in Hegel's master-slave dialectic, so the possessor becomes enslaved by her possessions. This relation leads inevitably to despair because in the end my own death will take everything from me.

In contrast to having, which is characterized by anxious self-obsession, being is characterized as a state of openness which Marcel calls *disponibilité* (availability or disposability). Availability is not meant to imply a emptiness, as in the case of an available dwelling (*local disponible*); nor should it be understood in the sense in which a tool is available for some use.[18] Availability, for Marcel, means "an aptitude to give oneself to anything which offers, and to bind oneself by the gift."[19] This handing oneself over should not be understood as a state of indifference to one's destiny or character. In availability we not only *undergo*, that is, are open to, whatever fate offers, but make whatever is given our own "by somehow recreating it from within."[20] This recreation from within is an act of binding, or committing oneself to an appeal addressed to me, and one to which I am only open to in availability. In its most obvious form, availability is "associated with the claim of another concrete human being upon us and with that form of love that renders us open to this claim, namely, *caritas* ('charity')."[21] It is not, however, restricted to this, but is a general state of being open to whatever unforeseen opportunities the future has to offer.

The association of hope with this positive relation to the future may lead one to think of hope as a form of optimism—a belief that, in the end, everything will turn out for the good. But Marcel stresses that we should distinguish genuine hope from optimism. Optimism involves a certain distance from the world and from others which is alien to hope as he conceives it. The optimist, he writes, adopts the standpoint of the spectator; it is a theoretical attitude in which the individual withdraws from his or her involvement in the world and with others and looks on as an outsider.[22] In hope, however, one does not withdraw to this external position, for it is a way of sustaining one's everyday mode of involvement with others in a situation which threatens to distort this.[23] Indeed, we shall see that, for Marcel, hope is inaccessible from such a detached standpoint.

But, it may be asked, if hope does not presuppose adherence to a false belief about the possibility of redemption, and is not a form of optimism, then how does it secure one's integrity against the temptation to despair? In order to answer this question we need to consider the way in which time is experienced by those who live in hope, and in what way this involves some form of communion.

## 3. Time

In despair, time is experienced as closed and as enclosing. In hope, however, time is experienced as the medium of a creative process: "He who hopes, inasmuch as his hope is real and not to be reduced to a mere platonic wish, seems to himself to be involved in some kind of a process."[24] I have already referred to a confidence in something like this process in our discussion of being patient with another person, and of availability. Here this notion is developed with reference to the experience of time and the temporal it involves. From the perspective of established experience time is seen as bringing nothing new, "as though the future, drained of its substance and of its mystery, were no longer to be anything but a place of pure repetition."[25] From this perspective, therefore, those who hope against the odds will seem irrational. But what sustains the hopeful is not a calculation of possibilities, but the experience of time as a creative process, involving the immanent possibility of a break with established experience. In hope, one does not pin down the future in advance in terms of what one can imagine or calculate. Hope is, as Otto Bollnow puts it, "availability for the gift of the future, which exceeds all expectations and all calculations."[26] It involves an experience of being as overflowing an inventory of facts and states of affairs that can be inferred from such facts. It is, to use Marcel's terms, to experience the mystery of being. Whatever being means, Marcel maintains, its "essence" cannot be reduced to a catalog of facts. Its nature can only be known negatively as the overflowing of any such inventory. Despair can thus be characterized as "the shock felt by the mind when it meets with 'there is no more.'"[27] What sustains the hopeful, therefore, is an experience of time and the temporal. The experience of time and the temporal which is peculiar to the hopeful does not sustain hope in the way in which evidence sustains a hypothesis. Marcel's idea is not that we first experience time, or the temporal, in a certain way, and then, on the basis of this, are able to hope. Rather, this distinctive experience of time is the reverse side of hope. So far as we hope we experience time in this way, and so far as we experience time in this way, we hope.

This makes it difficult to see how we achieve hope, but Marcel maintains that hope is no more an achievement than love is. As I have already noted in passing, hope is, for Marcel, a gift, something offered to us. Nonetheless, it is something which depends upon us. For "we can refuse hope just as we can refuse love."[28] The analogy with love is useful here, for so far as we think of hope as a gift, we may be tempted to think of it as something deeply mysterious and mystical. Once we realize that it is a gift only in the sense in which love is a gift, we should realize that hope is no more mysterious and mystical than love.

Marcel does not, therefore, think that significant hopes are, or need be, justified by the evidence which is available to a disinterested spectator, that is, by an inventory of facts. It may be that certain specific hopes are constrained by such evidence, but not the genuine hope with which he is concerned. But, it may be asked whether we have a right to hope when the reasons for doing so are insufficient or completely lacking. Isn't such hope irrational, and to that extent objectionable? Marcel's first response to this leads us down a dead end. At first he seems to maintain that so far as we continue to hope, we take it that there is sufficient reason to do so.[29] Since it is *not possible* to hope when we assume that the reasons for doing so are insufficient, or absent, the question of whether we may hope in these circumstances does not arise. But if this is his view, then he must maintain that the reasons which are regarded by the subject as sufficient are not reasons of probability, that is, they are not reasons which could be seen from an external, detached perspective. As we have seen, Marcel does not think that significant hopes are justified by evidence which is available to a disinterested spectator. Thus, if he thinks that to hope implies the conviction that the reasons for hope are sufficient, he must maintain that the reasons which are taken by the subject to be sufficient are not reasons which are accessible from the spectator's point of view. Here, then, Marcel's response to the question of whether one may hope where the reasons for doing so are insufficient or absent, seems to be to maintain that the question is irrelevant. It is irrelevant because it is not possible to hope where we believe the reasons for doing so are insufficient or absent. It may be that from the standpoint of the spectator, it will sometimes appear as if there is little or no reason. This is because the sort of reasons which are available to the spectator are not the ones on which hope is based. These are available only to the hopeful.

If this is Marcel's response to the question of whether we may hope where the reasons for doing so are insufficient or absent, then it is not a good response. At the point at which the reasons for hope become accessible, they would become redundant. If hope is not an achievement of the subject, but something like a gift, then we will not need reasons to get ourselves into this condition (because it is not a condition into which we get ourselves). We do not, however, need these reasons once we are in this state. We only need reasons to hope in the absence of hope. Thus, to the extent that these supposed reasons would become accessible to us, they would become redundant.

Reason exists, however, to think that when Marcel states that hope presupposes the assumption that there is sufficient reason to do so he is not expressing his own view. These claims do not fit with his view that the issue of reasons only arises so far as we detach ourselves from our hope.[30] Furthermore, Marcel makes it clear that when he states that hope involves the assumption that the reasons for doing so are sufficient, he is considering hope as it is understood according to the standard account. If one understands hope in this way, then it will be absurd to hope when one believes there is no reason to do so, since hope is partly defined in terms of beliefs about such reasons. He writes, "that here the meaning of the word hope has been completely distorted."[31] So when he states that hope involves a belief that there is sufficient reason to hope, he is not expressing his own view, but the standard view of hope which, he believes, does not capture its true nature.

A different response to the question of whether we may hope when the reasons for doing so are insufficient is suggested when Marcel states that "we shall have to deny that the words 'reasons for hoping' have any meaning whatsoever."[32] He here rejects the view that hope is based on any reasons, be they available to an impartial spectator or only to the hopeful themselves. His view thus seems to be that it is not the case that hope implies that the subject believes there is sufficient reason for doing so, for genuine hope is not based upon reasons at all.

Although it may be true that so far as we hope we do not raise the issue of whether there is reason to do so, it may be that we should raise this issue, and that our hope should be constrained by reasons available to an impartial observer. Marcel maintains that to the extent that hope against the odds is based upon love, it is beyond the realm of objectively calculable probabilities and the norms which govern such calculation. This brings us to the third way in which hope is contrasted with despair, and to the heart of Marcel's defense of hope against the charge of irrationality.

## 4. Love

To illustrate this point, Marcel considers the example of a woman who persists in hoping that she will see her son again, despite the fact that all of the evidence suggests that he is dead, and that she will never see him again.[33] If the woman bases her hope on a judgment about the probabilities of seeing her son again her hope will appear irrational. Marcel maintains, however, it is nonetheless legitimate for the woman to hope, so long as her hope isn't expressed as a judgment about probabilities. He writes,

> Sofar as the hope of the mother is expressed as an objective judgment, "It is possible that John will come back," we have the right to say: "No, objectively speaking, the return must be considered as impossible." But at the root of the mother's objective judgment, which, as such, cannot be accepted, she has within her a loving thought which repudiates or transcends the facts, and it seems as though there is something absurd or even scandalous in disputing her right to hope, that is to say to love, against all hope.[34]

The woman's hope cannot legitimately be arrived at by a process of rational deliberation based on facts available from an external perspective, for these facts imply that there is no hope. From an external perspective, therefore, the woman's hope will be regarded as irrational and thus illegitimate. But the woman's hope may not be arrived at by a calculation, or miscalculation, of probabilities, it may be a simple expression of her love for her son. As such, her hope embodies the simple affirmation, "You are coming back." And this "you are coming back" is, Marcel writes, "beyond the reach of objective criticism."[35] It is beyond the reach of objective criticism because it is outside of the space of probabilistic reasons.

When our hope takes this form, Marcel states it is both absurd and objectionable to raise the question of the permissibility of hoping against the odds. It is absurd because such criticism is wholly inappropriate. It is as if one were to object to someone loving another person on the ground that insufficient reason exists to do so. When someone states that there are no reasons which support my love for another, or even that the reasons there are (say, reasons of self-interest) militate against this love, I do not conclude that my love is irrational, but I realize that this person does not really understand what love is. If he did he wouldn't treat as if it were something one arrives at, or should arrive at, by a process of deliberation; as if love were, or ought to be, the conclusion of a special kind of practical syllogism. Marcel wants to make the same point about genuine hope when it is an expression of love. So far as the mother's hope expresses her love for her son—that is, so far as it expresses the simple affirmation, "You are coming back"—the fact that every reason exists to abandon hope will not make her hope irrational. In this form, it is not the sort of thing that is appropriately arrived at by a process of deliberation, or calculation. This thought may be expressed by stating that such hope lacks a rationality value, or, to put this in more Nietzschean terms, it can be said to be beyond rationality and irrationality. Bernard Williams may also have had something like this in mind when he said that the husband's act of saving his wife in preference to a stranger is "beyond justification."[36]

It is more difficult to capture what is objectionable about the thought that the mother must account for her hoping against the odds. It would clearly be objectionable if someone who had this thought sought to persuade the woman to give up hope. But this does not seem to be Marcel's worry. His worry is more about the sort of outlook someone who has this thought embodies, rather than about any particular act he or she may do as a consequence of having such an outlook. What I think Marcel finds objectionable in someone who believes that the woman has no right to continue to hope for her son is the type of detachment from ordinary human relations which would enable one to hold this belief. There is, Marcel maintains, a kind of arrogance and aggressive self-complacency involved in such a stance which is objectionable on its own account, but is all the more so if the demand for reasons is misplaced.[37]

It may be objected to this that, at some point, it will become desirable for someone to attempt to persuade the woman to give up her hope for her son. It may be that after a time, her inability to let go will begin to oppress her. There comes a point, it may be said, where one must give up hope and get on with one's life. This objection fails to distinguish the anxious form of non-acceptance implicit in revolt from the patient type of non-acceptance involved in hope. The type of non-acceptance implicit in revolt involves a destructive, oppressive fascination with one's fate. If the mother's refusal to accept that she will never see her son again takes this form, then it will be right, after a certain period of time, to attempt to persuade her to "let go." But since Marcel explicitly distinguishes the type of non-acceptance of hope from this form of refusal, this objection will not hold if the mother continues patiently to hope against the odds. For this form of non-acceptance does not destroy one's everyday form of participation in the world and with others, but is the way in which such participation is sustained.

In hope, therefore, we transcend the conditions governing calculation. But Marcel does not think that all hope is beyond justification. His view is rather that we only transcends the norms governing calculation of probabilities to the extent that our hope is based on love rather than on desire: "Hope only escapes from a particular metaphysical ruling on condition that it transcends desire—that is to say, that it does not remain centered upon the subject himself."[38] This is not to say that all significant hope is altruistic rather than egoistic, or that all desires are ultimately egoistic, but is to conceive of hope primarily as a relation between me and another, rather than as one between me and some desired object. Hope is not primarily *for something*, but *in someone*. The word "primarily" is important here. To say that hope is not *primarily* for something, is not to say that such hope lacks an object. The contrast between desire-based hope and genuine hope is not one between intentional and non-intentional hope. For, as I have already noted, Marcel maintains that all significant hope is a hope for salvation. What is distinctive about this type of hope is that the relation between me and the hoped-for object is mediated by a relation to another person, namely, the one in whom I place my hope. It thus involves an interpersonal relation in a way in which desire-based hopes do not. A useful analogy may be drawn here with Sartre's account of shame. The other, before whom I am ashamed, is not the intentional object of my shame. Rather, I am the object of this state. But I can only be an intentional object to myself in shame so far as my shame is mediated by the other. Similarly, although genuine hope has an object, it only has this object through a relation with another in whom I hope. Marcel describes this relation as a relation of communion.

This communion is a form of "I-thou" relation which cannot be accommodated within any subject-object schema. In this relation the other is encountered not merely as an object for me, but as a subject, that is, as a presence or being whose reality transcends the objectivity given.[39] Sartre's notion of an objectifying relation to oneself via the look of the other, which is discussed in the next chapter, is certainly a possibility, according to Marcel. It is, however, a phenomenon which can be transcended. Such transcendence is only conceived of as impossible so far as one assumes the universality of subject-object relations and attempts to squeeze the phenomenon of communion into this straitjacket.

Genuine hope is not only partly constituted by communion. This relation also constitutes the object of such hope: "Hope is essentially the availability of a soul which has entered intimately enough into the experience of communion to accomplish in the teeth of will and knowledge the transcendent act—the act of establishing the vital regeneration of which this experience affords both the pledge and the first-fruits."[40] The bedrock on which hope rests is the relationship of love, or what Marcel calls the experience of communion. This experience makes possible "the transcendent act," the act of moving beyond the realm of justification based on calculations of probability. Communion not only underpins this act, but is that to which all significant hope is oriented. The communion which constitutes the precondition of hope, therefore, is also its *telos*, or better, an intimation of its *telos*.

> If it is true that man's trial is infinite in its varieties and can assume the innumerable forms under which we know privation, exile, or captivity, it is no less certain that by a symmetrical but inverted process, each one of us can rise by his own special path from the humble forms of communion... to a communion which is both more intimate and more abundant, of which hope can be equally regarded as the foreshadowing or the outcome.[41]

Thus, Marcel maintains, the most adequate expression of genuine hope is, "I hope in thee for us."[42] The "hope in thee" is a form of communion, and the "us" which is hoped for is this same communion perfected.

### 5. Re-Evaluating Hope

Hope is thus described as a patient refusal to anticipate our destiny, as the experience of time as full of real possibility, and as both constituted by and oriented toward a communion with others. In outlining Marcel's account of hope, I have left a lot out. Most notably, I have not said anything about how God figures in this account. But although Christianity is important for Marcel's account of hope, I do not think his view depends upon a belief in a

Christian God. It is not so much that the account of hope Marcel offers is a Christian account, but that the Christian account draws on a general experience of hope which is available to all: "Christianity gives a specific character to a relatively special context of data that can also be accessible to non-Christians."[43]

Although I have not covered every aspect of Marcel's account of hope, I think I have included enough for us to get a sense of his alternative to the standard account, and to see the way in which this removes the major obstacle to a positive evaluation of hope generated by the standard account. The major obstacle to such an evaluation is that so far as hope is conceived of as involving a belief about probabilities, the sort of hopes we have been considering will appear illusory, irrational, and to that extent objectionable. By separating hope from beliefs about probabilities, Marcel can place hope beyond the reach of the norms governing the calculation of probabilities. If accepted, therefore, his account removes the main obstacle to a positive evaluation of hope generated by the standard account.

## Notes

1. See, *e.g.*, Thomas Hobbes, *Leviathan,* bk. 1, ch. 6 (Harmondsworth: Penguin, 1982); Descartes, *The Passions of the Soul* in The *Philosophical Writings of Descartes*, 1, trans. John Cottingham, Robert Stoothoff, and Dugald Murdoch (Cambridge, England: Cambridge University Press: 1988), p. 398; David Hume, *A Treatise of Human Nature*, edited by J. A. Selby Bigge (Oxford: Oxford University Press, 1978), bk 2, sec. 9. See also J. P. Day, "Hope," *American Philosophical Quarterly*, 6 (1969), pp. 89-102.

2. Gabriel Marcel, *Homo Viator: Introduction to a Metaphysic of Hope*, trans. Emma Craufurd (London: Victor Gollancz, 1951), p. 30.

3. *Ibid.*, p. 36.
4. *Ibid.*, pp. 37-38.
5. *Ibid.*, p. 60.
6. *Ibid.*, p. 60.
7. *Ibid.*, p. 38.
8. *Ibid.*
9. *Ibid.*
10. *Ibid.*, p. 39.
11. *Ibid.*
12. *Ibid.*, p. 40.
13. *Ibid.*, p. 32.
14. *Ibid.*
15. *Ibid.*, p. 46.
16. *Ibid.*

17. Marcel, *Being and Having*, trans. Katherine Farrer (Westminster: Dacre, 1949), p. 163.
18. See Otto Bollnow, "Marcel's Concept of Availability," in The *Philosophy of Gabriel Marcel*, eds. Paul Schilpp and Lewis Hahn (La Salle, Ill.: Open Court, 1984), pp. 182-183.
19. Marcel, *Homo Viator*, p. 23.
20. Marcel, *Being and Having*, p. 117.
21. Bollnow, "Marcel's Concept of Availability," p. 185.
22. Marcel, *Homo Viator*, p. 34.
23. *Ibid.*, p. 35.
24. *Ibid.*
25. *Ibid.*, p. 60.
26. Bollnow, "Marcel's Concept of Availability," p. 192.
27. Marcel, *Being and Having*, p. 102.
28. Marcel, *Homo Viator*, p. 63.
29. *Ibid.*, p. 64.
30. *Ibid.*
31. *Ibid.*, p. 65.
32. *Ibid.*
33. *Ibid.*
34. *Ibid.*
35. *Ibid.*, p. 66.
36. Bernard Williams, "Persons, Character, and Morality," in his *Moral Luck: Philosophical Papers 1973-1980* (Cambridge, England: Cambridge University Press, 1981), p. 18.
37. Marcel, *Homo Viator*, p. 33.
38. *Ibid.*, p. 66.
39. See John Glen, "Marcel and Sartre," in *The Philosophy of Gabriel Marcel*, p. 529ff.
40. Marcel, *Homo Viator*, p. 67.
41. *Ibid.*, p. 60.
42. *Ibid.*
43. Marcel, "Marcel's Concept of Availability: Reply to Otto Friedrich Bollnow," in *The Philosophy of Gabriel Marcel*, p. 200.

# Eight

# SARTRE, SEXUAL DESIRE, AND RELATIONS WITH OTHERS

## James Giles

One of the best-known aspects of Sartre's existential philosophy is his account of relations with others given at the end of Part Three of *Being and Nothingness*. Here Sartre presents a detailed and subtle description of the diverse forms that human interaction can take. However, what seems to be most familiar is not the account itself, but rather the conclusion Sartre draws from his discussion, namely, that because of their inherent inconsistencies, all human relations must ultimately collapse in failure. The universality of this assertion is supposed to be mitigated somewhat by his well-known footnote which vaguely refers to "the possibility of an ethics of deliverance and salvation,"[1] but such a disclaimer does not sit well with the numerous other arguments in *Being and Nothingness* that bad faith is inevitable and that conflict is the fundamental meaning of human interaction. There is the posthumously published *Notebooks for an Ethics* which some have seen as an attempt to construct the sort of ethics Sartre refers to in his footnote. However, as Terry Keefe points out in Chapter Four, it is not at all clear that the two accounts are compatible. And indeed, Sartre's choosing not to publish his notebooks seems to suggest he saw them as not being able to carry out the radical transformation deemed necessary to overcome the failure of human relations.

Because, then, of the immense implications of the claim that all relations are based on self-destructive inconsistencies, it is understandable that such a claim would draw more attention than would the nature of the interpersonal theory on which it is based. In this chapter, however, I want to explore the interpersonal theory itself to see where its insights and difficulties lie, and what modifications it might need if it is to be viable as a theory of human relations.

For Sartre, the analysis of human interaction must begin with a phenomenological analysis of that aspect of existence he calls "being-for-others," namely, the being or existence of a consciousness in relation to other consciousnesses. According to Sartre, being-for-others involves a fundamental problem. This problem begins with the fact that consciousness, or being-for-itself, is aware of itself and, consequently, is aware that it is not—and never can be—part of the material world; in other words, that it cannot be part of "being-in-itself." This is an unsettling awareness, for it means that being-for-itself can never have the definite or completed nature that being-in-itself possesses. This is because while being-in-itself has nothing to do with the meaning or creation of its own existence, consciousness freely chooses to exist and is forever engaged in projects of creating its own meaning, of positing values, and of pursuing its goals. Consequently, being-for-itself is responsible for the meaning of its own existence in a way that being-in-itself is not. Consciousness experiences anguish in this responsibility, because it means that there is nobody to blame for my existence save myself.[2] Consciousness or being-for-itself thus longs for the completed and reponsibility-free existence of being-in-itself. And yet, at the same time, consciousness also has what Sartre calls "facticity" or a factual existence—that is, relations to a past, a body, or the simply the fact of being there, each of which is an instance of being-in-itself. These instances of being-in-itself to which consciousness *is* related are thus experienced as a threat to the freedom of consciousness and its ability to engage in projects and pursue its goals. As a result, consciousness also attempts to escape its factual existence in order to continue to choose its own goals; or, in Sartre's words, to be its own foundation: "Thus the for-itself is both a flight and a pursuit; it flees the in-itself and at the same time pursues it."[3] Therefore, consciousness, which all the while wants to continue as consciousness, nevertheless seeks to escape its own condition in an attempt to become being-in-itself. Consciousness wants to become, as Sartre puts it, an "in-itself-for-itself." This attempt of consciousness is, however, based on a confusion, for being-for-itself can never become being-in-itself. To do so would be for it no longer to be consciousness. As a result, all such attempts are doomed to failure from the start.

This attempt of consciousness, says Sartre, explains why the existence of other people is so crucial to us and touches each of us to our inner depths. For it is through other persons that we can pursue the attempt to "objectify" ourelves; in other words, to make ourselves into being-in-itself. It means that the other person who experiences me—by the fact she experiences me—turns me into an object upon which she gazes. The problem, however, is that although I am in some sense aware that the other person objectifies me in this way, I am also aware that the object I am for the other person is something that must always escape me. That is, I can never experience that objectified me as another person experiences it, since it only exists as part of the other person's consciousness, and it is forever beyond my grasp. In his earlier work, *The Transcendence of the Ego*, Sartre explains this elusiveness of another consciousness by saying that the consciousness of another person is "radically impenetrable." Thus, "I cannot *conceive* Peter's consciousness without making an object of it (since I do not conceive it as being *my consciousness*). I cannot conceive it because I would have to think of it as pure interiority and as transcendence *at the same time*, which is impossible."[4] Consequently, as Sartre puts it in *Being and Nothingness*, "the objectivity of my flight I experience as an alienation that I can never transcend or know."[5] Yet, says Sartre, by the sole fact that the other person confers that object-like status on my flight, I must turn back to meet it and assume various attitudes toward it. Although Sartre does not fully explain why I "must" assume such attitudes here, what he may have in mind is the uneasiness caused by the awareness that another person is perceiving me in a false way, perceiving me as an object (which in another sense is precisely what I want). Sartre also says of the other person, "I realize him through uneasiness; through him I feel myself perpetually in danger."[6] I thus feel compelled to react to, or assume an attitude toward, the other person's perception or constitution of me. I could simply be indifferent to the other person, but for Sartre even indifference is an assumed attitude, an attitude in which I try to hide from the objectifying look of the other by trying not to notice him or her. The attitudes I assume in such cases are the framework of my relations with others.

According to Sartre, these attitudes, or ways of relating to others, fall into two primary types, each of which can be further divided into various sub-attitudes. The first primary attitude involves the attempt to assimilate the other into oneself, while the second involves the attempt to reduce the other to an object. Under the heading, "First Attitude toward Others," Sartre lists the sub-heading, "Love, Language, Masochism." Despite its appearance under the heading, from the discussion which follows, "language" is not to be seen as a separate attitude toward others. It is rather that aspect of being-for-others which is presupposed in all interactions. This means that it is love and masochism, two attempts to assimilate the other person into oneself, which comprise the first attitude. Under the second attitude, Sartre lists "Indifference, Desire, Hate, Sadism," each of which is supposed to be a separate attempt to reduce the other to an object.

Although Sartre calls one of these primary attitudes, "the first attitude," and the other, "the second," he is quick to tell us that neither is really first or second. Instead, they occur in a circle, or, as we might more accurately say, they oscillate back and forth. Thus, because of the failure of my attempt to assimilate the other into myself, I could find myself reacting to this failure by trying to look upon the other person and transform him or her into an object. The failure of this attitude might then occasion my swinging back to the other attitude. And the same holds true for the sub-attitudes within each primary attitude. Thus, the failure of my attempt to love someone might lead me to masochism. Likewise, within the second attitude, the failure of one sub-attitude can give rise to another. Here the failure of my attempt to objectify the other person through the attitude of, say, desire, by which Sartre means sexual desire, can give rise to an attempt to objectify the other through sadism.

This, then, is the general picture of Sartre's account of relations with others, an account which helps us to focus on the intricacies and dynamics of human relations. Many of the interchanges of love, for example, become clearer when we see that they involve the attempt to assimilate the other into oneself (see Thomas Jones's discussion in the next chapter). Further, someone's love or sexual relationship can easily pass into a masochistic or sadistic enterprise, as the numerous accounts of partner-abuse testify. However, closer scrutiny reveals various difficulties in the structure of Sartre's theory. For there are different places throughout the discussion where Sartre gives a particular account of a certain aspect of interpersonal relations, only later to call what he says into question by then giving another account which is evidently at odds with the first. Thus, although Sartre tells us that the first set of primary attitudes—love and masochism—represent an attempt to assimilate the other into oneself, he later makes clear that his account of masochism does not fit this description: "Its ideal will then be the opposite of that which we have just described [that is, love]; instead of projecting the absorbing of the Other while preserving in him his otherness, I shall project causing myself to be absorbed by the Other and losing myself in his subjectivity in order to get rid of my own."[7] Thus, while love is supposed to be the attempt to assimilate the other into oneself, masochism is the attempt to deny one's own subjectivity by trying to have it incorporated into the other. As Sartre says, these two attitudes toward others are opposite: one attitude is to be the assimilator, the other attitude is to be the assimilated. It is therefore unclear why Sartre sees love and masochism as being instances of the same attitude.

A similar problem appears when we come to Sartre's description of hate. Although Sartre initially tells us that there are only two primary attitudes, and that hate is an instance of the second, that is, hate is the attempt to reduce the other person to an object, he later says that hate is *not* one of the primary attitudes and is thus a separate "third" attitude.[8] Although Sartre does not say why hate is to be seen as a distinct attitude in itself, one possible explanation is because hate has more to it than the attempt to transform or be transformed into an object. Hate, says Sartre, "wishes to destroy this object in order by the same stroke to overcome the transcendence which haunts it."[9] Someone who hates another is not satisfied with reducing the other person to an object in the way that someone who is indifferent or sadistic might be, for the real goal is the elimination of the other person. Here we find the place where consciousness no longer has a use for the other person; hate "implies a fundamental resignation; the for-itself abandons its claim to realize any union with the Other; it gives up using the Other as an instrument to recover its own being-in-itself."[10]

Since these inconsistencies seem fairly obvious, it is peculiar that so many of Sartre's commentators have failed to notice them. Thus Mary Warnock,[11] Monika Langer,[12] and Linda A. Bell, to name but a few, all give detailed descriptions of Sartre's account of concrete relations with others without so much as batting an eye these problems. Bell, for example, seems quite happy to cite Sartre's claim that hate is a third original attitude and in the same breath discuss it as though it were in the same category as indifference.[13] Although it is difficult to say why these problems have largely gone unnoticed, one of the reasons, I suspect, is because, as I mentioned earlier, most of the energy and attention here has been focused on the general problem of whether human relations are, as Sartre says, failures. Consequently, the more specific question about the basic structure of his theory gets ignored.

These difficulties with Sartre's theory, however, may not be so serious. Rather than saying that only two primary attitudes toward others exist, Sartre could simply accept from the outset that more than two exist. Instead of all relations with others being reducible to either the attempt to make the other part of oneself, or the attempt to make the other into an object, Sartre could also allow that there are the further attitudes of trying to make oneself part of the other (masochism), and trying to destroy the other (hate). Or again, rather than saying that the second attitude is the attempt to make the other into an object, a description which stops short of and thus excludes his account of hate, he could say that the second attitude merely involves the attempt to get rid of the other person's consciousness by acting on the other person. This would be broad enough to include indifference, sadism, and hate. The problem is that once we start adding new attitudes to the two primary ones, or stretching the description of one so that it includes others, the clarity of a simple two-attitude system becomes obscured and the relations between the various attitudes become more difficult to explain.

More serious difficulties occur when we come to Sartre's discussion of sexual desire and its relation to the other attitudes. At first, sexual desire appears as just one more attitude among others; that is, it is said to be an instance of the second attitude, the attempt to reduce the other to an object. This attitude, like all the other attitudes, is the response to the failure of a previous attitude, ultimately fails itself, and so provokes a further attitude, namely, sadism. But at the end of his discussion of sadism, Sartre suddenly tells us that *all* the attitudes are sexual attitudes. This dramatically changes the whole picture. This now means that the failure of sexual desire does not lead to sadism: sadism is already a form of sexual desire. Further, the failure of masochism does not really provoke sexual desire; it too is already sexual desire. The whole story of a circle of attitudes and the place of sexual desire within them now becomes quite unclear.

Again, the difficulties here seem to have slipped by most commentators and even given rise to confusions in their own accounts. Thus Langer argues that, for Sartre, sexual desire is accompanied by the permanent danger of degeneration into masochism and the constant threat of sadism. This is because, she tells us, of the "inherent instability of [sexual] desire."[14] But if sexual desire is unstable, then it seems it should be in danger of degenerating into a non-sexual attitude. That is, if Langer is right, then masochism and sadism should be non-sexual attitudes. But as just shown, Sartre says that all the attitudes are sexual. And if this is true, then, contrary to what Langer says, sexual desire seems a remarkably stable condition. Similar confusions appear in Bell's discussion. Bell claims that the failures of "love and desire...are of greater significance for Sartre than might otherwise be imagined, since, as he tells us these attitudes are fundamental and are integrated into all attitudes toward the other, the latter being 'only enrichments of these two original attitudes (and a third—hate.'"[15] But Sartre does not say that "love and desire" are "integrated into all attitudes toward the other." Although this might fit with his later claims about sexual desire, it certainly does not fit with what he says about love. Love is quite plainly, for Sartre, only an instance of the first attitude. Further, Sartre does not claim, as Bell says he does, that all other attitudes are only enrichments of "love and desire" (and hate). Again, although he later says that all the attitudes are sexual (not "enrichments" of the sexual attitude), what he says in the quote given by Bell is that all other attitudes are only enrichments of the two primary attitudes, namely, the attempt to assimilate the other into oneself, and the attempt to reduce the other to an object. Bell seems here to have confused love and desire with the primary attitudes.

In order to see where the difficulties lie with Sartre's account of the relation between sexual desire and the other attitudes—difficulties that have led to much confusion in the secondary literature—let us start by looking at what Sartre says about the nature of sexual desire itself. First, Sartre tells us, sexual desire is not something which consciousness experiences passively; instead, it is something which consciousness freely chooses to express. This state which consciousness enters into can be understood in terms of its object, meaning, and motive. The object of desire, that is, the object which is sexually desired, is the physical body of the other person. But, Sartre says, it is more complicated than this. For we do not simply desire a body in and by itself, but we desire a conscious or potentially conscious body situated in the world. Even though someone may be asleep and so lack consciousness, one can still desire that person because "sleep appears on the ground of consciousness...a living body as an organic totality in situation with consciousness at the horizon: such is the object to which desire *is addressed*."[16] This desire is different from other desires, however; for in sexual desire "facticity invades consciousness" and consciousness seems to cease in its continual efforts to escape its own body. It now seeks to subordinate itself to its own body while at the same time seeing another body as desirable.[17]

But what, asks Sartre, is the meaning of this sexual desire? Or, as he also asks, why does consciousness seek to make itself a body, and what does it expect from this desire? The answer, he says, is that sexual desire is the desire to possess or appropriate, to caress, grasp, and draw over against my own body, the other person's body "as flesh," in order that this appropriation reveals my body to me as flesh. By "flesh" Sartre means the body as "an isolated object maintaining external relations with other *thises*" or the body appearing "as the pure contingency of the present"[18]; in other words, the body removed from its situation.

Since sexual desire is a choice, it must have a motive. To understand this motive we must see that within the process of sexual desire there appears a dilemma. A primordial reaction to being looked at by another person, says Sartre, is to realize that one is being seen as an object by the other person. If, in an attempt to avoid being seen as an object, I respond by trying to look at the person as an object, then I lose the awareness of the other as a freedom which seemed to give me the objectivity I long for all the while. It is, says Sartre, "as if I wished to get hold of a man who runs away and leaves only his coat in my hands. It is the coat, the outer shell which I possess. I shall never get hold of more than a body."[19] If, however, I try to avoid looking at the other as an object and so preserve her as a freedom, then once again my efforts must come to naught. For in this instance, I have constituted the other person as something which is completely beyond my grasp. If I do this, then I cannot avoid the awareness that the meaning of my actions will be decided by something beyond my awareness and control.

Sexual desire is a response to this dilemma; it is an attempt to enchant my way out of the situation, an attempt to have it both ways. Thus, when I try to grasp the other in the only way I can, as an object, I also try to use this grasping to "ensnare" or possess the other person's freedom: "so the Other's For-itself must come to play on the surface of his body, and be extended all through his body; and by touching his body I should finally touch the Other's free subjectivity."[20] This impossible ideal, says Sartre, is what sexual possession is really about. In sexual desire, one wants to possess the body of the other person, but only, says Sartre, so far as the body becomes identified with the person's consciousness.

Does sexual desire necessarily imply that one wants to possess the other person? Although this seems true for some forms of sexual desire, it also seems true that in other forms one desires primarily *to be* possessed; that is, to become an object for the other person to appropriate "as flesh." In such a form of sexual desire, what a person wants is *to be* caressed, grasped, and embraced by the other person, rather than to perform such acts. Sartre seems aware of this passive type of sexual desire when he says that in sexual desire, "I make myself flesh so as to fascinate the Other by my nakedness and to provoke in her the desire for my flesh."[21] The problem is that he is no longer just referring to the desire to be appropriated, but to the quite different case where what I desire is that the other person *desire* to appropriate my flesh. Here the object of my desire is the other person's desire to appropriate my flesh, not the simple appropriation of my flesh. These two types of desires are distinct; for although someone can desire that another person *desires* to caress and stroke his or her body, someone can also desire that another person caress and stroke him or her and yet not care whether the other person desires to do so. Although this sort of desire probably occurs in various types of sexual encounters and relationships, a good example would be where a male client has sexual desires toward a female prostitute and wants to have his body caressed and fondled by her, and is yet quite unconcerned about whether the prostitute desires to do so. Although the motivation behind seeking out a prostitute is varied and often complex, the attempt to satisfy one's sexual desires without having to concern oneself about the other person's desires is a likely enough reason for someone's engaging a prostitute. As one of the clients says in Lewis Diana's study of prostitution, "This woman wants nothing, asks nothing, needs nothing. I don't need to please her or be concerned about whether she's enjoying it. I can do what I want and please myself."[22] There might be some instances in which the client of the prostitute might fantasize or even fool himself into thinking that the prostitute whom he wants to caress him desires to caress him, but it seems quite unlikely that such fantasies or beliefs need always be present. Consequently, although sexual desire toward another person might be accompanied and even be intensified by the desire "to provoke in her the desire for my flesh," such a desire would not be a necessary component of sexual desire.[23]

The fact that Sartre overlooks the sort of sexual desire which does not make references to the other person's desires is indicative of a shortcoming with his account. It suggests that rather than giving a general account of the nature of sexual desire, Sartre is only focusing on one type of sexual desire. This is further evident when he says, "the communion of desire" (*la communion du désir*) is realized when "each consciousness by incarnating itself has realized the incarnation of the other...by each caress I experience my own flesh and the Other's flesh through my flesh, and am conscious that this flesh which I feel and which I appropriate through my flesh is flesh-realized-by-the-Other."[24] Although it is unclear what Sartre means by "communion of desire," he appears to be referring to a state of sexual interaction wherein a reciprocity is achieved in which each person becomes aware of the other's flesh and his or her own flesh by caressing and being caressed (it should be clear that Sartre does not have in mind a sort of communion referred to by Marcel wherein a person might actually experience another as a subject—see Stratton-Lake's discussion in Chapter Seven. For Sartre, as we have seen, the other person must always be experienced as an object.) While it might be true that some persons' sexual desires aim at this sort of "communion" of awarenesses, it seems equally true that there are other persons, or even the same persons on different occasions—whose sexual desires do not have such an aim. A person might, for example, be fascinated by or feel attracted to another person's body and simply desire to experience through his or her own flesh the other person's body as flesh, and not be too bothered about whether the person thus comes to experience his or her own body as flesh as well. Or, conversely, one's primary goal might be to get the other person to experience his or her own body as flesh, through massaging, stroking, or caressing the other person's body, and have no desire to experience one's own body similarly. It would be difficult to argue that such desires, because of their lack of desire for reciprocity, were not really sexual desires. Consequently, Sartre's account is not adequate because it brings in too many elements that are non-essential to sexual desire. The result is that many types of sexual desire escape his definition. Perhaps it is an awareness of this problem that leads Sartre later to try to extend his account of sexual desire by finally asserting that all the attitudes are sexual.

But this assertion gives rise to problems of its own. For if all the attitudes to others are in fact instances of sexual desire, then sexual desire cannot be a separate attitude (that is, it cannot be, as Sartre starts out by saying it is, only an instance of the second attitude), but must be an attitude or feature somehow present in or accompanying all our attitudes. Yet, Sartre's account of sexual desire is quite distinct from his accounts of the other attitudes. For example, the feature of sexual desire which Sartre focuses on in his first account, the appropriation of flesh, is evidently absent in his account of the other attitudes. But if it is this "desire for the appropriation of flesh," according to Sartre's account, appears only in the attitude of sexual desire, then this feature, which is clearly a sexual one, imparts to sexual desire its essential quality. If this is true, it is quite unclear how Sartre's account supports the claim that all attitudes to others are sexual. A second problem is that, even if all the attitudes are really sexual, one must still be able to show not only what makes them all sexual, but, what it is that makes one or some of them more obviously sexual than others. Being able to distinguish between an overtly sexual and an apparently non-sexual interest that one might have in another person is essential to make sense of the varieties of human interaction. Sartre's account, however, does not enable such a distinction to be drawn.

What, then, are Sartre's reasons for asserting that all our attitudes to others are sexual? In an attempt to support this claim Sartre says they are sexual "not because of the existence of a certain *libido* which would slip in everywhere but simply because the attitudes we have described are the fundamental projects by which the For-itself *realizes* its being-for-others and tries to transcend this factual situation."[25] This hardly seems a sufficient ground for claiming that all our attitudes are sexual. Sexual desire might involve the attempt to realize our being-for-others and transcend the factual situation, but it is far from obvious that there is something essentially sexual about such a project. Although such a project might be a necessary condition for sexual desire, it is not clear that it is a sufficient one. Why cannot we attempt to realize our being-for-others and transcend our factual situation through mere friendship, indifference, or aggression? The reply that to do so would be engaging in a sexual attitude seems to be little more than begging the question. We still need an explanation of why this project is essentially a sexual one.

One of the difficulties is when Sartre comes to argue that all the attitudes are sexual, he does so by dismissing the role played by the body, something that was central to his earlier account, and asserting that sexual desire is essentially a project of realization and transcendence. His reason for rejecting the reference to the body as a necessary feature of sexual desire is that, in themselves, physiological and bodily events lack human significance. This rejection is what is behind Sartre's dismissal of Freud's concept of libido; that is, the concept of a unified physiological drive or energy that lies at the basis of the various instances of sexual desire (though this is only one way of understanding Freud. On another interpretation Sartre's position is not as distinct from Freud's as he would like it to be.[26]) In themselves, such biological entities or events are devoid of significance and, as a result, cannot be the essence of sexual desire. The bodily events or actions involved in sexual desire, for example, the lubrication of the vagina, the erection of the penis, the act of sexual intercourse, and other sexual acts, therefore have only a contingent relation to sexual desire. This contingency of the physical is, for Sartre, not something that holds only for sexual desire, but is rather true for all aspects of human existence. This point is also the basis of Sartre's theory of the emotions. Consequently, in his earlier work *The Emotions*, he says, "every human fact is in essence significative. If you remove its signification you remove its nature as a human fact." Considering then physiological accounts of the emotions, he says, "we shall not lose ourselves in the study of physiological facts, precisely because, taken by themselves and in isolation, they signify *almost* nothing."[27] Likewise, in *Being and Nothingness,* he tells us, "our physiological structure only causes the symbolic expression, on the level of absolute contingency, of the fact that we are the permanent possibility of assuming one or the other of these [sexual] attitudes."[28]

Unfortunately, although Sartre's arguments for the non-physical nature of the emotions, that they are primarily ways of apprehending objects in the world, and therefore cannot be essentially physiological events, have a certain force to them, his arguments for the contingent relationship between the body and sexual desire are not so convincing. It may be true that the tumescence of the sex organs or other physiological events cannot, as Sartre says, fully explain sexual desire; this does not mean, however, that all bodily activities have a purely contingent relationship to sexual desire. A necessary component of sexual desire is the desire to do something physical (if not in reality then at least in fantasy) with a person's body. Sartre, however, argues against this view, claiming that the desire for "doing" is not part of sexual desire. To support this conclusion he starts by saying, "it would be wholly inaccurate to say that desire is a desire for 'physical possession' of the desired object—if by 'possess' we mean here 'to make love to.'" For, says Sartre,

> desire by itself by no means implies the sexual act; desire does not thematically posit it, does not even suggest it in outline, as one sees when it is a question of the desire of very young children or of adults who are ignorant of the "technique" of love. Similarly, desire is not a desire of any special amorous practice; this is sufficiently proved by the diversity of sexual practices which vary within social groups. In general desire is not desire of doing. The "doing" is after the event, is added on to the desire from the outside and necessitates a period of apprenticeship.[29]

Several things are wrong with this argument. First, the fact that sexual desire might not imply the sexual act, by which Sartre means sexual intercourse, does not allow the conclusion that sexual desire does not imply some form of sexual act; that is, some form of sexual "doing." As Sartre mentions, a wide variety of sexual practices are engaged in and, consequently, sexual desire can carry with it a desire for any of these sexual practices. But this is hardly the same thing as saying sexual desire does not imply some form of sexual practice or sexual "doing"; for at least one thing that all sexual practices have in common is that they are each some form of doing. The same could be said about Sartre's other point, that the sexual desires of young children and ignorant adults do not suggest sexual intercourse "even in outline." This does not show that the sexual desires of such persons do not refer to some form of sexual act. Indeed, the way that we know that young children have sexual desires is by observing their physical sexual "doings": masturbation, exploring each others bodies, and playing sexual games. It is also worthwhile to note here that, despite what Sartre says, some children's sexual desires might well suggest "in outline" sexual intercourse. In cultures where children's sexual behavior is not suppressed by adults, sexual games resembling intercourse are common at least as early as ages five and six.[30] Sartre begins with the observation that no one particular physical act is the goal of sexual desire, and then he concludes that sexual desire does not imply any physical act. But this is like arguing that because hunger does not imply eating any particular food, it is not really a desire for eating. Yet, the essence of hunger is a desire for eating. Likewise, at the heart of sexual desire is the desire for some form of intimate bodily interaction with another person. Were someone to say she sexually desired another person, and yet at the same time insist that she had no desire for any form of bodily intimacy with that person, we would probably think that she did not really understand the meaning of the term "sexual desire." People often have sexual desires which at the same time they find repulsive, which make them feel guilt, or which, for various other reasons, they are afraid to express or perhaps dare only fantasize about. This only shows that, in addition to their sexual desires, people often have countervailing desires which prevent the attempt to satisfy the sexual desires. It does not show that sexual desire does not imply a bodily action. Therefore, to say that the "doing" comes after the event and is only contingently related to sexual desire appears wrong. The conclusion which should be drawn from Sartre's premises is that sexual desire must imply a type of action that is common to all these desires, and that each particular sexual act is merely a contingent way of carrying out that action. One must then find the action or actions that are common to or at least implied in all forms of sexual desire (I argue elsewhere that what makes a desire sexual are the desires for baring and caressing[31]). The conclusion thus must be that Sartre has not shown that all the attitudes are sexual.

Does this mean that Sartre is wrong in trying to argue that a fundamental sexuality lies behind all relations with others? Not necessarily; for once it is accepted that reference to the body is a basic feature of sexual desire, then Sartre's view about the sexual nature of human relations finds the support it needs in another way. To see this, we must turn to the ontogenic dimension of human relations and examine the origin of these relations.

We can start by noting that for each person the first relationship is typically with a primary care-giver, normally, the mother. This relationship is important for several reasons. From the infant's perspective, it is important not only because it is the relationship in which its every need is taken care of and thus its life is sustained, but also because it offers the infant a first glimpse of what another person is, and of what it is to interact with another person. Because of the infant's lack of certain abilities, its vulnerability, its need to be cared for, and the mother's usual desire to bestow such care and express her feelings toward her new child, the infant's relationship with the mother will tend to be one in which it typically receives much warm physical contact, including kissing, touching, caressing, cuddling, and holding, along with much mutual gazing, smiling, and vocal murmurings. It is not surprising that investigators have noted points of similarity between the intensely intimate and physical relationship between a mother and infant, and later adult sexual relations, relations which also involve all these intimate behaviors. According to sexologist and therapist Helen Singer Kaplan, these early interactions are "inadvertently mildly erotically arousing to infants and young children, and sensuously pleasurable for their parents, most especially the mothers," and "these experiences form the psychologic origins of normal sexual fantasies and desires."[32] Kaplan's other point here about the parents' and especially the mother's erotic bond to the child also offers support for Sartre's position. The erotic bond's relation to breast-feeding is underlined by the fact that many women report erotic sensations, occasionally leading to orgasm, during breast-feeding.[33] For Freud too the mother and infant relationship plays a decisive role in the process of psychosexual development, that is, the developmental process through which a maturing child comes eventually to acquire its gender identity, sexual orientation, and adult sexual desires. According to Freud, these early mother–infant interactions are the basis for later sexual interactions. Thus, he says, "sucking at the mother's breast is the starting-point of the whole sexual life, the unmatched prototype of every later sexual satisfaction, to which phantasy often enough recurs in times of need."[34]

Many people might want to take exception to the view that anything is sexual about an infant's breast-feeding behavior. Thus Zella Luria, Susan Friedman, and Michael D. Rose say of Freud's view, "as real as these oral pleasures are, only confirmed Freudians feel free to call them sexual, because the Freudian definition of sexual encompasses any sensual pleasure."[35] Remarkably enough, Luria *et al.* nowhere tell us exactly what the alleged difference is between sexual and sensual pleasures. They imply, however, that it is the non-involvement of the genitals which makes oral pleasures sensual rather than sexual; that is, sexual pleasure must involve genital pleasure. But if this is their view, it is inadequate for various reasons. First, other parts of the body, not least the mouth and lips, are also erogenously sensitive and thus, for many people (of all ages), are the focus of what would normally be called sexual pleasure. Second, oral and other body pleasures, even for infants, are frequently intertwined with genital pleasure. Indeed, Luria *et al.* themselves refer to the case of an infant who would "clamp her thighs together rhythmically while sucking hard on a nipple."[36] As a result, it might well prove difficult if not impossible conceptually to separate such experiences and hold that one sort is sexual while the other is not.

Breast-feeding for the infant is not just the receiving of oral pleasure or nourishment from the mother. Breast-feeding also typically involves bodily contact, with extended periods of caressing, cuddling, holding, and other intimate behaviors. Thus when Freud says that were an infant able to speak he would no doubt tell us that the most important thing in his world is sucking at his mother's breast,[37] Freud is probably right. But this does not mean that it would be the milk or the oral stimulation alone which the infant would see as being the only or even the most important thing about engaging in this activity. For in thus receiving its nourishment it is, at the same time, also being held against a warm breast and embraced and cuddled in an intimate way. Such physical interaction with the mother, although connected with the taking of nourishment, seems to satisfy a need for bodily contact which is quite independent of the need for nourishment. This much is also suggested by Harry Harlow's well-known studies with non-human primates. Here infant rhesus monkeys were shown to prefer to cling to a non-nourishing but soft cloth-covered mother-substitute rather than to a wire-framed one with a milk-dispensing nipple. It is also suggestive that Harlow discovered that infant monkeys who had been deprived of early contact with their mothers had immense difficulties in later establishing adult sexual relations.[38]

None of this is to say that a mother–infant relationship is of precisely the same kind as an adult sexual relationship, for obviously many differences exist. Among other things, the infant is psychologically and physically underdeveloped and is thus dependent on the mother for all its needs in a way that is not normally true of one adult sexual partner's relation to another, though, as research has shown, the infant is nevertheless quite active in determining the mother's behavior.[39] Such differences, however, do not seem to affect the points made about the essentially sexual aspects of the mother–infant relationship. Also, that the mother–infant relationship is a sexual one does not mean there is no difference between a caring and loving mother–infant relationship and one which might be sexually abusive or exploitative. In the former case the mother is foremost a care-giver who is primarily concerned with tending to the infant's needs and giving it her affection, while in the latter case the infant is being sexually exploited by the mother for her own ulterior purposes (see L. Alan Sroufe's and June Fleeson's discussion of "seductive maternal behavior."[40])

But if the infant's first relationship is a prototype for later sexual relations, it is also the prototype for *all* later relationships. As was just said, in these primal interactions an infant first learns both what to expect from an interpersonal relationship, and, as a result of this, how to behave interpersonally. Consequently, all of a person's later relationships will be, at a basic level, a development of his or her first relationship. This development is described by the psychiatrist Eric Berne as a process through which a person's original need for physical contact and stimulation eventually allows itself to be satisfied, to some degree, by mere recognition from others. Thus, says Berne,

> after the period of intimacy with the mother is over, the individual for the rest of his life is confronted with a dilemma upon whose horns his destiny and survival are continually being tossed. One horn is the social, psychological and biological forces which stand in the way of continued physical intimacy in the infantile style; the other is his perpetual striving for its attainment. Under most conditions he will compromise. He learns to do with more subtle, even symbolic, forms of handling, until the merest nod of recognition may serve the purpose to some extent, although his original craving for physical contact may remain unabated.[41]

Here we see how the primal relationship can also lie at the origin of what are normally thought of as non-sexual relationships. What Berne is saying is that the desire to regain the physical intimacy that characterized the first relationship, the touching, holding, caressing, is a desire which also motivates engagement in non-physically-intimate relationships. This does not mean that the only purpose of interpersonal relationships is the achievement of physical intimacy or even its symbolic substitutes, for relationships are inherently complex and there are numerous other levels on which different goals are being pursued and needs satisfied. What it does mean is that the prototype of every relationship will be the primary relationship, and, as a result, the content of the desires which were of central importance in the primary relationship will continue to be crucial, and consequently still operating, in both later intimate and non-intimate relationships. The difference is that in the non-intimate relationships obstacles exist which preclude the possibility of the relationship becoming one of physical intimacy. Consequently, the person is here forced to interact and find satisfaction in non-physical ways. Even in an overtly sexual relationship continued physical intimacy in the purely "infantile style" will still not be possible, for the reasons Berne gives. Nevertheless it will be much closer to being achieved than in the non-physical relationship. Here too various features of the primary intimate relationship will be still be discernible. As Sroufe and Fleeson put it, relationship history is carried forward. This is because the infant's early attachment or relationship to the primary care-giver ultimately becomes "internalized" as an organizational blueprint for later relationships. It becomes part of the infant as its organizational principle for relating to others. Thus, say Sroufe and Fleeson, "this transition from dyadic organization to self-organization is of fundamental importance for it profoundly shapes the direction of future relationships. The young child seeks and explores new relationships within the framework of expectations for self and other that emerges from the primary relationship."[42]

Although Sroufe and Fleeson, like other psychologists working in this area, are mostly interested in how particular infant–mother attachment styles (for example, secure, anxious, or avoidant) reappear in later relationships, it is possible to look at the relation between the early and later relationships in a more basic way. Despite their differences, the majority of mother–infant relations share something basic in common. This, as I have argued, is the essentially sexual quality of the relationship. If it is true that particular aspects of relationship histories are carried forward, then it seems equally true that basic aspects of relationship histories are also carried forward. For different styles of mother–infant relationships are, for all their differences, still mother–infant relationships. If a basic quality of the mother–infant relationship is its sexual quality, then this sexual quality will likely be carried forward to new relationships. As was mentioned earlier, numerous factors will prevent most of a person's later relationships from becoming physically intimate and overtly sexual. But the original desires, which must now be satisfied differently, continue nonetheless.

Here, then, we are able to make sense of Sartre's claim that all the attitudes are sexual. They are all sexual simply because they carry with them and are consequently organized around the essentially sexual features of the primary relationship. Thus when Sartre says that the different attitudes "all include as their skeleton—so to speak—sexual relations,"[43] the way to make sense of this claim is to see that the skeleton being referred to can only be the framework of the primary relationship. This interpretation not only allows us to make sense of Sartre's claim but also helps to illuminate his general account of later adult relations. It will be recalled, for example, that according to Sartre there are two primary ways of relating to others, namely, the attempt to assimilate the other into oneself, and the attempt to reduce the other to an object. But why, one wants to ask, is it these specific attitudes that are the primary ones? If we turn again to the structure of the infant's relation to the mother, an answer to this question is forthcoming. For in breast-feeding, which as Freud suggests is central to the infant's world, one of the things that happens *is* precisely an assimilation of the other into oneself. That is, in drinking milk from the mother's breast the infant is physically assimilating part of the mother, the first and prototypic other, into itself. This instance of actual physical assimilation of the other is also accompanied by less tangible forms of assimilation: absorbing the mother's warmth and smells, hearing her voice, and so on.

Because this relation of assimilation begins immediately following birth, it is likely that as the infant first becomes aware of the mother it is simultaneous with the awareness of continually assimilating the mother into itself. Because of the primariness of this early mode of relating to the other, we can easily see how such a structure could become, as Sartre says, one of the basic modes of relating to others, a mode which, as Sartre also says, can take many forms.

The question of when exactly the infant first becomes aware of the mother as distinct from itself is one in which there is much disagreement. The psychoanalyst, Margaret Mahler, for example, argues that the new-born infant is probably not aware of a distinction between itself and the mother, and that this awareness only begins to appear during the second month of life when the infant enters what she calls the symbiotic phase. Here the infant begins to develop a dim awareness of the mother or her breast as a separate entity, though a separate entity with which it nevertheless shares a common boundary.[44] Other psychologists, like D. N. Stern and Milton Klein, have argued that Mahler is wrong and that the rudimentary abilities to distinguish between self and other are already present in the neonate.[45] Although there might well be some problems with Mahler's account, it is obvious that, even if the neonate does have some awareness of its distinctness from the mother, this awareness can only be at a primal or basic level. Consequently, the infant does progress, as Mahler says, from a more-or-less symbiotic state with the mother toward what she calls separation and individuation. That is, as the infant develops, it tends to see itself as more and more distinct from the mother. This progression helps to explain the origin of Sartre's second attitude to others, namely, the attempt to reduce the other to an object.

This attitude can be found in its rudimentary form in Mahler's next stage of the separation-individuation process. In this "differentiation" subphase, which occurs at about four to five months, the infant makes its first tentative movements to separate itself off from the mother. This attempt at separation has its origins in the infant's increasing control over and therefore more interest in its sensory abilities. These gradually developing abilities now enable the infant to constitute the mother as more of a distinct object, not only distinct from itself but also from other objects. Here the infant begins to display a "checking back to the mother" behavior, wherein it alternately gazes at various objects and then back at the mother as though it were comparing the "not-mother's" appearance with the mother's. This increasing awareness of the mother as a distinct object finds dramatic expression in the "practicing" period (nine to 12 months) when, relying on its maturing motor skills, the infant actively seeks to separate itself in space from the mother.[46] It is not difficult to see in these behaviors an early form of the attempt to make the other into an object. Part of what it means to make the other into an object is to see the other as something which can be compared with other objects, and as something from which one is separate. There remains, as shown above, the problems of which specific attitudes fall under which of the two primary attitudes and whether all attitudes can be subsumed under one of these two. Yet such an analysis gives more sense to Sartre's account by showing how his general picture of primary attitudes has a basis in human development. It is also perhaps worth noting here that this ontogenic account of the sexual background of human relations helps to throw light on the claims of Michel Foucault—a thinker who was heavily influenced by Sartre—about the role of sexuality in power relations. Sexuality, says Foucault, is one of the elements in such relations that is "endowed with the greatest instrumentality: useful for the greatest number of maneuvers and capable of serving as a point of support, as a linchpin, for the most varied of strategies."[47] The problem is that, just as Sartre has difficulty accounting for the pervasiveness of the sexual attitude, Foucault likewise fails to explain satisfactorily why sexuality should be so basic to power relations. Rather than attempt to give such an explanation, he instead chooses to analyze the ways or strategies in which sexuality has been deployed. But why is sexuality particularly well suited to this sort of deployment? The ontogenic theory gives an obvious answer to this question: it is because the sexual quality of the primary relation is carried forward into all relations that sexuality is readily accessible and capable of being exploited in all relations.

Another feature of the ontogenic approach to interpersonal relations is that it not only gives sense to the notion that sexuality accompanies and imbues all of our relations, but also enables one to explain the distinction between overtly sexual relations and apparently non-sexual relations, something Sartre's treatment of the matter did not do. The distinction between the two is, as we have seen, that in the first case the structure of the relationship is much closer to the original primary relationship than it is in the second case. That is, an overtly sexual relationship will typically involve all those physically-intimate behaviors that first made their appearance in the mother–infant relationship. Here, consequently, the desires for intimate caressing and bodily joining will explicitly seek their fulfillment. However, in the non-overtly-sexual relationship, such physical intimacy will, for several reasons, not be possible. Consequently, the desires for such intimacy, which constitute the framework of all relationships, must, as Berne says, seek their fulfillment in subtler ways.

An object may be raised here that this account paints a picture of human relations where all our interactions with others are fueled by an implicit if not explicit desire for overtly-sexual interaction, and such a picture is plainly false. Although we could imagine various of our non-sexual relationships becoming, under particular circumstances, sexual relationships, there are nevertheless those relationships where we feel no sexual interest in the other person, and indeed might even feel disgust to contemplate the idea. However, it is important ask oneself where such disgust comes from. To what extent is the disgust felt in these situations the product of internalized social restraints? In Sartre's words, "behind the prohibitions of morality and taboos of society the original structure remains, at least in that particular form of 'trouble' which is sexual disgust."[48] Interpolating the ontogenic theory into this remark, we could say that the "original structure" which remains behind the taboos is the structure of the primary relationship, and the "trouble" of sexual disgust is just the sexual desires for physical intimacy coming into conflict with deeply-held fears, prohibitions, and taboos. Such an account supports Sartre's view of the centrality of sexual desire in human relations, though it only does so by turning to the ontogenic dimension of human relations, a dimension which Sartre seems too willing to overlook.

## Notes

1. Jean-Paul Sartre, *Being and Nothingness: An Essay in Phenomenological Ontology*, trans. Hazel E. Barnes (London: Methuen, 1956), p. 421.

2. *Ibid.*, p. 381.
3. *Ibid.*, p. 362.
4. Jean-Paul Sartre, *The Transcendence of the Ego: An Existentialist Theory of Consciousness*, trans. Forrest Williams and Robert Kirkpatrick (New York: Farrar, Straus and Giroux, 1957), p. 96.
5. Sartre, *Being and Nothingness*, p. 362.
6. *Ibid.*, p. 275.
7. *Ibid.*, p. 377.
8. *Ibid.*, p. 407.
9. *Ibid.*, p. 411.
10. *Ibid.*, p. 410.
11. Mary Warnock, *Existentialism* (Oxford: Oxford University Press, 1971).
12. Monika Langer, "Sartre and Merleau-Ponty: A Reappraisal," in *The Philosophy of Jean-Paul Sartre*, ed. Paul Arthur Schilpp (La Salle, Illinois: Open Court, 1981).
13. Linda A. Bell, *Sartre's Ethics of Authenticity* (London: University of Alabama Press, 1989), p. 81.
14. Langer, "Sartre and Merleau-Ponty," p. 316.
15. Bell, *Sartre's Ethics of Authenticity*, p. 81.
16. Sartre, *Being and Nothingness*, p. 386.
17. *Ibid.*, p. 388.
18. *Ibid.*, p. 389.
19. *Ibid.*, p. 393.
20. *Ibid.*, p. 394.
21. *Ibid.*, p. 396.
22. Lewis Diana, *The Prostitute and her Clients: Your Pleasure is her Business* (Springfield: Charles C. Thomas, 1985), p. 191. See also M. Simpson and T. Schill, "Patrons of Massage Parlors: Some Facts and Figures," *Archives of Sexual Behavior*, 6:6 (November 1977), pp. 521-525.
23. See James Giles, "A Theory of Love and Sexual Desire," *Journal for the Theory of Social Behaviour*, 24:4 (December 1994), pp. 339-357.
24. Sartre, *Being and Nothingness*, p. 396.
25. *Ibid.*, p. 407.
26. See Lee Brown and Alan Hausman, "Mechanism, Intentionality, and the Unconscious: A Comparison of Sartre and Freud," and also Ivan Soll, "Sartre's Rejection of the Unconscious," both in *The Philosophy of Jean-Paul Sartre*, ed. Paul Arthur Schilpp.
27. Jean-Paul Sartre, *The Emotions: Outline of a Theory*, trans. Bernard Fretchman (New York: Carol Publishing, 1993), pp. 16-17. Also translated under the title *Sketch For a Theory of the Emotions*.
28. Sartre, *Being and Nothingness*, p. 406.
29. *Ibid.*, p. 385.
30. See Bronislaw Malinowski, *The Sexual Lives of Savages in North-western Melanesia* (London: G. Routledge & Sons, 1929) and John Money, J. E. Cawte, G. N. Bianche, and B. Nurcombe, "Sex Training and Tradition in Arnhem Land," in *Exploring Human Sexuality*, eds. Donn Byrne and Lois Byrne (New York: Harper &

Row, 1977), pp. 79-88.

31. See Giles, "A Theory of Love and Sexual Desire," See also Giles, *A Theory of Sexual Desire* (forthcoming).

32. Helen Singer Kaplan, *The Sexual Desire Disorders: Dysfunctional Regulation of Sexual Motivation* (New York: Brunner/Mazel, 1995), p. 41.

33. See Daphna Ayalah and Isaac J. Weinstock, *Breasts: Women Speak about Their Breasts and Their Lives* (London: Hutchinson, 1979).

34. Sigmund Freud, *Introductory Lectures on Psycho-Analysis* (1916-1917), in *The Standard Edition of the Complete Psychological Works of Sigmund Freud*, ed. James Strachey, 16 (London: Hogarth Press, 1986), p. 314.

35. Zella Luria, Susan Friedman, and Michael D. Rose, *Human Sexuality* (New York: John Wiley & Sons, 1987), p. 344.

36. *Ibid.*

37. Freud, *Introductory Lectures*, p. 314.

38. See H. F. Harlow, "The Development of Affectional Patterns in Infant Monkeys," in *Determinants of Infant Behavior*, ed. B. M. Foss, 1 (New York: John Wiley & Sons, 1961).

39. T. Berry Brazelton, Edward Tronick, Laura Adamson, Heidelise Als, and Susan Wise, "Early Mother–infant Reciprocity," in *Parent–Infant Interaction*, Ciba Foundation Symposium 33 (New Series) (Amsterdam: Associated Scientific Publishers, 1975), pp. 137-154.

40. L. Alan Sroufe and June Fleeson, "Attachment and the Construction of Relationships" in *Relationships and Development*, eds. Willard W. Hartup and Zick Rubin (London: Lawrence Erlbaum Associates, 1986), pp. 64-67.

41. Eric Berne, *Games People Play: The Psychology of Human Relationships* (New York: Grove Press), p. 14.

42. Sroufe and Fleeson, "Attachment," p. 52.

43. Sartre, *Being and Nothingness*, p. 407.

44. Margaret S. Mahler, Fred Pine, and Anni Bergman, *The Psychological Birth of the Human Infant: Symbiosis and Individuation* (New York: Basic Books, 1975), p. 45.

45. D. N. Stern, "The Early Development of Schemas of Self, of Other, and of various Experiences of 'Self with Other,'" in *Reflections on Self-psychology*, ed. S. Kaplan (New York: International Universities Press, 1985); Milton Klein, "Mahler's Autistic and Symbiotic Phases: An Exposition and Evaluation," *Psychoanalysis and Contemporary Thought*, 4 (1981), pp. 69-100. Also see James Giles, *No Self to be Found: The Search for Personal Identity* (Lanham: University Press of America, 1997), ch. 5.

46. Mahler *et al.*, *Psychological Birth of the Human Infant*, p. 55.

47. Michel Foucault, *The History of Sexuality: An Introduction*, trans. Robert Hurley (Harmondsworth: Penguin, 1990), p. 103.

# Nine

# USELESS PASSIONS?

## Thomas Jones

In the previous chapter the structure of Sartre's general view of relations with others was examined and various difficulties inherent in that account were pointed out. In this chapter, I want to narrow the focus and have a look at one particular attitude discussed in the early existential philosophy of Sartre; this is the attitude of love. My aim will be to explore and criticize Sartre's view. But rather than do so in the manner of textual analysis, I will examine his view in the context of a consideration of love as a concrete problem for the existing individual. I want to ascertain how Sartre's view of love might help in orienting and directing us in the area of thinking about love; by "love" I mean the lived experience, about which questions can be raised regarding pre-theoretical assumptions and styles of engagement at both individual and cultural levels. Again, I must emphasize that my concerns here are with the existential view of love as presented primarily in *Being and Nothingness*. Although it is true that Sartre later attempted to modify his view of human relations in *Notebooks for an Ethics*, it is, as has been pointed out in earlier chapters, debatable whether this attempt was successful or even compatible with his earlier account.

My opening observation, which is hardly contentious, given the nature of the Sartrean account of love, is that it is hard really to hear that account; it opens up in a challenging fashion some basic features of our relationships with others, and discovers bad faith or self-deception in a certain attitude to others that we call "love." We live in a culture which confers an exalted value upon the state of being in love, but Sartre's critique of love radically challenges the assumptions inherent in this valuing.

It is relevant to raise the question of love, and Sartre's answer to it, as a concrete problem for the existing individual, rather than as a matter of Sartrean scholarship, since there can be little doubt *that* we love and that we already "know" what love is (although the meaning of this "love" is precisely the issue we are raising). This is to say that, as we consider the question of love and Sartre's view on it, we exist as already involved in human relationships; and among these, *love*-relationships have a special place for our sense of what we are and what our existence is about. I think we can take this to be true in a general sense. There is no question, then, of raising the problem of love as if it were a matter of something about which we have no preconceptions or prejudices; for this reason, my strategy in approaching Sartre on love is not *first* to discuss his views in order that *later* I may consider how they are relevant to the lived problems of love. My contention is that the importance, and difficulties, of Sartre's view on love are most apparent if from the beginning we raise the problem of love as one that actually and already concerns us. What, then, is Sartre's view of love, and, if we can understand it, in what direction does it point us for the philosophical task of understanding love?

We do not raise such questions in a vacuum; for instance, one may suspect that the question as Sartre raised it was influenced by his reading of Freud, whose views on love (especially in *Civilization and Its Discontents*) bear comparison with Sartre's in their conclusions if not at all in their method. In general, however, little exists by way of a sustained modern philosophical tradition of questioning love, which means that, in discussing Sartre's view on love more generally, we need to cast around in the philosophical tradition for appropriate terms and concepts. We also need to make explicit the assumptions about love that we have acquired through living in our cultural situations, since these greatly affect our approach to thinking about love. To make that approach in a general way, I suggest that thinking about love (with which we are already involved) tends to shift between two different modes or poles: on the one hand, a concern with the facts about what love actually is, as we involve ourselves in loving (or trying to), and, on the other hand a concern with the values implied by those facts, that is, with what love should ideally be. That is, when we think about love, we often attempt to separate moral evaluation from factual description, and perhaps then attempt to bring them together in an abstract ideal which can guide further reflection. For instance, if someone one knows is involved in an extra-marital affair, one may think about love by first trying to come to an understanding of the connection between love and faithfulness or honesty, and consequently by trying to formulate an abstract ideal of love with which to reflect on the actual situation. A strength of Sartre's account of love, I contend, is that it utilizes the phenomenological method of thinking to cut through these abstractive tendencies, resulting in an account of love that remains on the plane of concrete, lived experience.

However, before we turn to Sartre to see these claims borne out, we need to clarify the use of this word "love." It is an unusually vague and ambiguous word in English, being used to denote a positive disposition toward things (ice-cream, tennis, sex), as well as being used to express feelings and attitudes toward another person of the most tender and intimate kind. "Love" is a word that is often, at least implicitly, used in a moral sense, to signify a general attitude or intention of regarding others positively even in the absence of positive feelings. Part of Sartre's intention in discussing love seems to be to get at the root of this ambiguity of meaning in everyday language use. He uses "love" to mean what he calls a basic attitude which we take up toward others, and he explains this basic attitude in ontological terms that suggest, without his explicitly specifying it, that he has in mind the kind of love between lovers as the basic exemplification of that attitude. The non-specificity of

Sartre's discussion is problematic because it is not entirely clear if what he says about love is also supposed to be true of relationships in which we would say that we loved someone, but which were not of the sort between lovers (for instance, relationships with parents and with close friends). Sartre would apparently want to include these instances of love in his general account, but this raises some problems, for instance, of how the attraction-fascination-seduction plot (which I will describe later) is supposed to work with one's parents. For the sake of this exposition, I will assume that Sartre's discussion of love is primarily about the love between lovers, as that instance of love that best allows us to explain love in general. The meaning of "love," then, which Sartre takes as primary is that of "being in love," and it is this meaning which I will discuss, although I will return to a more general consideration in the conclusion.

We may now look at Sartre's phenomenological approach to love. He discusses being in love as a phenomenon of human existence; love, as a conscious phenomenon, shares the characteristic of intentionality with all such phenomena; it intends an object. That object is the other whom I love, and love is therefore to be described in terms of this other. If this intentional relation of myself to the other in love is essential to the phenomenon, we can, following Sartre, make some important observations.

First, we can say that those explanations of being in love are incorrect which interpret it in terms of a procreative instinct or as related to physiological symptoms such as adrenaline rushes, or secretions of brain-hormones. These are explanations that take the intrapsychic and physiological-emotional phenomena of the experience to be its essence. These physiological changes do occur, and we sometimes do and say rash or amorous things in relation to others which could be linked to these changes, but although these phenomena are part of a description of the experience, as explanations, they ignore the fundamental phenomenological characteristic of being in love. This characteristic, fully evident in the lived experience of love, is that of consciousness aiming "across the world" (possibly via instinctual or physiological modifications of my being) toward the other with whom I am in love. Attempts to ascertain the essence of love in terms of "objective facts" of human biological nature assume a conceptual scheme that makes consciousness and action to some degree passive and determined effects of extra-conscious forces, and assumes a great deal about how adrenaline rushes, and so on, can *cause* modifications of conscious subjectivity. We should say, rather, that in phenomenological terms, objectively measurable and subjectively lived modifications of consciousness are precisely aspects of a conscious phenomenon; an upsurge of passion that aims across the world in which I exist, toward the other with whom I am in love. This other, through my relation to him or her, is the fundamental object intended by the phenomenon.

Second, love is not essentially any sort of psychological or emotional *state*; it is not that there are no such states (at least we experience them sometimes), but the perception or constitution of such states is itself a peculiar and complex reflective achievement. In *Sketch for a Theory of the Emotions*, for instance, Sartre interprets emotions as "magical transformations of the world" which seek to overcome difficulties encountered at a pre-reflective level of engagement[1] (see Elizabeth Murray Morelli's chapter on Sartre's view of reflective and pre-reflective consciousness). Moreover, in *Being and Nothingness*, Sartre takes up the theme developed in *The Transcendence of The Ego*, of the constitution of psychic states by a sort of magical process of discovering aspects of ourselves between the purely lived phenomena of subjectivity and the passivity of being an object for our own "accessory" reflections.[2] Hence, to view love as a state, emotional or psychological, is also to assume a conceptual scheme that is far from adequate, since it does not take account of how consciousness constantly *lends significance* to this "state," maintaining it in (magical) existence as "what I am feeling." It would be interesting to explore more fully Sartre's critical approach to psychology, as it concerns love, but for now we need only note that, in discussing love, he has in mind something that is essentially neither a passive reaction on the part of consciousness to non-conscious causal factors nor an emotional or psychological state undergone by consciousness. Indeed, to the extent that we reflect upon being in love as "this reaction/state I am undergoing/feeling," Sartre's discussion criticizes these concepts and conceptual assumptions as helping to maintain us in bad faith, for the sake of useless passions.

What Sartre means by "love," then, as an attitude that consciousness takes up toward the other, is something that aims across emotions and psychic states; in this attitude, emotions and psychic states are organized into the existential structure of being in love. Moreover, it is consciousness itself that does this organizing, through aiming at something to be attained for consciousness. This need not be any sort of reflective achievement, but is consciousness's (pre-reflective) way of being, "being-for-itself" in Sartre's terminology. It is difficult to evoke summarily the depth of meaning Sartre discovers in the concept of being-for-itself, but an important point for this discussion is that of the foundationlessness of consciousness. Consciousness is determined as what it is by negation; it is always consciousness *of* something which it is not; I can be conscious of being in love, for instance, only if a beloved exists who is not myself, is other. But, according to Sartre, consciousness is also the lived attempt to become its own foundation—to establish its own being as itself, a completion or fulfillment, in relation with what it is not. It is this quest that, Sartre concluded, is a "useless passion"[3]; being in love, as an existential structure within this useless quest, is doomed so far as it is implicated in it. It is up to each individual to reflect on his or her own experience to see if and how he or she takes up this attitude of love. But it seems that Sartre regards the paradigm of being in love, as Proust, for instance, describes it, as the exemplification of an organizing existential attitude.

Love, as Sartre describes it, is a basic attitude or primitive reaction to the other in our concrete relations with others.[4] It is basic in that it is one of two kinds of basic attitudes or reactions that we can take up in our concrete relations: the first aims at appropriating the other's consciousness in order that in the eyes of the other I am a consciousness recognized as such; the other (exemplified in what Sartre calls "desire") aims at capturing the other's consciousness so that my consciousness can do the looking. This complex set of strategies, which are complementary yet opposed, arises from the situation of being a consciousness in a world in which there are others. Sartre's aim in discussing "being-for-others" is to show that the "problem of other minds," as far as it concerns knowledge of other minds, is irresolvable; instead, he seeks to show how others are implicated in what we are, as a matter of fact, and on the basis of this ontological demonstration, he seeks to illuminate the human situation a little more clearly. However, he does this from the individualized and subjective perspective of the *cogito*, and it is this startingpoint that determines, among other things, an ignoring of cultural determinants of experience, a theme to which I will return.

Consciousness, as being-for-itself, is in its being that whereby *there is* a world; it is the "instantaneous nucleus," the absolute center, of an organized system of references to things which determines existence in a world, in a situation, and as a body. However, when another consciousness enters into the picture (which it does in fact, though not as a matter of logical necessity), this dynamic system of reference is radically decentered, since for the other I am an object in his or her world. Yet, if consciousness as being-for-itself implies the quest to be its own foundation, this radical decentering is a problem: I am no longer the one by whom there is a world (I am no longer the center of my world), since the other has made me aware of other consciousnesses for whom I am in no privileged position at all. We cannot go on being the center of the world when we encounter others; since I recognize other consciousnesses as such, but as *not-me*, with as much subjectivity and world-organizing efficacy as myself, there is no choice but to take up an attitude toward these alien presences in the world. Hence ensues conflict, which Sartre calls the essence of being-for-others.

At this point, we may fear that we have already left anything resembling concrete experience, and entered the bleak and unfriendly world of Sartre's novels. Further, we may feel that we maintain non-conflictual relationships with at least some people—did not Sartre himself do so, with Simone de

Beauvoir, for instance, or the co-editors of *Les Temps Modernes*? Indeed, for Beauvoir, as Margaret A. Simons argues in Chapter Five, it is just these sort of relationships—relationships of helping and generosity—that are the basis of our relations with others. These are important points, and ones which Maurice Merleau-Ponty also sought to solve in his search for a common ground of our being in the world with others. He did so in terms of the experience of the lived body (see Edmond Wright's discussion in Chapter Two) with its impersonal and ambiguous original intentionality, another theme to which I will return in connection with the criticism of Sartre's reliance on the individual *cogito*. At the least, the dimension of the social in lived experience implies some common ground for consciousnesses confronting each other. However, for the moment, I wish to remain faithful to Sartre's account of being-for-others. It may be, for instance, that in the sphere of love we human beings consistently and unreflectively attempt to appropriate other consciousnesses as free subjectivities that affirm us as the center of the world, that is, that justify our existences as ourselves; and we simply do not want to become aware of these patterns of bad faith (as they may turn out to be). Sartre's discussion of being-for-others brings out the possibility that the experience of being in love is *not* what we would wish it to be; it raises a problem over love at the point at which we least want it raised. We should heed this before moving beyond Sartre's possibly inadequate ontology of interpersonal relationships.

To move on to his account of love, Sartre does not discuss being in love in order to describe the lived experience. Instead, he interprets everything about the experience in terms of his basic ontological scheme. In this sense, he is not attempting a phenomenology of being in love, but instead an ontological interpretation of the phenomenon. In other words, his account is something like a transcendental argument that tries to determine the necessary conditions for the experience. In effect, though only implicitly, he strips away all the prejudices, both positive and negative, with which various thinkers have approached being in love, and points out a fundamental ontological structure. For instance, Schopenhauer interprets being in love as the Will's way of getting men and women to perpetuate the species, such that all the subjective ideas that lovers have about the experience are basically epiphenomenal (what we might call the "nature's con-trick argument," also put forward by psychologists and biologists).[5] This kind of argument should be seen as being negatively prejudicial in that it denies the crucial role of consciousness in the experience. In falling in love, according to Sartre, I take up an attitude toward the other in which all the projects through which I comport my existence toward this other aim at getting her to make me that whereby there is a world for her; I appropriate this alien consciousness, and get her to make me the center of the world, thereby attempting to ensure that what I am for her is in accordance with what I am for myself. In this way, my passion to be the foundation of my existence will ideally become freed from the alienating encounter with the other that perpetually threatens to usurp my freedom.

Therefore, Sartre gives a startling twist to the question of why we fall in love: not because of a natural tendency to seek out a mate for the procreation of the species, even less because I recognize a soul-mate with whom to share the adventure of life. But because this other is a threat to my freedom. This startling reversal of common perceptions of being in love typifies Sartre's discussion. I will rehearse his account of the experience of falling in love in order to see how he reaches the conclusion that love is doomed to fail; I will do so in terms of the drama of attraction-fascination-seduction that Sartre utilizes, seeking to elucidate the power of Sartre's account by evoking a recognizable description.

I meet someone to whom I am attracted, who exudes a certain promise that draws me like a magnet. I feel myself drawn and responding, with desire to make contact, to communicate. As I participate in this attraction, as I respond to the other, I feel that I am no longer "being myself"; I want the other to be drawn to me, to be attracted. I feel the weight of what I am in the eyes of the other, the distance between us, and I am filled with images swirling around my desire, of contact and communion, images which are the reversal of our actual distance. And when I see this person again, my excitement and desire makes my hands shake, my heart race, and with this glut of desire my mind melts into a maelstrom of wild thoughts—what to say? what to do? The excitement is addictive. I cannot stop thinking about, I cannot wait to see this person again, I plot meetings, conversations,...

We must not be misled by the apparent passivity of the feelings involved in falling in love: the overwhelming nature of falling in love indicates not an extra-conscious force but a lack of comprehension of what is happening, and what is happening is quite obviously a great temptation for the existing individual. I do not partly participate in an experience forced upon me from outside; I assent to an upwelling experience of my being which involves more than my conscious mind (reflective consciousness), which involves "body and heart too," in short, my whole being. Even the experience of a "troublesome" infatuation must not mislead us into thinking that falling in love is really passive: in this case, I distrust with my reason or with my conscience what other parts of my being are crying out for, actively desiring. It is for this reason that falling in love can be a painful experience: an internal conflict can be involved, with all the attendant tensions and worry.

Falling in love therefore seems to well up right from the depths; sometimes, the experience is one of being tossed about on a sea of violent emotion, with my powers of rational reflection swamped. Sometimes, the experience is that life has become wonderful as it never was before, my senses heightened, my history rewritten. I feel as if lit up by a new sun. With my whole being, I am drawn toward the person I am in love with: the attraction I feel toward this person seems to be the calling of soul to soul; I yearn for her presence, I interpret each word and gesture as signs of a deeper affinity. My mind is filled with the imagined realities of our communion beyond all these obstacles found between us of age, experience, or situation. My heart aches with the warm feeling that we are somehow already communicating on a level far beyond the everyday, as if I am remembering a forgotten homeland, as if we were always meant to meet, as if it is only this cruel world that keeps us apart,...

I want to go to the inner depths in intimate communication with my lover. I tell (or want to) the story of my life to my beloved, who listens, attentive and loving. I too, listen to her story. It leads ultimately to this love and resolves itself in our future together. All this is the fantasy that guides the experience, but it also points to the value implicitly attached to the attraction. This value is an ideal which lies at the far end of all my thoughts, feelings, imaginings: the ideal of lovers existing for each other. My lover will exist for me, I for my lover. By being for each other, what we are for ourselves will be what we are for each other, and the pre-reflectively apprehended conflict of self and other will be resolved in this co-existence. This is not necessarily an ideal I am aware of as such; falling in love is a project which I live through, and live with all my being. My powers of reflection may not necessarily be able to reach much clarity about my motivations at the time, but the interpretive startingpoint of an engaged consciousness implies that, if I was aware enough of what is happening, then the project and its ideal could become clear. The fact that the experience of falling in love is so intense that we rarely think clearly at all is not a reason to claim it is irrational or instinctive, but only an excuse to do so.

But can the ideal which motivates the project of falling in love be realized? Sartre's claim is that it is an unrealizable project, a primitive reaction to the other that endlessly and unsuccessfully tries to resolve the fundamental issue of what we are for others. However, we need to plot the course of falling in love further to understand the exact meaning of the failure of the project, for since it is clearly possible to fall in love, the project is not impossible. Its unrealizability is a matter of its never being able to reach the goal it sets itself.

Sartre describes fascination and seduction as further moments in the plot. Before our attraction develops into a relationship, I am intensely aware of myself in the eyes of the other, and in this intensity I try to engage all the powers of my wit, charm, and intelligence, to appear fascinating to the person with whom I am in love. This takes effort, and may involve worry, for I have little idea if this person is attracted to me, or what I am for this other. I try, through my words and gestures, to lead the other to an understanding of my hidden depths, my character, my worthiness. I might do things and go to places I would never have considered before, to capture the attention of my beloved. If we are mutually fascinated, we laugh together, talk intensely of ourselves, of our feelings, beliefs, and hopes, hanging on to each word as if entranced, paying avid attention the mutual fascination whirls on, past the initiation into relationship, be it the kiss or the mutual declaration of "I love you," to absorption in each other, a mutual seduction in which each person's world shifts and re-orients around this new center, so that lovers become lost in each other, devoted to each other, existing for each other.

So we are in love, and life seems wonderful. Now, what has happened to the ideal that motivated falling in love? Do we now exist for each other and find our being-for-ourselves and our being-for-others resolved in love? The answer depends on whether we choose to continue to exist for each other in this way. Now we are in love, and have attempted to realize the project in attraction, fascination, and seduction. We can continue to be attracted and fascinated by each other, and to this extent, falling in love continues to attempt to realize its ideal; but this remains a somewhat "metastable" situation. Sartre describes this metastability as the "triple destructibility" of love: first, it remains an ongoing ideal, and we deceive ourselves in thinking it is ever wholly achieved; second, at any moment a lover may awake from the trance-like absorption of lovers, and implicit consciousness of this means lovers feel perpetually insecure (and here begins jealousy and possessiveness); and third, being in love has as its aim an absolute guarantee of my existence by my lover, an aim always made relative by all the others in the world who make me what I am for them just as before.

This destructibility is founded on and reveals bad faith (the self-deception of being in love): existing for another means my alienating myself from what I am for myself in order to be for another. The other, moreover, whose freedom I have attempted to capture in order to resolve the issue of my being for others, is no longer the freedom that could guarantee my existence as myself: I can grasp only the semblance of my love's being-for-herself, an alienated image of that for which I reached. I know this in the way my love slips away from me in certain looks this person gives others, and in certain moments as my love slips into thought; as I move to follow in anguish or in wonder, my love moves only further away and is herself, in the finally irreducible otherness of her being. And in the mutuality of being in love, all this is as true of the other, in her own attempt to appropriate me for the sake of founding her being-for-others, as it is for me. Hence, being in love is mutual alienation, a magical way of being for each other, which, like all magic, is true only if we believe in it.

Falling in love, then, is successful to the extent that we, probably unreflectively, keep on being for each other through attraction, fascination, and seduction. The factuality or givenness of the mutual absorption is a "magical" phenomenon. The only given is the sheer and problematic difference of the other from me which falling in love tries to resolve, and being in love is the ongoing attempt to resolve the issue, and not the resolution itself. The ongoing attempt has no realizable end, and no declaration or proof of love can guarantee its future. Many lovers simply get bored of it all after some time, at which point they may engage in a renewed attempt to found being-for-itself in being-for-another with someone else.

Let us note some general features in all this. First, Sartre's account of love is obviously "anti-romantic" in a concrete sense; he denies that the ideal of romantic love is realizable and allows it no positive value. There are a couple of references in the account of love in *Being and Nothingness* to love as aiming at a fusing or uniting of consciousnesses, and the ideal of such a fusion lies at the heart of romantic love as an ideal of interpersonal relationship.[6] This puts Sartre into the philosophical tradition of discussing the ideal of such love, which begins with Plato. In the *Symposium*, Plato puts into the speech of Aristophanes an articulation of the archetypal romantic ideal. The comic playwright praises love by means of an outrageous myth of the original four-armed, four-legged, spherical beings, cut in half by Zeus to make us human beings, after these original creatures committed *hubris*. Aristophanes uses this myth to explain why people fall in love: they are seeking their "other half," in order to recover a wholeness that their lost original nature yearns for.[7] However, later in the dialogue, Plato has Diotima tell Socrates that the concept of lovers seeking their other half is not the truth. If it is true that love is desire, as Plato has it, and what we lack, and therefore desire, is the good, exemplified in the beauty of the person we are in love with, then we do not seek wholeness, or anything else, in love, unless that whole happens to be good.[8] Plato seems to be suggesting that being in love may appear to the lovers to be a fusion or uniting of beings in wholeness, but this description of an experience is not an explanation of love, but an obfuscation of the true motivations of lovers. In Sartrean terms, the myth of original wholeness is like an image of the quest of being-for-itself to be founded by its being-for-the-other in love. While Plato points to the confusion and limitation implicit in attributing true goodness to the beloved, Sartre indicates the magical and unrealizable character of the relationship.

Indeed, more common ground can be found between Plato's philosophy of love and Sartre's than first seems apparent, since Plato argues that love, as desire, implies a lack, in the case of being in love, a lack of beauty, which a lover seeks to recover through the person of the beloved. Sartre's account of love similarly interprets the project of being-for-itself as a passion to make up its lack (its self) and to be its own foundation, a project that being in love takes up through the intermediary of the other and a mutual being-for-each-other. Plato goes on to describe an itinerary of philosophical development toward the true goal of being in love ("absolute beauty") for which there is no complement in Sartre, but the similarities are interesting enough.

Sartre's anti-romantic approach to being in love also bears comparison to Martin Buber's approach in *I and Thou*,[9] and contrasts sharply with the attempt of one analytic philosopher, Mark Fisher's attempt to describe the good of personal love as a fusion of selves permeated by "humble benevolence."[10] Sartre's account of love offers grounds for questioning any account of love that posits the goal of fusion or uniting in love as realizable or authentic. Any form of love that implicitly or explicitly means "wanting to be loved," loving in order to appropriate the other, reveals the dialectic of that basic attitude toward the other which is ontologically doomed. In this sense, Sartre's account of love is broader in its scope than a critique of being in love in particular. Yet being in love, the passionate upsurge of my existence that seeks to appropriate the existence of the other, is without doubt the basic exemplification of that attitude to the other which in general we call "love." I suggest that we can notice in Sartre's ontological approach to the question of love a profound continuity with the myth of Tristan and Isolde, which is the archetypal romantic myth from which later European love-literature derives its basic pattern.[11] Just as, in the myth, the lovers are doomed to fall in love despite all the codes that regulated the sexual and social interactions of their cultural life, culminating in their deaths together as the outcome of their passion, so Sartre's account of love posits an attitude to which we are doomed by the factual necessities of being in the world in the midst of others, an attitude that culminates in the destruction of love through its own metastability, leaving consciousness no nearer the realization of the goal of its useless passion. The myth gives us images, whilst Sartre gives us ontology, but the underlying drama of seeming fate or apparent factual necessity gloriously exhausting itself in useless passion is common. It is up to each individual to reflect on his or her own experience to ascertain the degree to which we are committed to projects for which there is no hope of realization, to a tragedy for which we yet yearn.

However, this connection between Sartre and the quintessentially European myth of Tristan and Isolde shows up a specific *aporia* in Sartre's account of love: the way in which being in love is influenced by cultural factors that suggest to lovers much of what they are looking for in the experience, indeed, the whole idea of being in love may be a Western speciality and not a universal human interest. Sartre describes the use of language as a means to fascinate the other, through its ability to project an objective sense of one's self into the world for the sake of the person with whom one is in love, but it seems to me indisputable that far more than language is involved in the way lovers bridge the sheer contingency of their being-for-each-other in order to create themselves as necessary centers of reference for the other's existence. Along with language, lovers have the resources of discourse and paradigms with which to make themselves fascinating for each other. Discourses about love (systems of knowledge and meaning that encourage predictable styles of communication) formed through the long evolution of a cultural style of bad faith, and paradigms of love constantly reworked through literature and other media that communicate ways by which consciousnesses can create themselves, and perceive others, as fascinating objects. Being in love, then, depends more heavily upon a style of cultural being than upon the individualism of the for-itself's upsurge than Sartre seems to allow.

My point is that between the upsurge of the for-itself as a quest for the fullness of itself and the drama of the useless passion of love, there is a whole range of cultural factors in which terms lovers seek to expend their passion. But if this is the case, then the role of imagination in the meaning of love is more important than Sartre's ontological scenario suggests, since it is through the mediation of images pertaining to social life that love can take on form as both an experience and a value in concrete relations in a specific cultural context. This is to suggest that our individual perceptions of and feelings about the other constantly allude to and are informed by images current in cultural life, which condition the lived texture of the individual's conscious upsurge. This is an important point, since it relocates, though not completely, the site of bad faith from the individual to existence as it is informed in advance by imaginative structures in the culture in which the individual is emplaced.

Moreover, if we are more culturally-situated than the Sartre of *Being and Nothingness* admits, then it is quite possible that specifically modern Western images of love have infected Sartre's discussion of love with a set of assumptions that need to be made more explicit. One such assumption is that of love as something like a spiritual connection between human beings, for whom sexual desire is a contingent aim of passion. This lack of reconciliation between passion and desire has a long history in European culture, emanating originally from the development of the courtly love tradition of twelfth-century France. In this tradition, the sexual desire that was restrained by the moral and confessional ideology of medieval Christianity was sublimated into an imaginative world of passion and emotion. Although more recent thinking has attempted conceptually to reconnect passion with desire (for Schopenhauer, for example, the individual's passion is interpreted in terms of Ideas, while desire is a manifestation of Will), the attempt has tended to reduce one of the two to the other, leaving a gulf of understanding meanwhile. While Sartre's account of being in love is an acute reminder of the hopeless ideal of love, and while for him sexual desire is implicated as a complementary attitude to love in the circle of primitive reactions to the other in our concrete relations, the connection is similarly not made explicit.

The connection can be made more explicit, in a way that utilizes Sartre's account of sexual desire but links it in a new way to his account of love. Let us consider the role of sexual desire in the maintenance of the love-relationship, in a lived experience which combines imagination with actuality in an inculturated commitment to passion. In the attempt to appropriate the other as a consciousness for whom I am the center of his or her existence, thereby justifying my existence, sexual desire may arise as the further attempt to "incarnate the other as flesh," to bring all of the other's freedom on to the surfaces of the body, there captured and made safe. Whatever the merits of this account of sexual desire, it is clear that within the love-relationship this mutual incarnation of consciousness in desire, along with the following drama of pleasure and satiation, can take the role of a symbolic attainment of a union of human beings, a combination of image and actuality, a quasi-fusion of consciousnesses in mutual pleasure and within a strictly private world. Within this private world of lovers in the flesh, the whole plot of love appears (at least sometimes, or ideally) to reach a pitch of success and achievement that renders lovers blinded to the bad faith and unrealizability of love in the wider sphere of existence with others. We discover, then, in sexual desire, the most potent means by which lovers persevere in their passion.

However, if we have found that the drama of love is enriched as well as maintained in that of sexual desire, then it is possible to discuss more critically Sartre's consistent and counter-intuitive account of love as wholly conscious in its motivation. This is not to say that love is ever unconscious in its motivation, but that we may look to the origins of sexual desire in the impersonal life of the body for a more adequate account of being in love. To do so, we can take up Merleau-Ponty's cautious but insistent critique of Sartre as too heavily reliant on the sheer translucency of the *cogito*. Merleau-Ponty interprets consciousness as never wholly free from the original intentionality of the body, an impersonal and ambiguous upsurge of meaning that, in sexual desire, aims across the world to another body in its sexual dimension; sexual desire is therefore by no means wholly lucid in its project, but consciousness takes up the organic roots of its being into its own organization of its world.[12] If it is true that the bad faith of love is rooted in a blindness generated by sexual desire along with a cultural style of imagining the embodied processes of passion, Merleau-Ponty's account of that desire as an upwelling of the ambiguous life of bodily intentionality allows us to see Sartre's account of love in a broader light. It is a tragedy to which we are doomed, not just through the anguished individualism of the for-itself's upsurge, but also through the organization of the body's impersonal desires in a world where the other is never merely another body, in which the other to whom one is attracted is encountered through images that mediate both passion and desire. If the impersonal desire of the body is taken up into a cultural style of appropriating another's freedom in love, then we arrive at the myth of Tristan and Isolde, and the modern Western emphasis on, and tragedy of, love.

In criticizing Sartre's account of love, I have not meant to vitiate what appears to me to be its central insight: that falling in love involves a pre-reflective, usually unreflective, attempt to appropriate the other in order to found my own existence as myself in relation with this other. My points regarding the culturally-determined nature of love, and the connection between love, sex, and the impersonal life of the body, are designed to make more concrete the relevance of Sartre's account to the lived problems of love: that the trials and futilities of being in love relate to an ontological structure in which the unrealizability of love is ignored in bad faith.

However, I do not want to end this chapter with a mere recapitulation of Sartre's negative conclusions regarding love. Recall that we inferred that Sartre regards being in love as the exemplification of a basic attitude to the other, which we call "love." But it may be that this is mistaken, and that being in love is *not* the exemplification of love, which, as we noted, is both a word and a lived experience that applies to the relation of parent and child, friend and friend, as well as to that of lover and beloved. We can, for instance, utilize Aristotle's analysis of love (in Greek, *philia*, usually translated as "friendship") to present a different account.

Aristotle is quite prepared to admit that love for the most part appears as something like a basic attitude that aims at appropriating another for the sake of founding one's own existence: "Most people seem to want to be loved rather than to love, the reason being their desire for honour [*time*—esteem]... to be loved is felt to be the next thing to being honoured, which is the aim of most people."[13] This does not imply that being in love is the exemplification of this attitude; the specific organization of sexual desire and cultural imagination that determines the lived experience of this sort of love differentiates it from friendship, for instance, but does not necessarily imply that it underlies friendship (we might also note that the Greek paradigm of *Eros*, or "being in love," differed from the modern Western paradigm as we might expect in a culture-specific organization of sexual desire).[14] Hence, *contra* Freud, love as a conscious phenomenon of human experience may include and consist in the organization of sexual desire but nevertheless does not necessarily imply it; and, *contra* Sartre, love as a basic attitude to the other does not necessarily manifest as being in love.

Following Aristotle, we could take the basic exemplification of love to be more like friendship; in which case, neither the attraction-fascination-seduction plot of falling in love, nor the ontologically inevitable tragedy of passion wholly determines what it means to love. Aristotle develops a conception of "perfect friendship" that goes beyond wanting to be loved: "[perfect] friendship [*philia*, the general Greek word for "love"] seems to consist more in giving than in receiving affection....So if friendship consists more in loving than in being loved, and if people are commended for loving their friends, it seems that loving is the distinctive virtue of friends."[15] Whilst I make no claims about reconciling Aristotle's philosophy with that of Sartre, I wish to make the point that a positive conception of love may be possible even if we have appreciated Sartre's radical account of being in love as a useless passion. It also needs to be said that this positive conception does not exclude sexual love, but only a sexual love which is implicated in the project of fusing our existence with another, and which is hence in bad faith. However, Sartre's critique of love is invaluable in that it cuts through the grand cultural discourse of romantic love, and challenges us to raise the ethical question of love somewhere beyond our general and pre-theoretical assumptions.

## Notes

1. Jean-Paul Sartre, *Sketch for a Theory of the Emotions*, trans. Philip Mairet (London: Methuen, 1962), p. 63ff. Also translated under the title *The Emotions: Outline of a Theory*.

2. Jean-Paul Sartre, *Being and Nothingness: An Essay in Phenomenological Ontology*, trans. Hazel E. Barnes (London: Methuen, 1958), pp. 335ff., 356.

3. *Ibid.*, p. 615.

4. *Ibid.*, p. 361ff.

5. Arthur Schopenhauer, "On the Metaphysics of Sexual Love," in his *The World as Will and Idea*, ed. David Berman, trans. Jill Berman (London: J. M. Dent, 1995), supplement to bk. 4.

6. Sartre, *Being and Nothingness*, pp. 365, 376.

7. Plato, *Symposium*, trans. Robert Waterfield (Oxford: Oxford University Press, 1994), secs. 189c-193d.

8. *Ibid.*, secs. 205d-206a.

9. Martin Buber, *I and Thou*, trans. Ronald Gregor Smith (Edinburgh: T.&T. Clark, revis. edit., 1958). See esp. p. 87.

10. Mark Fisher, *Personal Love* (London: Duckworth, 1990), p. 26.

11. See Denis de Rougemont, *Love in the Western World*, trans. Montgomery Belgion (Princeton: Princeton University Press, 1983), and Robert Johnson, *The Psychology of Romantic Love* (Harmondsworth: Penguin, 1987).

12. See esp. Maurice Merleau-Ponty, *The Phenomenology of Perception*, trans. Colin Smith (London: Routledge and Kegan Paul, 1970), pt. 1, ch. 5.

13. Aristotle, *Ethics*, trans. J. A. K. Thompson (Harmondsworth: Penguin 1994), bk. 8.

14. See esp. Kenneth Dover, *Greek Homosexuality* (London: Duckworth, 1978).

15. Aristotle, *Ethics*, bk. 8.

# Ten

# STRUGGLING WITH THE OTHER: GENDER AND RACE IN THE YOUTHFUL WRITINGS OF CAMUS

## Christine Margerrison

While it is well known that Albert Camus was anxious to distance himself from the French existentialist movement, good reasons have always existed for drawing parallels as well as contrasts between his own perspectives and positions and those of other French writers like Jean-Paul Sartre, Simone de Beauvoir, and Gabriel Marcel. A broad strand of his thought and writings, however, is thoroughly distinctive and immediately recognizable, bringing together his particular origins and personal preoccupations, with human issues of the most general significance. It is a thread difficult to disentangle, but the central purpose of this chapter will be to show that elements often isolated by commentators have necessarily to be seen together. This strand can initially be located, for practical purposes, by pointing to the obvious and constant importance assumed in Camus's works by representations of the mother, other people, gender, and race. Since these *are* so intricately interrelated in Camus, and since "representations" can take a variety of forms and affective charges, the questions involved are deep and complex ones. One concerns the extent to which, at a general level, Camus's treatment of these matters may constitute the equivalent of, or a counterpart to, treatments of "the Other" in the works of his contemporaries. As a first—tentative—step toward providing a basis on which to try answering this and other questions, we need to examine, in particular, Camus's early, posthumously-published writings, which have so far received little attention from critics.

In the earliest writings, we see repeated attempts to draw a portrait of the young writer's mother—predictably unsuccessful, given his conviction that she is "incapable of the slightest thought." One fragment from these writings, probably written between 1934 and 1936, and probably part of an early novel which Camus was working on,[1] illustrates the difficulties of the young man in relation to this opaque and silent figure: "He saw again her face animated by the warmth of an indifferent conversation, he felt how much others felt her to be lively, and he was surprised that he found her so lifeless, almost an actress."[2] The woman is dead, yet others respond to her *as if* she were alive. It is only in the presence of others that she seems to act out the state of life, as the young child had discovered when, arriving home from school, he had found her alone and immobile in the half-light, staring "abnormally" at the floor.[3]

It is after Camus abandoned his first attempts at novel-writing that this fragment, along with extracts from "Voices from the Poor Quarter," was incorporated, in modified form, into the collection *Betwixt and Between,* published in 1937.[4] The extracts that remain from "Voices from the Poor Quarter"[5] demonstrate once more the problems the writer faced in portraying this figure. The first of these introduces "the voice of the woman who did not think," an apparent contradiction in terms except that we hardly hear her voice, which is eclipsed by that of the narrator. The poignancy of the question, "what is she thinking of, what is she thinking of just now?" is immediately stifled, as if too difficult to bear, by the statement "nothing."[6] A further portrait, in "the voice that was roused by music," confers a "tragic" dimension upon what she says by means of the music playing in the background and not her words themselves. When the woman leaves we read that "she does not exist any longer, since she is no longer there....She is going back into her darkness, after having briefly emerged because of the miracle of a stupid tune."[7]

Despite the descriptions of the mother, the concentration is not upon her but the effect of her presence upon the narrator. Indeed, this move is facilitated by the repeated insistence that "she does not think," a characteristic which will be attached to this figure throughout Camus's novelistic works. Given her silence, and her apparent indifference to her son, it begins to seem necessary that *she should not think:* otherwise, she might be capable of opinions or of judgments not only beyond the reach of the writer but beyond his control. It is this possibility which threatens to subvert the narrative voice in these early portraits.

Earlier in the first extract cited above, we have some indication of the way in which Camus is to solve the problem of this threatening consciousness. She is "nothing but an instrument," a "symbol" reflecting the life of poverty he had known.[8] This transformation of the mother into a symbol is to culminate in an equation between the maternal figure and French Algeria itself in Camus's last and unfinished novel, *The First Man*.[9] There she embodies the poverty, ignorance, and endurance which are transferred on to the entire French Algerian community. For the first time, her status as a European version of the Algerian *fatma* (a cleaning woman) is embraced and no longer the cause for ambivalence. On the level of symbol, she can be a representative of the equally poor, ignorant, nomadic, and "authentically Algerian" European settlers in order to take over the identity of the indigenous population. Again, for the first time, she is presented as potential mother of all those races born upon the Algerian soil, rather than, as in *The Plague*,[10] of the exclusively European male community. On the level of the individual woman, however, although a clear attempt at understanding has been, she remains an enigma with no apparent inner life, outside of history and the affairs of men.

It is not my intention to suggest that the transformation into symbol is an unproblematical process; on the contrary, as critics have often pointed out, the portrayal of this figure is laden with ambivalence.[11] In my view, this duality stems from her human and biological status as mother, which must be distinguished from her role as maternal stereotype. This is illustrated in the early writings with the recognition that "he knew that everything which made up his sensibility was that day when he had understood that he had been born of his mother and that she almost never thought." (I have adopted here the correction made by Lévi-Valensi, who reads in the manuscript the word "born" rather than "seen.")[12] Her quasi-animal status is clear in "Between Yes and No,"[13] a characteristic which links her there with the Arab café-owner and marks the difficult association between mother and racial identity. No resolution of this question is to be found in *The First Man*, for whereas she may be presented there as potential mother of all, her son remains—in the line of every Camusian hero, and in the words of Jean Sarocchi—"unpolluted by indigenous blood."[14]

I have concentrated on the early treatment of the mother figure and her transformation into a symbol because this serves as a template for relations with others in the fictional writings of Camus. It is the presentation of others as devoid of an autonomous consciousness or of an existence beyond the orbit of the central character which facilitates their manipulation in the literary works. Pointing out that others are experienced as a physical presence rather than an individual consciousness, Brian Fitch long ago concluded, "the world of Camus remains essentially an egocentric and solitary universe."[15]

Although I am in general agreement with this statement, I wish to investigate it in matters of gender and race. The "virile fraternity of the combatants of the plague" apparently cannot be united into the same category of others as that represented by "heterosexual love," as Fitch suggests.[16] The "virile fraternity" (which Camus seeks to establish from his earliest writings) is a source of strength, foundation of the collective "we" so important in the writer's novelistic works. By contrast, the sexuality of women is a potentially debilitating force which threatens to contaminate the pure male collectivity unless controlled by its transformation into a symbol of the "fruits of the earth" offered to men. It is not possible to speak of "others" as a uniform category in the works of Camus. The misleading effect of such a generalization is demonstrated through a consideration of the earliest writings, when the young Camus first attempts to come to terms with the existence of others in his works.

These writings date from 1932 to 1934, when Camus was between 18 and 21 years of age and was not only developing his talents, but seeking his subject matter while attempting to formulate his own role as artist. Most of the works from 1932 consist of essays on literature and philosophy and were published in the local review, *Sud*.[17] The remaining essays, although still concerned with the definition of art, are much more personal, revealing the young man's insecurities.[18] Inevitably, as he begins to write about the world around him, he is forced to confront the existence of others and to develop the means of translating this existence into the artistic universe he is creating.

Broadly speaking, these others may be divided into two main categories. The first group consists of the men of Camus's own French Algerian community (and often, by extension, the men of Europe), whose consciousness seems transparent and can be ultimately merged into the "egocentric universe" of which Fitch speaks. On these men the writer is to bestow his allegiance, and with them he identifies. Although a development occurs in Camus's youthful writings toward portraying the external non-egocentric world, this is associated specifically with this group, and reached at an early stage with "The Hospital of the Poor Quarter" in 1933.

The second group of others consists of all those excluded from this first category by virtue of their race or gender, and whose consciousness is perceived as opaque and possibly hostile. Although the mother, as maternal stereotype, is to function as symbol of the first group, her early treatment serves as a template with respect to the second group. During the same year that he writes "The Hospital of the Poor Quarter," Camus also confronts for the first time the indigenous population of Algeria in "The Moorish House." In December of the following year he gives a fairy story, "Melusina's Book," to his first wife and also dedicates a collection of writings, "Voices from the Poor Quarter," to her. While those works concerning the poor neighborhood present with a degree of realism the lives of its inhabitants, "Melusina" moves entirely into the realm of the imagination. In "The Moorish House," and "Melusina," two new sets of others can be discerned for the first time: these are the colonized population, and the woman as a sexual partner. Because of overlaps between these two, which I hope to demonstrate, I have placed them into the same category. I propose to trace these two lines of development in the youthful writings of Camus, and to suggest why he was to abandon his attempted depictions of this second group of others.

Far from showing a commitment to the immediate environment, these youthful works are permeated by a constant "wish for evasion." For the young Camus, the real world is sordid, and art is valorized as "the creation of a Dreamworld, attractive enough to hide from us the world in which we live and all its horrors."[19] The creation of such a universe gives the artist a privileged and God-like status, a status he seems willingly to embrace. In contrast to this self-assigned position, others in the external world are seen as a hostile and nebulous mass, a herd blindly following convention and living routine and ignorant lives. This distance between self and others is found in the series of writings from 1932, "Intuitions," which, although marked by a self-absorption, is the work in which Camus begins his confrontation with others. The first-person speaker in this work is faced with the choice between divinity or joining the community of other men with whom he feels allegiance. This conflict is enacted through the creation of a set of "internal others" who are aspects of the speaker's own consciousness and rehearse his uncertainties. Others external to this consciousness are portrayed as an abstract entity opposing his desires with the pressure of their expectations that he should conform.

The speaker, alone in his room, is visited by a succession of others who are projections of the self, the most significant of whom is the figure of the Fool who voices the speaker's conflict with respect to others. This consists of a mixture of contempt for these "stupid animals,"[20] and envy for their capacity to live without questioning or analyzing their lives: "I wander in this impasse and meet other wanderers who, like me, envy those who do not think and drink the sun in over there, in long draughts."[21] Intelligence is the cause of disunity both within the self and between self and world. Those without intelligence, on the other hand, are entirely at one with their surroundings. For this reason the Fool, like the speaker, has the wish "to be like everyone" and to have "a wife and children," earn his living, have "a name and the respect of good folk."[22] While his intelligence apparently bars the speaker from access to this kind of unity, it is a higher form which is available to both speaker and Fool, who says, "God does not know himself. This is why he is God. He created the world in his delirium and forgot it. And I, too, have been made divine by the ability to forget."[23] This section itself is entitled "Deliriums," so that the above quotation reflects the writer's aspirations: while seeking "oblivion," the artist has created a universe peopled with projections of his internal conflicts.

The external world of men is represented, but in an abstract way. In her comments on this early work Jacqueline Lévi-Valensi insists upon the presence of the real world—the barking of a dog, the slamming of a door, the physical presence of an old man whose description seems to root him in the external world.[24] Yet the movement of "Intuitions" is not directed outwards toward entry into the external world, but at a process in which that world is made imaginary and then incorporated into the consciousness of the speaker. This process of internalization simultaneously annihilates its threatening "otherness" while reinforcing the divine status of its creator, for as product of the imagination it can be dismissed at will. Such is the fate of that apparently real character, the old man. As he walks with the speaker in the outside world, his seeming solidity is cast into doubt when the objective reality of his age becomes merely an effect of the subjective imagination: "He had taken my hand and I felt very old skin beneath my fingers. At least, I thought it was old, and I would not have known how to say why."[25] In a following section, the fictional quality of this apparent reality is confirmed when, abruptly, "at the corner of a street, he left me. For he was only the 'me' that I had become accustomed to watching act beneath my eyes. He disappeared, as I had at last united the spectator and the actor in the same desire for the ideal and the infinite."[26] This comment picks up the recurrent theme of unification with the divine which reflects the strong influence of Nietzsche in these works. In *The Birth of Tragedy,* we read "only in so far as the genius is fused with the primal artist of the world in the act of artistic creation does he know anything of the eternal essence of art; for in that state he is wonderfully similar to the weird fairy-tale image of the creature that can turn its eyes around and look at itself; now he is at once subject and object, at once poet, actor and audience."[27] Through artistic creation the writer turns his eyes "round" to look not at others but at himself. For these reasons, I cannot agree with Lévi-Valensi's comment that "over the lyrical monologue these reveries favor dialogue time and again."[28] The outside world is represented as an anonymous mass rather than a collection of individuals with whom any dialogue is possible. The dialogue we witness is between self and selves, and in a movement toward a foregone conclusion, so that these "others" at times express the same conflicts as the speaker himself, while speaker and "others" alternately occupy superior and inferior positions in a shifting balance of power. Equilibrium is only reached through the swallowing up of these alternative selves in a procedure which reflects the relationship between the speaker and the external world. Initially perceived as "this world that I imagined at first confronting me as a whole," outside reality then becomes "suddenly composed of innumerable elements separated from one another but trying to regroup"[29] — like the speaker himself. Only when this perceived world disintegrates does the speaker begin to unify his fragmented self, but this unification becomes a form of self-universalization incorporating the outside world as an extension of the self. When the speaker finally comments that "I was not different from other men,"[30] it is not his own similarity with others that he is asserting, but their similarity with him.

Art becomes the medium through which reality can be approached yet simultaneously kept at a distance. In the role of artist, the writer becomes God in a universe of his own creation, thus able to confront in a controlled environment the conflicts engendered by the unwilling awareness of the existence of others. That the youthful writer only feels able to confront the existence of others from this exalted position is surely a sign not solely of egocentrism but of vulnerability. Moreover, if the young Camus exhibits a conflict between, on the one hand, a belief in his natural superiority, and, on the other hand, a wish to be a part of the community he apparently so despises, then this should be the cause for no surprise. The contrast is extreme between this future Nobel prize-winner and the men of Camus's own immediate community, who are, generally speaking, not only ill-educated and ignorant but also racist, and whose strongly pro-fascist tendencies have been described as traditional.[31]

Although in "Intuitions" the description of others remains vague, the indications are that these references are to the men of the French Algerian community. In relation specifically to this group, the writer first attains a form of resolution in the short piece entitled "The Hospital of the Poor Neighbourhood." In this work, Camus moves away from concentration on a single consciousness to the attempted depiction of others in a "real" world. Here, both direct and indirect speech are incorporated, giving their voices an apparent independence from their creator. The effect is of harmony and unity in face of a shared threat, the bacillus of tuberculosis.

This society, however, is another closed world isolated from the outside and those same everyday concerns spoken of in "Intuitions." The menace of tuberculosis is revealed as less of a danger to life than to the prospect of gaining a wife, children, or earning a wage, for his failure to fulfill these responsibilities had previously led one of these men to attempt suicide.[32] Likewise, the death of another is linked, not with his illness, but with his wife.[33] Indeed, it is the degree to which these men are removed from the domestic world of women and work which appears crucial in explaining the extent of the harmony between them. Notwithstanding the overwhelming reality of death, they are also separated from "real life" itself. While speaking often in their own voices, these remain anonymous and disembodied, speaking in unanimity. "The Hospital of the Poor Neighbourhood" creates a world apart characterized by a viewpoint in which men are interchangeable and women are set aside. I would suggest that this utopian dimension prefigures Camus's later novel, *The Plague*, where in the "hospital" of Oran a society of men isolated from the outside world likewise faces the threat of death from a bacillus, and, despite its internal differences, also manages to work in harmony.

Of interest is the fact that Camus wrote this piece in 1933, given the similarity of subject matter between this and the later "Voices of the Poor Neighbourhood" (1934). It would appear that the resolution of difference achieved here marks a significant stage in the evolution of Camus's treatment of others. This work begins to establish the communal identity in face of the world which can be traced through Camus's subsequent works, culminating in the "I rebel, therefore we are" of *The Rebel* [34] and finally resuscitated in *The First Man*. The solitary hero predominates as the case of Meursault will testify. But the society which condemns him and fails to understand is that of metropolitan France and not the men of his immediate community. In the earlier hero of "A Happy Death,"[35] Patrice Mersault—who also tends toward the same self-divinization spoken of in "Intuitions"—we nevertheless see a similar desire for acceptance in the community of men.

As early as 1933 Camus reaches a fragile accommodation with others in his writings, an accommodation to which he returns in 1934 with "Voices from the Poor Quarter." This suggests an explanation for the failed detour attempted in other works written around this time. The voices from the hospital can be successfully unified into one viewpoint representative of the "human condition" precisely because they are those of the men of Camus's own community. But this universalizing project founders when the young writer attempts a similar transformation with respect to others unlike himself; and despite claims to the contrary, these others represent an opaque consciousness which thus undermines the author's control.

This attempt to "people the universe with forms in [his] own likeness"[36] founders when Camus attempts to write about an Arab house in Algiers, for here he goes even further into the external world to confront the existence of the indigenous population of Algeria. Once more, this reality is not the subject of the work, but rather the role of the artist in transfiguring and stylizing this reality which is the central concern. His choice of subject matter is motivated by the wish to demonstrate a modification in his definition of art, as expressed in another text from 1933, "Art in Communion." There he asserts that dream, although integral to art, is also indissociable from reality. Art necessarily entails a remodeling or correction of reality in which the aesthetic object, chosen from daily life, is elevated above time and space.[37] Camus turns to the architecture of an Arab house for an example of the way in which the architect models the real building upon its "interior idea."[38] He asserts that the construction of such a house faithfully reflects "a desire for evasion...that responds precisely to the Oriental soul."[39] It is this theme which is developed in "The Moorish House."

In this work for the first time the young writer confronts an actual object existing in the external world, and hence the civilization he perceives behind it (Herbert Lottman records that this building was situated in the Jardin d'Essai, near Camus's own neighborhood of Belcourt[40]). The anthropomorphized house reflects less the interior idea of the building than an exterior idea of Arab aspirations and consciousness which replicates the narrator's own, and in which the theme of evasion from reality is projected on to "the Oriental soul." In his selection of Arab architecture as an illustration of his revised view of art, Camus has chosen a clear example of "otherness" existent in his everyday life. What he seeks to illustrate, however, is not difference, but the extent to which this external object is an extension of his own subjectivity.

That there are no others here besides the speaker himself is thus not surprising. The Arab house functions as metaphor for the self, and the speaker's tour round this building is a journey of *self*-discovery. In some respects, the colonial context facilitates such an enterprise. In his comments about the International Colonial Exhibition held in Paris in 1931, Christopher Miller remarks on the attempts to create an illusion of authenticity through the emphasis upon the "faithful reproduction" of reality: "As Michel Leiris pointed out, it is therefore ironic that the 'reproduction' of the Djenné temple was modeled on a building that the French in Africa had already rebuilt according to their own idea of 'Sudanese' architectural style: *reproductions of otherness always seem to reflect back on the self* (my emphasis)."⁴¹ "The Moorish House" conforms exactly to this description. The building itself was a reproduction—given that its architect, Léon Claro,⁴² was of European origin—and it was built *as* a symbol, to commemorate the centenary of the French conquest of Algeria. For those of European origin, it symbolized the conquest of an untamed land by a pioneering new race of fatherless men; while for the indigenous population, it was a symbol of their defeat. Moreover, the centenary celebrations had taken place in an atmosphere of self-congratulation and lavish spending which contrasts with attitudes toward the native population.⁴³ At a time when the call for independence was first being heard, we might speculate that this "Arab" house may have represented something other than the grandeur of the French colonizers to the indigenous population of the town.

Although "The Moorish House" is the first of the previously unpublished writings in which an addressee can be discerned, the writer is not directing himself to an indigenous audience as he speaks of the emotions engendered by a first tour round "these Arab houses."⁴⁴ This reference alone suggests that he is speaking to those familiar with, but not coming from, such buildings—an outside, yet likewise indigenous, European Algerian audience. The familiarity often claimed by this group was in fact nothing more than an illusion, and of no greater authenticity than this Arab house. Indeed, José Lenzini points out that there was little contact between the European and indigenous populations. Few Arabs lived in Belcourt, and not many Arab children went to school.⁴⁵ Lenzini reports that it was in 1930 that Camus discovered the Casbah, in the company of Jean de Maisonseul, a young student of architecture.⁴⁶ Although he probably learned something of Arab architecture, these forays seem to have been of a touristic nature, as the recollections of Camus's friend Blanche Balain bears out. Camus as observer may have remarked to her that "they are more civilized than we are," but he had no intimate knowledge of such a civilization.⁴⁷

This ambiguous position of the European of French Algeria suggests a further symbolism associated with the Arab house, and which Camus's text accurately reflects: the building provides an *illusion* of familiarity and authentic knowledge. Excluded in fact from this interior life, excluded from the women at its heart (or in its harem), how can the conquerors of the 1930 centenary assert ownership when they themselves are refused possession of that which they claim above all else to understand? As a building, then, the "Arab house" performs a dual and ambivalent function, symbolizing the *genuine* desire both to understand an alien population, and yet through such familiarity to occupy the position of rightful conqueror.

Camus's text is marked by a similar ambivalence in which claims of intimate knowledge are undermined by an otherness which seems to escape such knowledge. The move in "The Moorish House," similar to that of "Intuitions," is to incorporate the house into the speaker's emotional architecture, rendering it no longer a feature of the outside world and of a different civilization, but rather part of the self.

Paul Viallaneix insists that Camus "eliminates the picturesque,"[48] but the entire piece is constructed round an exoticism perhaps indistinguishable from the tourist-like enterprise in which the speaker is engaged. The exotic—implicit in the term "Moorish" and made explicit by references to seduction—fills the speaker with a feeling of power as he conforms to the Western image of the Oriental despot in his bored search after pleasure, allowing himself to be seduced by the promise of new diversions, yet knowing in advance that such hopes are in vain:

> At this hour when I no longer have any hope, I have yielded to the vain pride of building [the house], trusting all the same in the seductiveness of this new dream. I had said to it: 'Arrogant, conceited, jealous of the world you enclose, let me forget myself.' But from no longer wishing to forget, I hate it now. It will crumble: I was sustaining it on my faith and expectations, now vanished.[49]

Like the powerful despot seeking distraction, he is also at liberty to destroy what no longer has the power to seduce. This world is a secret one which would reject intrusion, yet dependent for its existence upon the creative power of the speaker, and subject to his whims.

This avowed loss of interest, combined with the vengeance about to be exacted, raises the suspicion that it is the choice of architecture itself and the unknowability of the civilization it represents which remain beyond the scope of the imagination. While claiming knowledge, the consciousness constantly evades confrontation with the reality of this world, retreating into a dream of ownership of that which it can know only externally. The narrative immediately withdraws from the possibility of an Arab town through the invocation not of its inhabitants but of its buildings and their discordant presence in face of the sea and sky. Violence, hostility, and rebellion are the adjectives associated with this anthropomorphized crowd of houses, but this aggression is translated into a form of metaphysical discord, an innate quality of the town itself in face of the natural world rather than a reaction against the speaker and his curiosity. Such is the insistence of the suspicion, however, that the speaker himself is the alien presence in this surprised and hostile environment that the reader is exhorted to forget the town in a contemplation of the sea beyond, blending with the stars upon the horizon, and above the vain efforts of the town to "disturb the fleeting harmony."[50] This theme of conflict builds in the following passages, to be embodied in a storm from which the speaker shelters in the park beyond the house, and a further evasion from this hostile environment is effected as he thinks about the Arab shops of the Casbah:

> At this hour I see blues and pinks again in the golden shops, then, like children, the magic fabrics of silver and silk, laughing without reason, made more delicate by the light. And the invariable polychromy of the insolent yellows, the pinks heedless of harmony, the blues forgetful of good taste, comes to life for me again intensely like a confused call, a harem made of fabrics, women with incoherent, comfortless ideas. Festive dresses hanging on flat mannequins with knowing, silly smiles.[51]

Here the sexuality only obliquely conjured up through the references to seduction in the context of power is made more explicit by the mention of the harem itself. My contention is that the fantasy of the harem underlies this piece of writing on the Arab house, a theme reinforced by the important role of sight in this work. The tour of the house, a form of sight-seeing, is an enforced revelation of the secretive other Oriental soul, an enterprise which invests power in the one who looks. Olivier Richon points out that:

> The harem is a place which excludes any foreign look. Western representations of the harem are then the fulfillment of the wish to uncover what is hidden....The harem is the exclusive domain of one being, the Despot. The order of the harem is organized around the limitless pleasure of the Master, above all his sexual pleasure which starts with his scopic privilege. Only the Prince has the privilege of seeing women....The Master's primal object of enjoyment and possession is not so much woman as women. With polygamy, he does not possess the other sex but its multiplicity. Multiplicity characterizes inferiority in respect of the uniqueness of the Despot: the amount of women will never match the uniqueness of the Master.[52]

Neither may the tourist, despite his claims to knowledge, be anything other than an inauthentic copy of the master, at least so far as the always unseen harem is concerned. As the depiction of the Algerian mistress in *The Stranger* implies, so here too what is unattainable is presented as a prostitute, and denigrated as not worth having. Just as the town is emptied of its inhabitants, so the women of the harem, forbidden to the foreign gaze, exist through fetishistic associations between them and the materials on sale in the shops. The discordant colors represent "women with incoherent and comfortless ideas" who are "flat mannequins with knowing, silly smiles," which suggests an insolent quality about these women, and yet one which will bring no comfort, a promise which promises no satisfactory outcome for the person who spies upon them. It is worth pointing out here that in this work the tropes of metaphor and metonymy conform to the analysis of colonial discourse made by Homi K. Bhabha. The Arab house itself is a metaphor of the narcissistic self, while the use of metonymy here (and in the reference to the Arab town) has the aggressive dimension identified by Bhabha.[53]

Whereas in other works the sordidness of the everyday so offends the young writer, in this setting the sordid acquires an exotic dimension in a context where the theme of sight is explicitly raised for the first time, and with overtones of voyeurism:

> And leaving the sickening melancholy of this garden, I imagine that I had surprised this orgy of colour in a dark, rough street, a street that I liked because it refused to carry me and only grudgingly permitted itself to be walked upon. Then I stopped in the evening, I did not know where to look, my eyes dazzled by the gaiety of the colour, the agitation of tones, my gaze jarred, jostled, shocked, and enraptured.[54]

Again, the speaker is assailed in the same way as the sea had earlier been by the houses — "jarred, jostled" by the power of the discordant colors. But here the emotions of the speaker are of a different nature: "shocked and enraptured," he is like a sexual voyeur who has seen more than he had expected to see.

I have suggested that this interior landscape devoid of humanity is in fantasy peopled by an Arab population which the speaker and those addressed in "The Moorish House" seek to penetrate and know. Further, at the heart of this world of others, the fantasy of the harem is embedded with its ambiguous image of the Arab woman who is simultaneously available yet forbidden. This sexual dimension pervades the quest of the speaker's itinerary through the house, with the sexual connotations of the subtitles "The Entrance," and "The Corridor," and of the house itself. In 1957 Camus cites the writer Custine, to the effect that Arab architecture is "the art of an effeminate people."[55] Despite the gap of over 20 years, this idea was commonplace in the Algeria of the 1930s and forms an important component of the orientalist discourse round which the present work is constructed. Female sexuality becomes a quality of the entire Arab world, in conjunction with the implicit theme of sexual conquest.

The allusion to the "hidden" Arab woman of the harem, and the associated disruption of the voyeuristic gaze, are not the only references in this work to a woman. Whereas this first reference is created through the device of metonymy, by contrast, the second mention of a woman is abruptly direct, in the form of an epigraph—a reference to another work by another writer, which has not been incorporated but "inserted without being integrated."[56] The epigraph is a line from Ibsen's *The Ghosts*, in which the son asks his mother, "Mother, give me the sun." Two images of woman are opposed in this text: the sexualized woman of race, "woven" into the text; and the mother figure, on its surface, out of context. In an atmosphere of clear ambivalence where claims to power are subverted by feelings of vulnerability, it is as if this sudden allusion to another mother and another son is a return to a certain and fixed point. Bhaba refers to the "myth of historical origination—racial purity, cultural priority," which is produced in relation to the colonial stereotype.[57] Such desire for origin, signified here by the return to the mother, is threatened, he suggests, by the differences of race and culture. In the case of "The Moorish House," the insertion of the epigraph performs a similar function in face of the "otherness" of a resistant population.

Lévi-Valensi argues that the introduction of the mother at this point marks the simultaneous birth of three major themes in the novelistic works: the mother, the sun, and the Algerian soil.[58] She makes no mention of the significance of the harem, concentrating instead upon the way in which this marginal appearance of the mother is set aside in favor of a description of the Algerian landscape, and in a move which makes nature and mother interchangeable. But here the turn to the mother follows the retreat from the harem as if to authenticate subsequent claims to possession of the Algerian soil. In this early work, where mention of the mother is made for the first time, we see the beginning of a development which is to signify, in a manner of speaking, "racial purity, cultural priority."

This is far from unambiguously the case here, for the theme of Ibsen's play concerns the question of inherited degeneration as the result of a sexually dissolute life. There, through biology the sins of the father are visited upon the son, and *via* the mother's body. The ambiguous symbolism of the epigraph indicates the beginnings of the development of the dual function of the mother figure as, on the one hand, a source of ambivalence with regard to her physical, human, and racial status; and, on the other hand, as maternal stereotype symbolizing the new melting-pot race of European men. I wish to underline the conflict between identity and biology, for—whatever his aspirations to the status of a god—man is always born of woman, one not of his choosing, and *via* that most animal of all forms of congress.

The most cursory reading of Camus's personal notebooks reveals the extent to which heterosexuality is regarded as a contaminant, a factor widely noted by scholars.[59] As the reference to the wife of Jean Perès in "The Hospital of the Poor Quarter" or the later celebration of masculinity in *Nuptials* make clear, the female body, not the male body, is the site of such ambivalence. The sexual insecurities discernible in "The Moorish House" are likewise present in the fairy-story "Melusina's Book,"[60] which Camus gave to his first wife, Simone, in December 1934. The couple had been married for six months at this time, and the work is marked by a personal and highly intimate tone which reflects its autobiographical nature. Whereas in "The Moorish House," the material for artistic elaboration had been an inanimate object, in this case the choice of subject matter is a living woman and sexual partner. In this sense, we can say that in his confrontation with others the young writer is moving gradually into a real world of others. At the same time, however, we must remember that this destination had been reached in the earlier "Hospital of the Poor Neighbourhood." In order to arrive back at this same point with "Voices from the Poor Neighbourhood," Camus has taken a detour via the Oriental soul and woman as sexual partner. In this view, such a trajectory might be seen more as a retreat than an advance, for in both cases what strikes one is the vulnerability and failure of control caused by the inability to depict the other.

"Melusina" also bears the imprint of "Art in Communion," which echoes the ending of the fairy story:

Must Art therefore be divine? No. But Art is a means of arriving at the divine. Some might reproach us for lowering Art, by considering it as a means. But means are sometimes more beautiful than ends and the quest more beautiful than the truth. Who has not dreamed of a book or a work of art that would be only a hopeful beginning, profoundly unfinished? There are other means as well besides Art: they are called faith and love.[61]

Like the Arab house, Melusina is the means of arriving at a communion in which she does not participate. Despite the apparent indication of the title, the subject of the fairy story is not Melusina but the narrator, his inventive powers, and his aspirations. Like a child with a doll's house, the narrator is God in his own small universe. Here for the first time, and as distinct from the implied reader of "The Moorish House," the reader is drawn into the text in a complicit "we" which creates a division in the text between "us" and others who belong to the mundane world of "everyday insolence." But this complicity is a necessary component of the power of the speaker, which demands the presence of a compliant and unspeaking "you" to whom he may address himself. A demonstration of his power is that he is able to predict and forestall the reactions and possible objections of the listener, whose gullibility is assumed as he or she is warned against giving credence to what others may say about fairy stories.[62]

I cannot agree with Lévi-Valensi's contention that in "Melusina" Camus unites dream and reality, no longer seeing them as opposed.[63] The theme of evasion from the world is continued in this work and not one of accommodation with the real world. Although the speaker insists that the fairy must have a human dimension, for "what good would a fairy be if there were nothing human about her?"⁶⁴ he makes no attempt to provide her with any "more human functions." She is transported into a world entirely of the imagination in which her only activities are to sing and to dance, actions which the speaker affirms are no longer qualities of man. Indeed, we are told, "if something external does not intervene, she may be occupied with herself alone, directing her mysticism to herself alone."⁶⁵ Her most important activity, then, will be to await the intervention of those destined never to arrive.

Melusina is no more than the object of a quest, a function confirmed by the refusal to grant her even a name: "the quest for names or titles supposes great inventive qualities. Which I don't have. Therefore, and in order to simplify, I'll call this fairy: She."⁶⁶ Paradoxically, then, she is neither fairy nor human. The signifier "She" signifies only the empty incarnation of the desires and fantasies of others, who seek precisely this absence. The quest is undertaken by the two other characters so far introduced into the story—a cat and a knight. Both seem to symbolize a conflict between sexual desire and a "higher" goal which can perhaps be identified as more truly "masculine." I use this term because such are the implications of the description of the knight, suggestive of a phallic power which is directed toward a higher destiny. The phallic imagery is easily discernible in the text: "But already beneath my pen, the knight is advancing, armed with his glory. He is following a path in the same wood. He is upright in his saddle, and the slant of his lance emphasizes his own rigidity."⁶⁷ The first words lend an inevitability to his march and its purposeful masculinity. The previous line had suggested that an element of choice existed about which character should intervene in order to rescue the fairy from her inherent narcissism. The choice makes itself, however—but only with the help of "my pen," whose phallic lines merge with those of knight and lance, thus producing an identification between writer and knight as one symbol of male authority is reflected and intensified by the other. But the knight is ultimately to choose a "grand highway" leading to the sky instead of the "little pathway" leading toward Melusina. There, "he can continue on his way without lowering his lance, as he would have had to on the little garden path."⁶⁸ The theme of the choice between an essentially masculine duty and the emasculating temptations of the seductive female which would weaken masculine power, as has been pointed out, permeates Camus's later writings.

Thus, sexual desire is retained and transformed to the greater glory of the knight and his destiny, from which the speaker is careful to protest his difference. But in the case of the cat, with whom the narrator later compares himself, this same desire is also likewise contained, and to the goal of its own pleasure, magnified and kept alive by abstention:

He is happy, for he is expecting happiness. I like him to be happy without knowing it. I should like him always thus. And since I wish it, with each step he takes, the distant foliage falls back in the same proportion. And without ever knowing it, our cat will live eternally in expectation and in fear. He will never reach the fairy: for how could he achieve her better than in anticipation? [69]

Necessarily, then, narrator and fairy do not share the same desires, for the satisfaction of his rests in the negation of hers, and this satisfaction gained through the frustration and control of her pleasure is evident elsewhere in the text. By herself, Melusina creates "man-stories."[70] The narrator comments that she would no doubt wish one of them to come along, yet this is what he refuses her. His control over her is an integral part of his pleasure, at the expense of any mutuality. Yet the presence in this text of another voice, albeit a silent one, may be destabilizing. The fact that a listener is incorporated into the fairy story offers the possibility of a dialogue, even though the narrative constantly closes off such possibilities. While this may be construed as an attempt to monopolize control, it entails at the same time a realization of the other's autonomy and that he or she may not share the other's interest.

That both fairy and narrator are posited as children in a fairy-tale land suggests the impossibility of sexual consummation. Although this may be seen as an effect of the narrator's will, the reverse may be the case. A feared impossibility of sexual consummation may have resulted in this compensatory world of childhood and the accompanying transference of pleasure into punitive abstention. This fear might be reflected in the portrayal of the knight. For the attempted entry of the knight into the "little pathway" may well represent the fear of the loss of male power. Likewise, the cat is frozen into seeking without ever having to act out his desires.

Not surprisingly, no external intervention takes place, for although the fairy's narcissism is an intrinsic part of her attraction it is a major obstacle to the possibility of her desiring anyone except herself. In spite of the narrator's earlier insistence, it is not at all clear that she has any need for external intervention. Her narcissism contains the threat that she simply would not be interested, a suspicion underlined by the choice of her name, Melusina. Half-woman, half-serpent, she is perhaps sufficient unto herself. Moreover, the hybrid body of the legendary Melusina bred only deformed children, a theme which echoes the epigraph of "The Moorish House." Thus, the apparent self-confidence of the text also reveals an insecurity which threatens to undermine the author's control.

The only intervention certain to have an effect is that of death, which allows a concentration upon the narrator himself. Thus, the attempted "we" is abandoned for a concentration upon the narrator as "child" who supersedes Melusina in the final section, "The Boats." Only after the death of the fairy does the child achieve a form of communion similar to that spoken of in "Art in Communion," a reference which confirms her status as—like art itself—the means of arriving at the divine.

"Melusina" is apparently the only example in the works of Camus where a woman is specifically addressed as listener, and the resulting "we" thus seems based upon an insecurity. Whereas Camus is able easily to incorporate others in his later works, this depends upon their implicit characterization as "men like himself." Over the course of these youthful works, we see a progressive move into the external world which is to culminate in "Voices from the Poor Quarter," a testimony to the lives of the poor European community of Camus's own neighborhood, Belcourt. In May 1935, Camus writes in his notebook: "A work of art is a confession, and I must bear witness. When I see things clearly, I have only one thing to say. It is in this life of poverty, among these vain or humble people, that I have most certainly touched what I feel is the true meaning of life."[71] Camus found his artistic role as "witness" or spokesman for his community, and adopted the perspective which is to remain with him throughout his life. In the 1939 essay, "Summer in Algiers" he remarks:

> Here, intelligence occupies nothing like the place it does in Italy. This race is uninterested in the mind. It worships and admires the body. From this it derives its strength, its naïve cynicism, and a puerile vanity that leads it to be severely criticized. People frequently criticize it for its mentality, that is to say for a particular mode of life and set of values. And it is true that a certain intensity of life involves some injustice. Here, nevertheless, is a people with no past, no tradition, and yet which is not lacking in poetry.[72]

This community, however, is an exclusive one. For *Nuptials* is written in praise of masculinity, while the reference to the people without a past indicates that the population for which Camus is speaking is the European one. The treatment of others in the youthful writings is a development toward this point, and from a stage where those aspects glorified in *Nuptials*—lack of intelligence and a rootedness in reality—had been the source of earlier conflict. Roger Quilliot suggests that the youthful writings mask an aspiration toward silence,[73] but it is appropriate to ask *whose* silence? The single narrative voice is based upon the silence of others, for the task of bearing witness on behalf of others *requires* their incapacity to speak for themselves.

I have pointed out two main categories of others in Camus's earliest works, and two opposing lines of development. Whereas the male European community is to people the fictional universe in Camus's subsequent works, the impasse of "The Moorish House" and "Melusina's Book" results in the abandonment of further attempts to focus upon this category of others. For this claim, I will offer only two final comments. After the failure of the early bid in "The Moorish House" to incorporate the indigenous population of Algeria as an extension of the self, Camus did not focus on this group again until the late 1950s, and in a move which coincides with his stated wish to return to the source of his creative powers.[74] As far as women are concerned, Camus remarked that he would be speaking of women *for the first time* in his projected novel *The First Man*, although it is not in their own right but for the important role they played in the development of the writer himself that their significance was to lie. In his previous works, he said, women had a mythical status.[75] While in agreement with the author on this point, I would add that Camus's fictional works never cease to be haunted by disquieting interconnections between sexuality and race. Such associations in his major and best-known works now need to be re-examined in the light of the complexities of the *Youthful Writings*.

## Notes

1. See Jacqueline Lévi-Valensi, *Genèse de l'œuvre romanesque*, unpublished thesis, Sorbonne, 1981, p. 321. See also her article, "La relation au réel dans le roman camusien," in *Albert Camus: Œuvre fermée, œuvre ouverte? Cahiers Albert Camus 5*, eds. Raymond Gay-Crosier and Jacqueline Lévi-Valensi (Paris: Gallimard, 1985), pp. 153-185.

2. Albert Camus, *Albert Camus: Essais, Bibliothèque de la Pléiade*, eds. Roger Quilliot and Louis Faucon (Paris: Gallimard, 1965), pp. 1215-1216. All translations are mine.

3. *Ibid.*, p. 1215.

4. Albert Camus, *Betwixt and Between*, trans. Philip Thody in *Albert Camus: Selected Essays and Notebooks* (Harmondsworth: Penguin Books, 1979).

5. Unless otherwise indicated, all of Camus's early writings referred to can be found in *Albert Camus: Youthful Writings: Cahiers II*: trans. Ellen Conroy Kennedy (Harmondsworth: Penguin, 1980), originally published as "Le Premier Camus': suivi de Écrits de jeunesse d'Albert Camus," *Cahiers Albert Camus 2* (Paris: Gallimard, 1973). Unless otherwise indicated, further references will be to the Penguin edition.

6. Albert Camus, *Youthful Writings*, p. 194

7. *Ibid.*, p. 200.

8. Camus, *Essais*, p. 1214.

9. Albert Camus, *Le Premier homme, Cahiers Albert Camus, 7* (Paris: Gallimard, 1994). Trans. David Hapgood as *The First Man* (London: Hamish Hamilton, 1995).

10. *The Plague*, trans. Stuart Gilbert (Harmondsworth: Penguin, 1960).

11. See, *e.g.*, Alain Costes, *Albert Camus et la parole manquante* (Paris: Payot, 1973), and Jean Gassin, *L'Univers symbolique d'Albert Camus: essai d'interprétation psychanalytique* (Paris: Minard, 1981).

12. Camus, *Essais*, p. 1213. (See "La relation au réel," p. 171.)
13. Camus, *Selected Essays*, pp. 38-46.
14. Jean Sarocchi, *Le Dernier Camus ou le premier homme* (Paris: Nizet, 1995), p. 155 (my translation).
15. Brian Fitch, *Le Sentiment d'étrangeté chez Malraux, Sartre, Camus, Simone de Beauvoir* (Paris: Minard, 1983), p. 217 (my translation).
16. *Ibid.*
17. See, *e.g.*, Camus, *Youthful Writings*: "A New Verlaine" (pp. 89-92); "Jehan Rictus, the Poet of Poverty" (pp. 93-100); "The Philosophy of the Century" (pp. 101-103); "Essay on Music" (pp. 104-122).
18. See Camus, *Youthful Writings*: "Intuitions" (pp. 123-135); "The Moorish House" (pp. 144-152), "Courage" (pp. 153-155); "Mediterranean" (pp. 156-158); "In the Presence of the Dead" (pp. 159-161); "Losing a Loved One" (pp. 162-164); "God's Dialogue with his Soul" (pp. 165-166); "Contradictions" (pp. 167); "The Hospital of the Poor Quarter" (pp. 168-170); "Art in Communion" (pp. 171-77); "Melusina's Book" (pp. 181-191); "Voices from the Poor Quarter" (pp. 192-204).
19. *Ibid.*, p. 105.
20. *Ibid.*, p. 127.
21. *Ibid.*, p. 125.
22. *Ibid.*
23. *Ibid.*, p. 127.
24. Lévi-Valensi, "La relation au réel," p. 161.
25. Camus, *Youthful Writings*, p. 131.
26. *Ibid.*, p. 133.
27. Friedrich Nietzsche, *The Birth of Tragedy out of the Spirit of Music*, trans. Shaun Whiteside, ed. Michael Tanner (Harmondsworth: Penguin, 1993), p. 32.
28. Lévi-Valensi, "La relation au réel," p. 161 (my translation).
29. Camus, *Youthful Writings*, p. 132.
30. *Ibid.*, p. 134.
31. See, *e.g.*, Charles-Robert Ageron, *Histoire de l'Algérie contemporaine*, 2 (Paris: P. U. F., 1979), pp. 362-378.
32. Camus, *Youthful Writings*, p. 169.
33. *Ibid.*, p. 242.
34. Albert Camus, *The Rebel*, trans. Anthony Bower (Harmondsworth: Penguin, 1981), p. 28 (translation amended).
35. Albert Camus, *A Happy Death*, trans. Richard Howard (New York: Vintage, 1973).
36. Camus, *Selected Essays*, p. 54.
37. Camus, *Youthful Writings*, p. 176.
38. *Ibid.*, p. 173.
39. *Ibid.*, p. 172.
40. Herbert Lottman, *Albert Camus: A Biography* (London: Weidenfeld and Nicholson, 1979), pp. 58-59. See also Paul Viallaneix's introduction to Camus, *Youthful Writings*, p. 49.
41. Christopher Miller, "Hallucinations of France and Africa in the Colonial Exhibition of 1931 and Ousmane Socé's *Mirages de Paris*," *Paragraph: A Journal of*

*Modern Critical Theory*, 18:1 (March, 1995), pp. 39-63 (see p. 50).

42. Olivier Todd, *Albert Camus, une vie* (Paris: Gallimard, 1996), p. 57.

43. Jacques Berque, *French North Africa: The Maghreb Between Two World Wars*, trans. Jean Stewart (London: Faber, 1967), p. 222. See also Ageron, *Histoire de l'Algérie*, ch. 2.

44. Camus, *Youthful Writings*, p. 147.

45. José Lenzini, *L'Algérie de Camus* (Aix-en-Provence: Édisud, 1987), p. 31.

46. *Ibid.*, p. 60.

47. *Ibid.*, p. 68.

48. Paul Viallaneix, "Introduction" in, *Youthful Writings*, p. 49.

49. Camus, *Youthful Writings*, p. 144.

50. *Ibid.*, p. 150.

51. *Ibid.*, p. 146.

52. Olivier Richon, "Representation, the Despot and the Harem: Some Questions Around an Academic Orientalist Painting by Lecomte-du-Nouÿ (1885)," in *Europe and its Others*, *Proceedings of the Essex Conference on the Sociology of Literature* (July, 1984), eds. Francis Barker, Peter Hulme, Margaret Iversen, and Diana Loxley (Colchester: University of Essex, 1985), p. 9.

53. Homi K. Bhabha, "Difference, Discrimination and the Discourse of Colonialism" in *The Politics of Theory*, *Proceedings of the Essex Conference on the Sociology of Literature* (July, 1982), eds. Francis Barker, Peter Hulme, Margaret Iversen, and Diana Loxley (Colchester: University of Essex, 1983), p. 204.

54. Camus, *Youthful Writings*, pp. 146-147.

55. Albert Camus, *Carnets III* (Paris: Gallimard, 1989), p. 202 (my translation).

56. Laurent Mailhot, "Le métatexte camusien," in *Œuvre fermée, œuvre ouverte?*, p. 296 (paraphrased).

57. Bhabha, "Discourse of Colonialism," p. 202.

58. Lévi-Valensi, "La relation au réel," p. 165.

59. See, *e.g.*, Alan J. Clayton, "Camus ou l'impossibilité d'aimer," *Revue des Lettres Modernes* in *Albert Camus*, 7, nos. 419-424 (1975), ed. Brian T. Fitch, pp. 9-34; Anthony Rizzuto, "Camus and a Society without Women," *Modern Language Studies*, 13:1 (1983), pp. 3-14; Édouard Morot-Sir, "L'esthétique d'Albert Camus: logique de la limite, mesure de la mystique," in *Œuvre Fermée, œuvre ouverte?*, pp. 93-113.

60. Camus, *Youthful Writings*, pp. 181-191.

61. *Ibid.*, p. 175.

62. *Ibid.*, p. 181.

63. Lévi-Valensi, "La relation au réel," p. 165.

64. Camus, *Youthful Writings*, p. 182.

66. *Ibid.*

66. *Ibid.*, p. 181.

67. *Ibid.*, p. 183. Translation amended

68. *Ibid.*, p. 185.

69. *Ibid.*, p. 186.

70. *Ibid.*, p. 182.

71. Camus, *Selected Essays*, p. 235.
72. *Ibid.*, p. 88.
73. Roger Quilliot, "Albert Camus ou les difficultés du langage," *Revue des Lettres Modernes* in *Albert Camus, 2*, nos. 212-216 (1969), ed. Brian T. Fitch, pp. 77-102.
74. See Camus, *Selected Essays*, pp. 17-27.
75. This confidence was made to Jean-Claude Brisville and reported by Olivier Todd in *Albert Camus, une vie*, p. 741.

# ABOUT THE CONTRIBUTORS

JAMES GILES is Acting Lecturer in Philosophy at the University of Copenhagen and Tutor at Madingley Hall, University of Cambridge. He has also taught at Roskilde University and Aalborg University, Denmark, the Hawaii College of Kansai Gaidai University, Japan, and the University of Edinburgh. He is author of *No Self to be Found: The Search for Personal Identity* (1997), *A Study in Phenomenalism* (1994), *A Theory of Sexual Desire* (forthcoming), and editor of *Kierkegaard and Freedom* (forthcoming).

THOMAS JONES was awarded his PhD from Lancaster University, England in 1995 for a thesis entitled *The Phenomenology of Love*. He has taught Indian Philosophy at the same university, later worked in the sales team of a Buddhist Right livelihood business in Cambridge, and is now working on a novel. He has published poetry, articles, and reviews in the Buddhist arts magazine *Urthona* and elsewhere, and has had his fiction read on British national radio.

TERRY KEEFE is Research Professor of French at Lancaster University. His publications include a general study of all of the writings of Simone de Beauvoir (1983), a book on existentialist fiction (1986), a monograph on two of Beauvoir's later works (1992), and a Macmillan "Modern Novelists" volume on Beauvoir (1998). He has also co-edited books on Zola and on existentialist autobiography.

MATTHEW KIERAN is Lecturer in Philosophy at the University of Leeds, England. He has published articles on aesthetics, ethics, and social philosophy, is the editor of *Media Ethics* (1998), and author of *Media Ethics: A Philosophical Approach* (1997).

CHRISTINE MARGERRISON has degrees in both Sociology and French Studies and was recently awarded a PhD by Lancaster University for her thesis on woman, race, and origins in the imaginative writings of Albert Camus. She is currently tutoring in French literature at the same university.

ELIZABETH MURRAY MORELLI is Professor in the Philosophy Department at Loyola Marymount University, California. She is the author of *Anxiety: A Study of the Affectivity of Moral Consciousness* (1986). With her husband Mark Morelli, she co-edited *Lonergan's Understanding and Being* (1980/1990) and *The Lonergan Reader* (1997).

MARGARET A. SIMONS is Professor in the Department of Philosophical Studies and Co-ordinator of the Women's Studies Program at Southern Illinois University at Edwardsville, and was editor of *Hypatia: A Journal of Feminist Philosophy* from 1985 to 1990. She is co-editor of *Hypatia Reborn* in *Feminist Philosophy* (1990), editor of *Feminist Interpretations of Simone de Beauvoir* (1995), and author of *Beauvoir and The Second Sex: Feminism, Race, and the Origins of Existentialism* (1998). She is currently co-editing (with Sylvie Le Bon de Beauvoir) a series of Beauvoir's philosophical texts in English translation.

JULIETTE SIMONT is Researcher at the National Fund for Scientific Research, Belgium. She is author of *Essai sur la quantité, la qualité, la relation, chez Kant, Hegel, Deleuze* (1997) and *Jean-Paul Sartre. Un demi-siècle de liberté* (1998). She has also published various articles about Sartre's philosophy, mostly in *Les Temps Moderns*.

PHILIP STRATTON-LAKE is Lecturer in Philosophy at the University of Reading, England. He has also taught at the University of Essex and at Keele University. He has published articles on Kant, Marcel, ethical intuitionism, and moral motivation, and is the Section Editor for German Idealism in the *Edinburgh Encyclopedia of Continental Philosophy*.

EDMOND WRIGHT has degrees in both Philosophy and English, is an honorary member of the Senior Common Room of Pembroke College, Oxford, and has recently been a Fellow at the Swedish College for the Advanced Study of the Social Sciences, Uppsala. He is the editor of *The Ironic Discourse* (1983), *New Representationalisms: Essays in the Philosophy of Perception* (1993), co-editor of *The Zizek Reader* (1997), and has published over forty articles on language, perception, and the philosophy of science, in *Mind*, *Philosophy*, *Synthese*, and other journals. He has also published two volumes of poetry.

# Index

Abraham, 100
Aesop, 33, 53
Algeria, 192, 194, 199, 202, 208
Alroy, Daniel, 45
anguish, 62-3, 100, 109, 112, 119, 156, 183, 187
anxiety, 142
apartheid, 68
Aquinas, Thomas, 118
Arab architecture, 198-99, 202
Arab house, 199, 201-2, 204
  metaphor for the self, 198
Aristotle, 1-2, 188-9
  *The Nicomachean Ethics*, 24
Arland, Marcel, 111
art, 75, 194, 198, 202, 204, 207
  objects, 131
atheistic existentialism, 2
Augustine, 19
Austin, J. L., 47
authenticity, 63-5, 70, 74, 77, 80, 89-90, 93-5, 113
Aztec Empire
  human sacrifices, 68, 70

bad faith, 15, 25, 63-5, 67-70, 72-3, 79, 87, 95, 108-9, 112-3
Balain, Blanche, 199
bare sensation, 37, 45-6
Barnes, Hazel, 24
Barrett, William, 12
Baruzi, Jean, 115-16, 118
Beauvoir, Simone de, 126, 191
  1927 diary, 107-21
  early philosophy, 87-105
  Kierkegaardian legacy, 108
  origins of philosophy, 107-21
  reaction to *War Diaries*, 92-3
  relationship with Sartre, 7, 61, 179-80
  *She Came To Stay*, 59-60, 108, 110, 115, 119, 121
  *The Ethics of Ambiguity*, 94, 109
  *The Second Sex*, 8, 88, 102-3, 116, 119, 121
  views on ethics, 72-3
  views on love, 110-12, 114-16, 118-21

  *When Things of the Spirit Come First*, 112
Beauvoir, Sylvie Le Bon de, 107
Bell, Linda A., 158-9, 160
Belsen, 67
Bergoffen, Debra, 109, 112, 116-18
Bergson, Henri, 11, 35, 50, 116
Berkeley, George, 1
Berne, Eric, 168-9
Bhabha, Homi K., 202
Biran, Maine de, 11
breast-feeding, 170
  erotic sensations, 167
Brehier, Émile, 43
Brentano, Franz, 2, 24
Brewster, Charles, 46
British Hegelianism, 2
British National Party, 68
Buber, Martin
  *I and Thou*, 185. *See also* relations with others, I-thou; Levinas, Emmanuel, I-thou
Burge, Tyler, 48

Callicles, 19
Capone, Al, 64
Camus, Albert, 2, 8, 13, 17, 60-3
  *Betwixt and Between*, 191-2
  first wife, 203
  *Nuptials*, 203, 207
  *The First Man*, 192, 193, 197
  *The Myth of Sisyphus*, 60
  *The Plague*, 192, 197
  *The Rebel*, 197
  woman as sexual partner, 17, 194, 204
  *Youthful Writings*, 191-208. See mother, descriptions in Camus
Catalano, Joseph S., 15, 22, 77, 79-81
chimpanzee
  special grin, 43
Christian existentialism, 2
Christianity, 151-2, 186
Claro, Léon, 199
Cleary, Chip, 38
*cogito*, 21, 24, 28, 179, 180, 187
communion, 142, 145, 150-1, 162,

181-2, 204, 207
desire, 162
consciousness, 1-2, 9-16, 43, 61-2, 90-1, 97, 104-111, 116, 119, 129, 193-8, 200
  intentionality, 59
  positional and non-positional, 23, 25-26
  pre-reflective, 22, 130, 178, 182, 188
  reflective, 19-30, 181
  self, 1, 20, 22-3, 28-30, 53, 72-3
  threatening, 192.
  unity, 39
  unreflective, 23-5. *See* Kierkegaard, reflective consciousness
culture, 7, 17, 12, 68, 70, 175
  imaginative structures, 186
  European, 188
  organization of sexual desire, 188
  race, 203
  sexual behavior not suppressed, 165

*Dasein*, 13, 88
Davidson, Donald, 48, 53
Descartes, René, 2-3, 10, 20, 26, 28
despair, 3, 15, 111-4, 117-8, 120-1, 140-6, 148
Dewey, John, 38
Diana, Lewis, 162
Dignaga, 35, 51
Donnellan, Keith, 48
Dretske, Fred 48
Dummett, Michael, 48
Dziemidok, Bohdan, 35

Edelman, Gerald, 44, 53-4
Eliot, George, 36
emotion, 9, 88, 110, 113, 117-9, 164, 177-8, 181, 186, 199-200, 202
empiricism, 37-8, 53
ethics, 9
  development of Beauvoir's view, 107, 109-10, 112-3, 117, 12

  development of Sartre's view, 89-106
  French existentialist, 12, 59-84
  virtue, 14, 16, 65, 121-2, 187
  *See* Sartre, critique of humanism; Sartre, creation of value
evil, 63-5, 67-73, 76, 84

femininity, 15, 102, 121
Fisher, Mark, 185
Fitch, Brian, 193-4
Fleeson, June, 168, 169
Foucault, Michel, 110, 171
freedom, 11, 14, 62-4, 67, 70-3, 75, 77, 79-80, 84, 90-1, 93-5, 97, 99-101, 101, 103-4, 108-21, 129-30, 132-6, 156, 161, 181, 183, 187-8
Frege, Gottlob, 48
French existentialism
  areas of inquiry, 9-10
  creation of value, 59-84
  Kierkegaardian ancestry, 2-3, 12
  lived experience, 8, 116
  school of 1-2, 7
French Marxism, 7
Freud, Sigmund, 164, 167, 170, 188
  *Civilization and its Discontents*, 176
Friedman, Susan, 167
Fullbrook, Edward, 90, 107-10, 113
Fullbrook, Kate, 90, 107-10, 113

Gadamer, Hans-Georg, 47
gender, 13, 14, 17, 167, 194, 196
generosity, 82, 109-10, 117, 119-21, 180
Gestalt, 37, 39, 43-5, 47, 49-51, 53. *See* psychologists, Gestalt
Gibson, James, J., 39
Gilligan, Carol, 15, 121
Glasersfeld, Ernst von, 42, 50
God, 90-2, 94-5, 100, 103-4, 111, 114, 117, 120, 151-2, 194-6, 203-4
  Beauvoir's loss of belief, 112
Golomb, Jacob, 15, 77-8

Graham, Gordon, 68
Gregory, Richard L., 49-50

harem, 199, 201-3
Harlow, Harry, 167-8
Harman, Gilbert, 37
hate, 157-60
Hegel, Georg Wilhelm Friedrich, 1-2, 12, 73, 145
Heidegger, Martin, 2, 13, 89
  *Sein und Zeit*, 88
Helmholtz, Herman von, 50
Himmler, Heinrich, 69
Hitler, Adolf, 69
Hobbes, Thomas, 76-7
Holocaust, 69
hope, 3, 10, 16, 61, 139-52, 183, 185, 200
Horgan, Terence, 48
humanism
  Kantian, 2. *See* Sartre, critique of humanism
Hume, David, 108
Humpty Dumpty, 34-5, 52
Husserl, Edmund, 12-13, 19, 20, 23-4, 109, 116
  determinable $x$, 51
  *The Idea of Phenomenology*, 27-8

Ibsen, Henrik 203
imagination, 28, 115-6, 186-8, 194-5, 200, 205
inner light, 45
intentionality, 1-2, 19-27, 29-30, 38, 108, 133, 177
internal others, 194
internal stereoscopic space, 45-6. *See* consciousness, intentionality
International Phonetic Alphabet, 35

James, William, 36, 48, 49, 52, 116
Johnson, Dr. Samuel, 1
joke, 34, 35, 40, 44, 48, 52-4
Judaism, 96
Julez, Bela, 45

Kant, Immanuel, 3, 14, 35, 37, 39, 60, 100, 108, 114
  *Third Critique*, 66
  universalizability, 71, 73-4
  *See* humanism, Kantian
Kaplan, Helen Singer, 166
Kierkegaard, Søren
  reflective consciousness, 19-20.
  *See* French existentialism, Kierkegaardian ancestry; Beauvoir, Simone de, Kierkegaardian legacy
Klaw, Barbara, 107
Klein, Milton, 170
Klu Klux Klan, 68
Knuckles, Frankie, 64
Kray brothers, 64
Kubrick, Stanley, 45

Lacan, Jacques, 53
Langer, Monika, 158, 159-60
Leibniz, Gottfried Wilhelm, 116
Leiris, Michel, 198
Lenzeni, José, 199
*Les Temps Modernes*, 108
Lévi-Valensi, Jacqueline, 193, 195, 196, 203, 204
Levinas, Emmanuel, 13
  I-thou, 52
Lewes, George Henry, 36
Liar Paradox, 40
Loar, Brian, 48
Lonergan, Bernard, 24-5, 27
Lottman, Herbert, 198
love, 16-17, 60-2, 82, 139, 145-6, 148-51, 193. *See* Sartre, views on love; Beauvoir, views on love
Lowe, Jonathan, 45
Luria, Zella, 167

"Magic Eye" pictures, 45-6
Mahler, Margaret, 170-1
Maisonseul, Jean de, 119
Marcel, Gabriel, 2-3, 94, 162, 191
  hope and virtue, 139-52,
  *Metaphysical Journal*, 8
Marx, Karl, 3
masochism, 104, 157-9

Matthews, Eric, 81
Maund, Barry, 45
McBride, William, L., 79
McClure, Roger, 51
McDowell, John, 37
Mead, George Herbert, 38
Merleau-Ponty, Maurice, 1, 3, 30
    influence on Beauvoir, 109, 118-19
    *Phenomenology of Perception*, 38, 43
    self-commitment, 70
    view of sensory, 33-54
    views on love, 187
Miller, Christopher, 198
Montaigne, Michel de, 10
Morris, Phyllis, 25
mother
    child relation, 79
    Merleau-Ponty's love, 118
    descriptions in Camus, 192-4, 203
    hope for son's return, 130-2, 148-50
    infant's relation, 148-54
Murdoch, Iris, 82, 95

Nazism, 64-5, 67-70
Nietzsche, Friedrich, 3, 12, 50, 126, 129, 149
    *The Birth of Tragedy*, 196
nothingness, 3, 15, 22, 81, 111-3, 120, 129-31,

oral pleasures, 167
Oriental soul, 198, 201, 204
otherness, 195, 198-99, 203

Pascal, Blaise, 7, 10, 12, 111
perception, 34-9, 43, 47, 49-50, 52, 60, 82, 139, 176, 179, 184
Plato, 84
    *Symposium*, 184-5
primordial experience, 37, 47
Princess Elizabeth of Bohemia, 3
psychologists, 42, 169-70, 180
    and biologists, 180

developmental and social, 16
feminist, 15, 16, 121
Gestalt, 14, 37
hypnagogic visions, 45
psychology, 13-4
    phenomenological, 89
Putnam, Hilary, 37, 53

Quilliot, Roger, 207
Quine, Willard, V., 48

race, 191-3, 199, 203, 207-8
rationalism, 38, 116, 118
Ravaisson-Mollien, Félix, 11
relations with others
    Camus's writings, 193
    Beauvoir's view, 107-21
    historical conditions, 79
    I-thou, 151
    Marcel's view, 143, 149, 151
    ontogenic dimension, 166-72
    Sartre's view, 94-7, 101, 103, 155-65. *See* love; hate; hope; masochism; mother, hope for son's return; mother, infant's relation; sadism; sexual harassment
rhesus monkeys, 167-8
Richon, Olivier, 201
Ricoeur, Paul, 47
Rimbaud, Arthur, 3
Rommetveit, Ragnar, 39-41, 43, 51
Rorty, Richard, 36
Rose, Michael D., 167
Rousseau, Jean-Jacques, 10
Royce, Josian, 44

sadism, 104, 157, 159-60
St. Vincent de Paul, 64
soap operas, 66
Sarocchi, Jean, 193
Sanches, Francisco, 10
Sartre, Jean-Paul
    *Anti-Semite and Jew*, 101-2
    *Being and Nothingness*, 20, 22-3, 25-8, 77, 87-8, 90, 93-104, 119, 128, 130, 135-6, 155-8,

164, 175, 178, 184, 186
creation of value, 59, 62
*Critique of Dialectic Reason,* 79, 130-5
critique of humanism, 125-36
*Existentialism and Humanism,* 100, 127-9
*Nausea,* 125-8, 135
*Notebooks for an Ethics,* 72, 82, 93-5, 103-5, 129, 131, 155, 175
phenomenologies, 1-3
relationship with Beauvoir, 7, 61, 179-80.
sexual desire, 155-72
*Sketch for a Theory of the Emotions,* 88, 164, 178
*The Emotions,* 164
*The Psychology of the Imagination,* 28
*The Roads to Freedom,* 127
*The Transcendence of the Ego,* 20, 24, 25, 156, 178
*The Words,* 30
*Truth and Existence,* 69
views on love, 157-8, 160, 165, 175-89
*War Diaries,* 88-95, 100, 126, 133. *See* ethics, development of Sartre's view; relations with others, Sartre's view; consciousness, pre-reflective; consciousness, reflective; consciousness, unreflective
Schank, Roger C., 38
Schelling, Friedrich Wilhelm Joseph von, 3
Schopenhauer, Arthur, 35, 50, 115, 186
Schutz, Alfred, 39-41, 43, 51
self, 1-3, 15, 22, 25, 77, 81, 88, 120-1, 141, 143, 185, 195-6, 199
authentic, 76
creation, 63
discovery, 198
embodiment, 132
moral, 80

and other, 119, 169-70, 182, 194
Sellars, Roy Wood, 36, 44, 50, 53
sensual pleasure, 167
sexual desire, 16, 157, 159-67, 172, 186-8, 205
sexual harassment, 83
Socrates, 84, 184
solaltrism, 121
solipsism, 108-10, 121
Speer, Albert, 67
Sroufe, L. Alan, 168, 169
stereoscopic squares, 45
Stoicism, 89
story, 38, 40-4, 48, 52-4
subjectivity, 2, 63, 73-4, 82, 109-10, 117-8, 158, 161, 177-9, 198

Tristan and Isolde, 185

Vaihinger, Hans, 92
Viallaneix, Paul, 200
Vintges, Karen, 109-10, 112, 115, 117
virtual-reality hood, 44
virtue. *See* ethics, virtue
void, 59, 111-3, 119

Warnock, Mary, 8, 158
Wiggins, David, 40, 52
Williams, Bernard, 149
Wittgenstein, Ludwig, 48
Woodfield, Richard, 49-50

**VIBS**

The **Value Inquiry Book Series** is co-sponsored by:

American Maritain Association
American Society for Value Inquiry
Association for Personalist Studies
Association for Process Philosophy of Education
Center for East European Dialogue and Development, Rochester Institute of Technology
Center for Professional and Applied Ethics, University of North Carolina at Charlotte
Centre for Cultural Research, Aarhus University
College of Education and Allied Professions, Bowling Green State University
Concerned Philosophers for Peace
Conference of Philosophical Societies
Institute of Philosophy of the High Council of Scientific Research, Spain
International Academy of Philosophy of the Principality of Liechtenstein
International Society for Universalism
Natural Law Society
Philosophical Society of Finland
Philosophy Born of Struggle Association
Philosophy Seminar, University of Mainz
R.S. Hartman Institute for Formal and Applied Axiology
Russian Philosophical Society
Society for Iberian and Latin-American Thought
Society for the Philosophic Study of Genocide and the Holocaust
Society for the Philosophy of Sex and Love
Yves R. Simon Institute.

Titles Published

1. Noel Balzer, *The Human Being as a Logical Thinker.*

2. Archie J. Bahm, *Axiology: The Science of Values.*

3. H. P. P. (Hennie) Lötter, *Justice for an Unjust Society.*

4. H. G. Callaway, *Context for Meaning and Analysis: A Critical Study in the Philosophy of Language.*

5. Benjamin S. Llamzon, *A Humane Case for Moral Intuition.*

6. James R. Watson, *Between Auschwitz and Tradition: Postmodern Reflections on the Task of Thinking.* A volume in **Holocaust and Genocide Studies.**

7. Robert S. Hartman, *Freedom to Live: The Robert Hartman Story,* edited by Arthur R. Ellis. A volume in **Hartman Institute Axiology Studies.**

8. Archie J. Bahm, *Ethics: The Science of Oughtness.*

9. George David Miller, *An Idiosyncratic Ethics; Or, the Lauramachean Ethics.*

10. Joseph P. DeMarco, *A Coherence Theory in Ethics.*

11. Frank G. Forrest, *Valuemetrics$^N$: The Science of Personal and Professional Ethics.* A volume in **Hartman Institute Axiology Studies.**

12. William Gerber, *The Meaning of Life: Insights of the World's Great Thinkers.*

13. Richard T. Hull, Editor, *A Quarter Century of Value Inquiry: Presidential Addresses of the American Society for Value Inquiry.* A volume in **Histories and Addresses of Philosophical Societies.**

14. William Gerber, *Nuggets of Wisdom from Great Jewish Thinkers: From Biblical Times to the Present.*

15. Sidney Axinn, *The Logic of Hope: Extensions of Kant's View of Religion.*

16. Messay Kebede, *Meaning and Development.*

17. Amihud Gilead, *The Platonic Odyssey: A Philosophical-Literary Inquiry into the Phaedo.*

18. Necip Fikri Alican, *Mill's Principle of Utility: A Defense of John Stuart Mill's Notorious Proof.* A volume in **Universal Justice**.

19. Michael H. Mitias, Editor, *Philosophy and Architecture.*

20. Roger T. Simonds, *Rational Individualism: The Perennial Philosophy of Legal Interpretation.* A volume in **Natural Law Studies**.

21. William Pencak, *The Conflict of Law and Justice in the Icelandic Sagas.*

22. Samuel M. Natale and Brian M. Rothschild, Editors, *Values, Work, Education: The Meanings of Work.*

23. N. Georgopoulos and Michael Heim, Editors, *Being Human in the Ultimate: Studies in the Thought of John M. Anderson.*

24. Robert Wesson and Patricia A. Williams, Editors, *Evolution and Human Values.*

25. Wim J. van der Steen, *Facts, Values, and Methodology: A New Approach to Ethics.*

26. Avi Sagi and Daniel Statman, *Religion and Morality.*

27. Albert William Levi, *The High Road of Humanity: The Seven Ethical Ages of Western Man*, edited by Donald Phillip Verene and Molly Black Verene.

28. Samuel M. Natale and Brian M. Rothschild, Editors, *Work Values: Education, Organization, and Religious Concerns.*

29. Laurence F. Bove and Laura Duhan Kaplan, Editors, *From the Eye of the Storm: Regional Conflicts and the Philosophy of Peace.* A volume in **Philosophy of Peace.**

30. Robin Attfield, *Value, Obligation, and Meta-Ethics.*

31. William Gerber, *The Deepest Questions You Can Ask About God: As Answered by the World's Great Thinkers.*

32. Daniel Statman, *Moral Dilemmas.*

33. Rem B. Edwards, Editor, *Formal Axiology and Its Critics*. A volume in **Hartman Institute Axiology Studies.**

34. George David Miller and Conrad P. Pritscher, *On Education and Values: In Praise of Pariahs and Nomads.* A volume in **Philosophy of Education.**

35. Paul S. Penner, *Altruistic Behavior: An Inquiry into Motivation.*

36. Corbin Fowler, *Morality for Moderns.*

37. Giambattista Vico, *The Art of Rhetoric (Institutiones Oratoriae, 1711-1741)*, from the definitive Latin text and notes, Italian commentary and introduction by Giuliano Crifo, translated and edited by Giorgio A. Pinton and Arthur W. Shippee. A volume in **Values in Italian Philosophy.**

38. W. H. Werkmeister, *Martin Heidegger on the Way*, edited by Richard T. Hull. A volume in **Werkmeister Studies.**

39. Phillip Stambovsky, *Myth and the Limits of Reason.*

40. Samantha Brennan, Tracy Isaacs, and Michael Milde, Editors, *A Question of Values: New Canadian Perspectives in Ethics and Political Philosophy.*

41. Peter A. Redpath, *Cartesian Nightmare: An Introduction to Transcendental Sophistry.* A volume in **Studies in the History of Western Philosophy.**

42. Clark Butler, *History as the Story of Freedom: Philosophy in Intercultural Context,* with Responses by sixteen scholars.

43. Dennis Rohatyn, *Philosophy History Sophistry.*

44. Leon Shaskolsky Sheleff, *Social Cohesion and Legal Coercion: A Critique of Weber, Durkheim, and Marx.* Afterword by Virginia Black.

45. Alan Soble, Editor, *Sex, Love, and Friendship: Studies of the Society for the Philosophy of Sex and Love, 1977-1992.* A volume in **Histories and Addresses of Philosophical Societies.**

46. Peter A. Redpath, *Wisdom's Odyssey: From Philosophy to Transcendental Sophistry.* A volume in **Studies in the History of Western Philosophy.**

47. Albert A. Anderson, *Universal Justice: A Dialectical Approach.* A volume in **Universal Justice.**

48. Pio Colonnello, *The Philosophy of Jose Gaos.* Translated from Italian by Peter Cocozzella. Edited by Myra Moss. Introduction by Giovanni Gullace. A volume in **Values in Italian Philosophy.**

49. Laura Duhan Kaplan and Laurence F. Bove, Editors, Philosophical Perspectives on Power and Domination: Theories and Practices. A volume in **Philosophy of Peace.**

50. Gregory F. Mellema, *Collective Responsibility.*

51. Josef Seifert, *What Is Life? The Originality, Irreducibility, and Value of Life.* A volume in **Central-European Value Studies.**

52. William Gerber, *Anatomy of What We Value Most.*

53. Armando Molina, *Our Ways: Values and Character,* edited by Rem B. Edwards. A volume in **Hartman Institute Axiology Studies.**

54. Kathleen J. Wininger, *Nietzsche's Reclamation of Philosophy.* A volume in **Central-European Value Studies.**

55. Thomas Magnell, Editor, *Explorations of Value.*

56. HPP (Hennie) Lötter, Injustice, *Violence, and Peace: The Case of South Africa.* A volume in **Philosophy of Peace.**

57. Lennart Nordenfelt, *Talking About Health: A Philosophical Dialogue.* A volume in **Nordic Value Studies.**

58. Jon Mills and Janusz A. Polanowski, *The Ontology of Prejudice.* A volume in **Philosophy and Psychology.**

59. Leena Vilkka, *The Intrinsic Value of Nature.*

60. Palmer Talbutt, Jr., *Rough Dialectics: Sorokin's Philosophy of Value,* with Contributions by Lawrence T. Nichols and Pitirim A. Sorokin.

61. C. L. Sheng, *A Utilitarian General Theory of Value.*

62. George David Miller, *Negotiating Toward Truth: The Extinction of Teachers and Students.* Epilogue by Mark Roelof Eleveld. A volume in **Philosophy of Education.**

63. William Gerber, *Love, Poetry, and Immortality: Luminous Insights of the World's Great Thinkers*.

64. Dane R. Gordon, Editor, *Philosophy in Post-Communist Europe*. A volume in **Post-Communist European Thought.**

65. Dane R. Gordon and Józef Niżnik, Editors, Criticism and Defense of Rationality in Contemporary Philosophy. A volume in **Post-Communist European Thought.**

66. John R. Shook, *Pragmatism: An Annotated Bibliography, 1898-1940*. With Contributions by E. Paul Colella, Lesley Friedman, Frank X. Ryan, and Ignas K. Skrupskelis.

67. Lansana Keita, *The Human Project and the Temptations of Science*.

68. Michael M. Kazanjian, *Phenomenology and Education: Cosmology, Co-Being, and Core Curriculum*. A volume in **Philosophy of Education.**

69. James W. Vice, *The Reopening of the American Mind: On Skepticism and Constitutionalism*.

70. Sarah Bishop Merrill, *Defining Personhood: Toward the Ethics of Quality in Clinical Care*.

71. Dane R. Gordon, *Philosophy and Vision*.

72. Alan Milchman and Alan Rosenberg, Editors, *Postmodernism and the Holocaust*. A volume in **Holocaust and Genocide Studies.**

73. Peter A. Redpath, *Masquerade of the Dream Walkers: Prophetic Theology from the Cartesians to Hegel*. A volume in **Studies in the History of Western Philosophy.**

74. Malcolm D. Evans, *Whitehead and Philosophy of Education: The Seamless Coat of Learning*. A volume in **Philosophy of Education.**

75. Warren E. Steinkraus, *Taking Religious Claims Seriously: A Philosophy of Religion*, edited by Michael H. Mitias. A volume in **Universal Justice.**

76. Thomas Magnell, Editor, *Values and Education*.

77. Kenneth A. Bryson, *Persons and Immortality*. A volume in **Natural Law Studies.**

78. Steven V. Hicks, *International Law and the Possibility of a Just World Order: An Essay on Hegel's Universalism*. A volume in **Universal Justice**.

79. E.F. Kaelin, *Texts on Texts and Textuality: A Phenomenology of Literary Art*, edited by Ellen J. Burns.

80. Amihud Gilead, *Saving Possibilities: A Study in Philosophical Psychology*, A volume in **Philosophy and Psychology**.

81. André Mineau, *The Making of the Holocaust: Ideology and Ethics in the Systems Perspective*. A volume in **Holocaust and Genocide Studies**.

82. Howard P. Kainz, *Politically Incorrect Dialogues: Topics Not Discussed in Polite Circles*.

83. Veikko Launis, Juhani Pietarinen, and Juha Räikkä, Editors, *Genes and Morality: New Essays*. A volume in **Nordic Value Studies**.

84. Steven Schroeder, *The Metaphysics of Cooperation: A Study of F. D. Maurice*.

85. Caroline Joan ("Kay") S. Picart, *Thomas Mann and Friedrich Nietzsche: Eroticism, Death, Music, and Laughter*. A volume in **Central-European Value Studies**.

86. G. John M. Abbarno, Editor, **The Ethics of Homelessness: Philosophical Perspectives.**

87. James Giles, Editor, *French Existentialism: Consciousness, Ethics, and Relations with Others*. A volume in **Nordic Value Studies**.